Living with Floods in a Mobile Southeast Asia

This book contributes to a better understanding of the relationship between migration, vulnerability, resilience and social justice associated with flooding across diverse environmental, social and policy contexts in Southeast Asia. It challenges simplistic analyses of flooding as a singular driver of migration, and instead considers the often complex ways in which floods figure in migration-based livelihoods and amongst already mobile populations.

Developing a conceptual framework based on a 'mobile political ecology' the authors pay particular attention to the multidimensionality, temporalities and geographies of mobility and vulnerability. The focus is on identifying the environmental, social, institutional and political factors that produce and perpetuate vulnerabilities that provide context to capacities (or lack thereof) of individuals and households. These include: the sociopolitical dynamics of floods, flood hazards and risky environments, the characteristics of migration and migrant-based livelihoods and the policy environments through which these take shape.

Organised around a series of eight empirical urban and rural case studies in Cambodia, Indonesia, Laos, Malaysia, Myanmar, the Philippines, Thailand and Vietnam, where lives are marked by mobility and by floods associated with the region's monsoonal climate, the book concludes by synthesising the insights of the case studies, and suggests future policy directions. Together, the chapters highlight critical policy questions around the governance of migration, institutionalised disaster response strategies and broader development agendas.

Carl Middleton is Assistant Professor and Director of the Center for Social Development Studies in the Faculty of Political Science, Chulalongkorn University, Thailand.

Rebecca Elmhirst is Reader in Human Geography and Deputy Head of the School of Environment and Technology at the University of Brighton, UK.

Supang Chantavanich is Professor Emeritus at the Faculty of Political Science, Institute of Asian Studies, and adviser to the Asian Research Center for Migration, Chulalongkorn University, Thailand.

Routledge Studies in Development, Mobilities and Migration

This series is dedicated to the growing and important area of mobilities and migration within Development Studies. It promotes innovative and interdisciplinary research targeted at a global readership.

The series welcomes submissions from established and junior authors on cutting-edge and high-level research on key topics that feature in global news and public debate.

These include the Arab spring; famine in the Horn of Africa; riots; environmental migration; development-induced displacement and resettlement; livelihood transformations; people-trafficking; health and infectious diseases; employment; South-South migration; population growth; children's well-being; marriage and family; food security; the global financial crisis; drugs wars; and other contemporary crises.

Crisis and Migration
Critical Perspectives
Edited by Anna Lindley

South-South Educational Migration, Humanitarianism and Development
Views from the Caribbean, North Africa and the Middle East
Elena Fiddian-Qasmiyeh

Organizational Perspectives on Environmental Migration
Edited by François Gemenne and Kerstin Rosenow-Williams

A Gendered Approach to the Syrian Refugee Crisis
Edited by Jane Freedman, Zeynep Kivilcim and Nurcan Ozgur Baklacıoğlu

South-South Migration
Emerging Patterns, Opportunities and Risks
Edited by Patricia Short, Moazzem Hossain and M. Adil Khan

Living with Floods in a Mobile Southeast Asia
A Political Ecology of Vulnerability, Migration and Environmental Change
Edited by Carl Middleton, Rebecca Elmhirst and Supang Chantavanich

Living with Floods in a Mobile Southeast Asia
A Political Ecology of Vulnerability, Migration and Environmental Change

Edited by Carl Middleton, Rebecca Elmhirst and Supang Chantavanich

First published 2018
by Routledge
2 Park Square, Milton Park, Abingdon, Oxon OX14 4RN

and by Routledge
711 Third Avenue, New York, NY 10017

Routledge is an imprint of the Taylor & Francis Group, an informa business

© 2018 selection and editorial matter, Carl Middleton, Rebecca Elmhirst and Supang Chantavanich; individual chapters, the contributors

The right of Carl Middleton, Rebecca Elmhirst and Supang Chantavanich to be identified as the authors of the editorial material, and of the authors for their individual chapters, has been asserted in accordance with sections 77 and 78 of the Copyright, Designs and Patents Act 1988.

All rights reserved. No part of this book may be reprinted or reproduced or utilised in any form or by any electronic, mechanical, or other means, now known or hereafter invented, including photocopying and recording, or in any information storage or retrieval system, without permission in writing from the publishers.

Trademark notice: Product or corporate names may be trademarks or registered trademarks, and are used only for identification and explanation without intent to infringe.

British Library Cataloguing-in-Publication Data
A catalogue record for this book is available from the British Library

Library of Congress Cataloging-in-Publication Data
A catalog record for this book has been requested

ISBN: 978-1-138-79324-8 (hbk)
ISBN: 978-1-315-76143-5 (ebk)

Typeset in Goudy
by Apex CoVantage, LLC

Front cover image by Rachanon Intharaksa

Printed and bound by CPI Group (UK) Ltd, Croydon, CR0 4YY

Contents

List of acronyms vii
Author biographies ix
Acknowledgements xiii

1 Migration and floods in Southeast Asia: a mobile political ecology of vulnerability, resilience and social justice   1
   REBECCA ELMHIRST, CARL MIDDLETON AND BERNADETTE P. RESURRECCIÓN

2 Living with the flood: a political ecology of fishing, farming, and migration around Tonle Sap Lake, Cambodia   22
   CARL MIDDLETON AND BORIN UN

3 Migrants seeking out and living with floods: a case study of Mingalar Kwet Thet settlement, Yangon, Myanmar   42
   MAXIME BOUTRY

4 Risky spaces, vulnerable households, and mobile lives in Laos: *Quo vadis* flooding and migration?   63
   ALBERT SALAMANCA, OUTHAI SOUKKHY, JOSHUA RIGG AND JACQUELINE ERNEROT

5 Living with and against floods in Bangkok and Thailand's central plain   89
   NARUEMON THABCHUMPON AND NARUMON ARUNOTAI

6 Generating vulnerability to floods: poor urban migrants and the state in Metro Manila, Philippines   105
   EDSEL E. SAJOR, BERNADETTE P. RESURRECCIÓN AND SHARON FELIZA ANN P. MACAGBA

7 Responses to flooding: Migrants' perspectives in Hanoi, Vietnam   127
   NGUYEN TUAN ANH AND PHAM QUANG MINH

8 Flooding in a city of migrants: ethnicity and entitlement in
   Bandar Lampung, Indonesia   146
   REBECCA ELMHIRST AND ARI DARMASTUTI

9 Vulnerabilities of local people and migrants due to flooding in
   Malaysia: identifying gaps for better management   167
   MOHAMMAD IMAM HASAN REZA, ER AH CHOY AND JOY JACQUELINE PEREIRA

10 Floods and migrants: synthesis and implications for policy   188
   LOUIS LEBEL, SUPANG CHANTAVANICH AND WERASIT SITTITRAI

   Index   198

Acronyms

ACCCRN	Asian Cities Climate Change Resilience Network
BAPPENAS	Badan Perencanaan Pembangunan Nasional (National Development Planning Board [Indonesia])
BMA	Bangkok Metropolitan Administration
CCT	Conditional cash transfer
CDEV	Community-driven enterprise development
DID	Department of Irrigation and Drainage (Malaysia)
DPWH	Department of Public Works and Highways (Philippines)
DRR	Disaster risk reduction
DSWD	Department of Social Welfare and Development (Philippines)
FDA	Foundation for Development Alternatives
FROC	Flood Relief Operations Centre (Thailand)
ID	Identification card
IOM	International Organization of Migration
ISRP	Informal Sector Relocation Program (Philippines)
IWRM	Integrated Water Resources Management
JICA	Japan International Cooperation Agency
Lao PDR	Lao People's Democratic Republic
MMDA	Metro Manila Development Authority
MMK	Myanmar kyat
MOF	Ministry of Finance (Malaysia)
MoAI	Ministry of Agriculture and Irrigation (Myanmar)
NGO	Nongovernmental organization
NHA	National Housing Authority of Thailand
NSC	National Security Council (Malaysia)
NSCB	National Statistics Coordination Board (Philippines)
NSO	National Statistics Office (Philippines)
NT2	Nam Theun 2 Dam
RASKIN	Beras untuk orang miskin (rice for the poor) (Indonesia)
RGC	Royal Government of Cambodia
RM	Malaysian ringgit
ROSCA	Rotating Savings and Credit Association (Laos)
Rp	Indonesian rupiah

SLORC	State Law and Order Restoration Council (Myanmar)
SLP	Sustainable Livelihood Program (Philippines)
SPDC	State Peace and Development Council (Myanmar)
THB	Thai baht
USDP	Union Solidarity Development Party (Myanmar)
VCI	Vulnerability and capacity index
VND	Vietnamese dong
YCDC	Yangon City Development Committee

Author biographies

Narumon Arunotai is an anthropologist at Chulalongkorn University Social Research Institute (CUSRI). She is the head of the Research Unit on Cultural Dynamics and Ethnicity. Her main research areas are on cultural heritage and adaptation, indigenous knowledge and disaster risk reduction, indigenous peoples and alternative development and community rights and collaborative resource management.

Maxime Boutry obtained a PhD in social anthropology and ethnology at the School for Higher Studies in Social Sciences (EHESS, Paris) in 2007. His research seeks to explore forms of continuity in the sociocultural changes affecting Burmese society through the study of 'frontiers' (borderlands, transition spaces). He is a research associate with the Centre for Asian Studies (CASE-CNRS), and he also works in applied anthropology in the fields of migration, land tenure and development.

Supang Chantavanich Professor Emeritus at the Faculty of Political Science at Chulalongkorn University, and adviser to the Asian Research Center for Migration. Dr. Supang received her PhD in sociology from the University of Grenoble in France and has over 25 years of experience leading and advising research projects and influencing migration policy on displacement and migration in Thailand. In her early experience, she examined issues such as asylum and resettlement of Indochinese refugees in the 1980s, and social and economic considerations of repatriation and responses to trafficking in person along the borders. More recently Dr. Supang has focused on the migration and development nexus where she examines the interplay between environment and migration, labour migration, human trafficking and private-sector labour practices.

Er Ah Choy is a professor in the Faculty of Social Sciences and Humanities, Universiti Kebangsaan Malaysia. Currently, she also holds the post of Associate Dean of Quality Assurance, Audit and Ranking within the faculty. Er's expertise is in the area of environmental policy and management. Er's sectoral foci are on the oil palm and palm oil chain and ecotourism chain. This also includes communities that are directly and indirectly involved with these chains. In addition, this also has extended to the realm of public health with particular focus on policy pertaining to dengue.

Ari Darmastuti is a lecturer and chairperson of the Masters Programme of Government Science in the Faculty of Social and Political Sciences, University of Lampung, Indonesia. Her research interests focus on gender and environment, politics and women's human rights.

Rebecca Elmhirst is a reader in human geography at the University of Brighton, UK. Her research interests lie in feminist political ecology, and the gender dimensions of natural resource governance, displacement and migration in Indonesia.

Jacqueline Ernerot is an environmental adviser at the SIDA Helpdesk for Environment and Climate Change at the Swedish University of Agricultural Sciences (SLU) in Uppsala, Sweden. Her research interests include global environmental change, the linkages between disaster risk reduction, gender and development and sustainable livelihoods in both developed and developing countries. Jacqueline holds a BA in geography from Stockholm University, Sweden, and a MSc in rural development and natural resource management from SLU.

Louis Lebel is the director of the Unit for Social and Environmental Research (USER) in the Faculty of Social Sciences, Chiang Mai University. His research includes water governance, sustainable aquaculture, climate change adaptation, science and technology studies, public health and environmental politics. He is coeditor of the journal *Global Environmental Change* and subject editor for the journals *WIREs Climate Change* and *Ecology & Society*.

Sharon Feliza Ann P. Macagba is an Environmental Planner and Assistant Professor at the Department of Community and Environmental Resource Planning of the College of Human Ecology, University of the Philippines Los Banos (UPLB). Her research interests include urban environmental management; community-based planning; indigenous knowledge and culture and local planning; and, disaster risk reduction management issues.

Carl Middleton is Assistant Professor and Deputy Director for Research Affairs on the MA in International Development Studies (MAIDS) Program, and Director of the Center for Social Development Studies (CSDS), in the Faculty of Political Science, Chulalongkorn University, Thailand. His research interests orientate around the politics and policy of the environment in Southeast Asia, with a particular focus on environmental justice and the political ecology of water and energy.

Nguyen Tuan Anh is an associate professor at the Faculty of Sociology, University of Social Sciences and Humanities, Vietnam National University, Hanoi.

The emphasis in Nguyen Tuan Anh's work is on kinship relations and social and economic change in villages in northern Vietnam, although he has recently extended his research to livelihood adaptations in the context of climate change.

Joy Jacqueline Pereira is Professor and Principal Research Fellow at Universiti Kebangsaan Malaysia's Southeast Asia Disaster Prevention Research Initiative (SEADPRI-UKM) and Fellow of the Academy of Sciences Malaysia. She is Vice-Chair of the Intergovernmental Panel on Climate Change (IPCC) Working Group 2 on Impacts, Adaptation and Vulnerability and a member of the UN-ISDR Asia Science, Technology and Academic Group (ASTAAG).

Pham Quang Minh is Professor of history and politics at the University of Social Sciences and Humanities (USSH), Vietnam National University (VNU), Hanoi. After receiving his PhD in Southeast Asian studies from Humboldt University in Berlin, Germany, in 2002, he became Deputy Dean, and then Dean of the Faculty of International Studies. In 2012, he was promoted to Vice Rector, and in January 2016 he was promoted to the president of USSH, VNU-Hanoi. His main teaching and research interests, among the other things, are world politics, international relations of the Asia-Pacific region and Vietnam's foreign policy.

Bernadette P. Resurrección is Senior Research Fellow at the Stockholm Environment Institute (SEI) and coleader of SEI's global Gender and Social Equity Programme. For more than 15 years, she has researched on gender, natural resource management, livelihoods, climate change adaptation, disasters and mobility in Vietnam, the Philippines, Thailand and Cambodia. Her current research interests include studying gender professionals in techno-scientific, development and environment research and policy fields, as well as disaster and large-scale economic land concession displacements from a feminist political ecology perspective.

Mohammad Imam Hasan Reza is a senior fellow in the Southeast Asia Disaster Prevention Research Initiative (SEADPRI), Institute for Environment and Development (LESTARI), Universiti Kebangsaan Malaysia. His research encompasses integrating knowledge of ecological and environmental processes with multifaceted socioeconomic factors in the Southeast Asian region, with a particular focus on environmental management, decision support systems, disaster management and sustainability.

Joshua Rigg is a PhD candidate at SOAS University of London, currently researching the politics of political transition in Tunisia.

Edsel E. Sajor is currently an associate professorial lecturer in the Faculty of Political Science at De La Salle University, Manila, and an adjunct associate professor of the Asian Institute of Technology, Bangkok. His research interests are in urban environmental management, urban governance, peri-urban development and cities and climate change studies in the Philippines, Thailand, Indonesia and Vietnam.

Albert Salamanca is a senior research fellow at the Stockholm Environment Institute (SEI) where he leads its research cluster on climate change adaptation and manages its initiative Transforming Development and Disaster Risk. He is also involved in other SEI initiatives on climate services and climate finance. His research interests include adaptation to global environmental change, sustainable livelihoods, de-agrarianisation, migration and disaster risk reduction. Albert has a PhD from Durham University (UK).

Werasit Sittitrai is Assistant Professor and currently an advisor on strategy at the Office of National Research Council of Thailand, and a board member of the Thailand Environment Institute Foundation. He is also the vice-president and founding member of the AIDS Society for Asia and the Pacific Foundation, and until recently was chair of UNAIDS Monitoring and Evaluation Reference Group (MERG), UNAIDS, Geneva. Previously, he was Director of the Department of Policy and Strategy at the Thai Red Cross Society, and for 10 years, he held high-level positions in UNAIDS, Geneva. Werasit received his PhD from the University of Hawaii, USA. His areas of expertise include disease prevention and control, behavioural research, organisation reengineering and disaster preparedness and response, as well as policy and strategy development and evaluation.

Outhai Soukkhy is Deputy Director of the Northern Agriculture and Forestry College (NAFC), and a consultant for NAFC's 27 farms that cover agronomy, livestock and fishery, agribusiness and forestry. He is also responsible for student income generation and administration. His research interests orientate around hydropower, agriculture production and agriculture land use in Southeast Asia.

Naruemon Thabchumpon is an assistant professor in politics and director of the Master of Arts in International Development Studies (MAIDS) at the Faculty of Political Science of Chulalongkorn University. Recently, she was appointed the director of the Asian Research Centre for Migration (ARCM) of the Institute of Asian Studies, Chulalongkorn University. She is the author of numerous publications with a focus on the roles of civil society in relation to democracy and development in the Association of Southeast Asian Nations (ASEAN).

Borin Un is a research fellow with a focus on water governance, natural resource management and livelihood development policies in Cambodia. Since 2011, Borin has conducted several studies on sustainable fishery and agricultural management around Tonle Sap Lake. His main research interest is the emergence of migration and livelihood transitions around Tonle Sap Lake.

Acknowledgements

This book emerged spontaneously amongst a group of researchers who joined a conference on environmental change and migration at Chulalongkorn University, organised by the Asian Research Center for Migration in December 2011. The long-planned conference was almost cancelled due to the severe flooding in Thailand at that time, which created a particular salience for the conference's theme, and resulted in the conception of our study on mobile political ecologies of flooding in Southeast Asia.

The project that subsequently emerged was generously supported by the Rockefeller Foundation, for which we are very grateful. In particular, we would like to thank Pariphan Uawithya and Busaba Tejagupta for their support and patience for the project.

At the Stockholm Environment Institute (SEI)–Asia Center, we would like to thank Annette Huber-Lee, Eric Kemp-Benedict, Chayanis Krittasudthacheewa, Albert Salamanca, Miaojie Sun and Papassara Kunjara for their contribution and support. The Laos case study, together with building a database for compilation of our quantitative data, was kindly supported by the SEI–Asia Center. Additional support was provided by SEI's Initiative on Transforming Development and Disaster Risk to enable a wider dissemination of this book and support its goal of promoting transformative thinking in understanding how risks are created within development.

At Earthscan-Routledge, we would like to sincerely thank our commissioning editor, Tim Hardwick, and editors, Ashley Wright and Amy Johnston. We genuinely appreciate their patient support and gentle encouragement over the prolonged duration of producing this book.

Within the Asian Research Center for Migration, we would like to thank Aungkana Kamonpetch and Suda Santisewekul for their administrative support for the project. For expertly producing and revising the maps in this book, we would like to thank Joy A. Anacta.

Finally, we would like to thank all of the interviewees, including community leaders and members, government officials and civil society groups, who shared their time and insights in undertaking our research. We hope that the outcome of our work has contributed towards a deeper and more nuanced understanding of the challenges and opportunities faced by migrants experiencing flooding and other forms of environmental change, and will furthermore help inform public policies in support of them.

1 Migration and floods in Southeast Asia

A mobile political ecology of vulnerability, resilience and social justice

Rebecca Elmhirst, Carl Middleton and Bernadette P. Resurrección

Introduction

Flooding is a common experience in monsoonal regions of Southeast Asia, where diverse flood regimes have for centuries shaped agrarian and fisheries-based livelihoods. From the pronounced seasonality of wet-season rice cultivation through to the rhythms of the flood pulse of the region's mighty rivers that links agriculture and wild-capture fisheries across extensive wetlands, the movement of water has historically played an important part in shaping the seasonal movement of people. However, in recent public discourse, the link between flooding and migration is most often made with regard to catastrophic flood events. News images and personal experience of frequent and intense weather-related flood events in the region's low-lying megacity and delta regions in recent years has contributed to a perceived link between extreme environmental events and mass migration through displacement. Such perceptions have been lent authority by high-profile expert reports around the impacts of climate change and its likely effects on migration flows, such as Myers (2002), and in the early meetings of the Intergovernmental Panel on Climate Change, where it was argued that projected sea-level rise would place a third of the population of Southeast Asia at risk of coastal flooding (Hugo and Bardsley, 2014).

The spectre of flood-induced mass displacement, particularly when associated with climate change, remains firmly established within public discourse (CNN, 2012). Images relayed via the world's media of the devastating impact of various types of catastrophic floods – for example, Cyclone Nargis in the Ayeyarwady Division of Myanmar in May 2008, countrywide flooding in Thailand including of Bangkok in late 2011 and Typhoon Haiyan in the Philippines in November 2013 – have served to cement the link between catastrophic floods, mass displacement and unplanned distress migration in the public imagination. Yet, this focus on mass displacement frames migration in largely negative terms. Mobility is seen as a failure of adaptation to a changing environment, with both transborder and internal population mobility even regarded by some as a security issue, 'lying within the realm of the military and the protection of sovereignty' (Ransan-Cooper et al., 2015: 110).

Yet, other kinds of stories linking migration and this catastrophic type of flood do emerge, and these point to the need for a more nuanced and plural account of migration and mobility in relation to flood disasters. For example, shortly after Typhoon Haiyan, it became evident that Filipino migrants working abroad were finding ways of helping those back home who were affected by the disaster, bringing to bear not only their economic remittances but also their cultural and political capital in holding those responsible for the official disaster response to account (Mosuela and Matias, 2014). Thus, complex and seemingly contradictory links between migration and flood-related vulnerabilities emerged from this and similar events.

Recent influential comparative studies, many focusing on climate change rather than floods *per se*, have sought to challenge simplistic and inaccurate assessments of the links between environmental hazards and accelerated rates of cross-border and transnational migration (Black et al., 2011; Warner and Afifi, 2014; Adger et al., 2015). Much of this work has drawn attention to the role of migration as an adaptive response, rather than a failure to adapt (e.g. Tacoli, 2009; Bardsley and Hugo, 2010; Dun, 2011). Migrants are reframed from being hazard victims to being 'adaptive agents' (Ransan-Cooper et al., 2015): a framing which is very much linked to wider discourses around livelihood diversification where migration is seen as a resilience-building strategy (de Haas, 2012; Rigg and Oven, 2015). Indeed, it is argued that 'immobility' is more of a problem in the face of environmental change, where 'trapped' populations (i.e. those without the resources needed to move out of harm's way) are especially vulnerable to catastrophic environmental events (Black et al., 2011; Findlay, 2012). Moreover, strong measures to regulate and limit population movement and minimize entitlements of those who have migrated or who are able to be mobile may also undermine livelihoods in very specific and frequently unjust ways (Tacoli, 2009; Black et al., 2011). Some warn that framing migrants as adaptive agents can also feed into an apolitical and neoliberal discourse of self-help and self-improvement, without addressing wider questions of social justice and structures of social and political power that 'make' different categories of migrants (Oliver-Smith, 2012; Felli and Castree, 2012). Indeed, even as simplistic views of migration are being challenged in recent work, the environment and human-environment relations remain relatively undertheorised and depoliticised (Greiner and Sakdapolrak, 2015).

In Southeast Asia, donor attention is being directed towards building resilience to climate change–related hazards (including flood hazards) in rural and urban areas (Bulkeley et al., 2011; ADB, 2011; Rockefeller Foundation, 2016), and this is taking place in tandem with (and in response to) a growing evidence base demonstrating changes to the region's hydrological cycle and extreme weather patterns that are predicted to further impact on the region's livelihoods (Zhaung et al., 2013). The Association of Southeast Asian Nations (ASEAN) too is seeking to shape a common policy framework for dealing with events such as flood disasters (di Floristella, 2015). However, for such projects and policy on flood mitigation and disaster preparedness to be effective and socially just, a multidimensional and qualified framing of migration is required.

Given these developments, the purpose of this book it to respond to the need for a nuanced understanding of the connections between flooding and migration in Southeast Asia. Our aim is to complicate simple readings of environmental change – in particular, flooding – as a singular driver of migration by exploring a diversity of flood-migration-vulnerability assemblages. Thus, we aim also to sensitise flood-hazard policy agendas to the complexities of migration and mobility in Southeast Asia.

In this chapter, we propose a 'mobile political ecology' conceptual framework for understanding how migration links to vulnerability and resilience across diverse environmental, social and policy contexts. Our conceptualisation has been developed, tested and refined through the undertaking of a diverse set of rural and urban empirical studies in Cambodia, Myanmar, Laos, Thailand, the Philippines, Vietnam, Indonesia and Malaysia set out in Chapters 2 to 9 of this book. The policy implications are discussed in Chapter 10.

In the next two sections, we briefly outline migration followed by flooding in Southeast Asia. We then introduce and critically review the organising concepts of our conceptual approach, namely vulnerability, resilience and political ecology. Next, we consider flooding and migration as a nexus to propose our conceptual lens of 'mobile political ecology'. We then outline the book's methodological approach of 'progressive contextualisation' to trace vulnerability in migration-flood contexts. Finally, having established the conceptual lens and methodology, we briefly summarise the empirical cases presented in subsequent chapters.

Migration and mobility in Southeast Asia

A starting point for this book is recognition of the diversity of forms of migration in Southeast Asia: a region long characterised by population mobility, including local, cross-border and transnational migration. Migration-based livelihoods in contemporary Southeast Asia are now made possible by increasingly accessible forms of geographical mobility, including rural-urban, rural-rural and transnational (Elmhirst, 2008; Rigg, 2012). Whilst some migration is exceptional, brought about by economic, environmental and sociopolitical shocks, much movement in the region occurs as everyday practice: short term, long term or permanent, or as circular, involving seasonal movements between different localities. Everyday mobilities form part of a broader effort to spread risk and adjust to long-term livelihood stresses, but they may also occur as part of individual or household aspirational strategies.

Increasingly, livelihoods are conducted on a multilocal basis, whereby households distribute their labour across multiple locations in order to maximise incomes and minimise risk (Rigg, 2012).[1] Multilocal livelihoods are held together and facilitated by social networks and, in some instances, are established as part of livelihood routines, for example as reflected in the seasonality of agricultural labour demand. Whilst income diversification is seen as a key strategy for mitigating livelihood risks, shocks and stresses,[2] multilocal livelihoods allow people to spread environmental, economic and political risk across different spaces, including in the context of more frequent flooding and uncertainty (Resurrección and Sajor, 2015).

Reflecting the aforementioned, this book adheres to a framing that gives emphasis to migration as an 'already significant phenomenon' (Black et al., 2011: 2), rather than as an isolated, one-off response to flood events.

Floods in Southeast Asia

A second starting point of this book is to develop a more nuanced approach towards floods in Southeast Asia. Rather than assuming floods equate with catastrophe, we see floods as extremely varied and can be negative or positive in impact. Diverse experiences of floods reflect in part the complex nature of flooding in the region, where flood events include seasonal floodplain inundation, irregular riverbank overflow, flash floods in urban areas, landslides and flash floods in mountain areas, coastal floods and tsunamis (Lebel and Sinh, 2009).

The experience of these different types of flooding varies distinctly between groups of people according to their livelihood, location, socioeconomic status and level of political voice. For example, farmers and fishers in rural areas hold a very different relationship with floods to those who live and work in urban or peri-urban areas. In some places, floods are beneficial and bring means to livelihood, as is the case around Cambodia's Tonle Sap Lake where fishers and farmers depend on the annual flood cycle for the vitality of the wild-capture fisheries and floodplain agriculture (Middleton, 2012).

Flood events can also be destructive, however, in both rural and urban areas. Destructive floods disproportionately affect those from lower socioeconomic groups with less political power (Wisner et al., 1994). The effects of floods can be mitigated or exacerbated by institutionalised disaster-response strategies (or the lack thereof), as well as shaped by broader long-term development planning policies and decisions. As Lebel et al. (2011) have shrewdly observed, risk reduction for some can result in risk redistribution to others.

More broadly, the region's development pathway has 'produced' floods. Thus, rather than see a flood as a wholly natural phenomenon, we recognise that policy decisions and their consequences – for example around urban growth, industrial and infrastructure development, deforestation and land and coastal degradation – contribute to the nature and frequency of floods. This perspective aligns with relational approaches to nature that have coalesced within the field of political ecology that this book adopts. Political ecology points towards the social and political processes that produce 'risky environments' and recognises 'nature' as a material force (Wisner et al., 1994; Pelling, 2003; Braun, 2006; Collins, 2009; Marks, 2015).

Thus, a second core concern when conceptualising migration and floods is to ensure that the complexities of floods, as socionatural phenomena, are sufficiently appreciated, and that a simple overemphasis on floods as catastrophic 'natural hazards' is avoided. Moreover, we seek to emphasise that people's 'vulnerability' to flooding often reflects a larger story of socioeconomic and political inequality.

Linking migration and mobility to a political ecology of floods

A conceptually sound approach towards the multiple ways floods intersect with migration in different Southeast Asian contexts must hold in play both the complexities of migration and mobility, and the complexities of floods as socionatural phenomena. In this section, we outline our organising concepts for a 'mobile political ecology', namely vulnerability, resilience and political ecology. Given the plural definitions and approaches in each of these terms, we undertake a brief critical engagement with existing literature to arrive at our use of these concepts.

Vulnerability

Vulnerability – 'the social precarity found on the ground when hazards arrive' (Ribot, 2014: 667) – is useful as a central organising concept, as it provides a lens for viewing the intersections between flooding and migration. 'Vulnerability' is a concept that holds sway for migration researchers, as well as for those researching the impacts of natural hazards such as floods, and as such, is a conceptual boundary object through which the two aspects of our book – floods and migration – may converge.

'Vulnerability science' has emerged as a catch-all phrase that includes a wide range of natural and social scientific approaches to vulnerability, which share a desire to understand 'what makes people, places, and societies vulnerable to a range of environmental threats' (Cutter, 2003: 9). Whilst Wisner et al. (1994: 11) define vulnerability as 'the characteristics of a person or group and their situation that influence their capacity to anticipate, cope with, resist and recover from the impact of a natural hazard', there have been many iterations, reflecting particular ideological positions and different disciplinary concerns (Adger, 2006). These include human capital or neoliberal approaches that regard vulnerability as an outcome or a quality held by individuals, which contrasts with perspectives that emphasize the processes that produce vulnerability (e.g. capital accumulation, property relations and social and political marginalisation) (Pelling, 2003; Collins, 2009). Furthermore, there are a range of approaches that reflect different disciplinary backgrounds, with dominant approaches including those from a hazards tradition, which focuses on the political economy of environmental risks and human responses (Wisner et al., 1994), and a sustainable livelihoods, entitlements and capabilities-based approach. The latter perspective draws on Sen (1997) to focus on the social realm of institutions, well-being and household assets or capacities (Bebbington, 1999; Kabeer et al., 2010), a perspective that has also been taken up by migration scholars (e.g. Julca, 2011). Recent debate has focused on the ways in which the hazard tradition does not deal explicitly with human agency, capabilities and the role of institutions (including social capital, social networks, institutions associated with governance), whilst livelihoods, entitlements, capabilities-based approaches underplay the materiality of nature and ecological or physical risk (Adger, 2006).

Tacoli (2009) outlines a 'livelihoods approach' to migration, in which mobility may be part of a wider household or individual strategy to reduce vulnerability and diversify income sources, including as a response to environmental, economic or political shocks and stresses (see also McDowell and de Haan, 1997). This framing gives particular emphasis to the capitals (assets or capacities) of individuals and households, and the ability to realise the benefits of these, as critical in shaping the shape and success (or otherwise) of livelihood strategies. These include human capital (labour resources, skills, health and education), financial capital (including remittances and access to credit) and social and political capital (which mediate access to material assets and to institutions, such as government or traditional authorities).

The chances of reducing vulnerabilities through migration depend in part on the characteristics (or 'the capitals') of those migrating, and also on forms of governance that either facilitate or inhibit mobility – for example, immigration controls, household registration systems and the capacities of migrants to draw on new social networks in areas to which they have relocated. However, 'capitals' or assets in the place of origin (e.g. social networks, knowledge or employment skills) may have limited purchase in the area of destination. Heikkilä (2005) refers to this as 'mobile vulnerability', which reflects the cultural nature of migrant vulnerability, deriving from stereotypes, prejudices, ignorance and institutional discrimination, that produces spatial vulnerabilities for those regarded as 'out of place' and therefore unable to access to limited resources, whether this is housing, employment or access to state services. Furthermore, entitlements may be nontransferable between different geographical locations. In other words, when people move to new places, their identity as migrants can lead to their access to social, political, economic and environmental resources becoming uneven and problematic. These 'citizenship effects' are not restricted to cross-border or transnational migration but may also be apparent in internal migration contexts, particularly in ethnically diverse countries, where the precariousness of livelihoods for migrants in urban areas may be quite marked.

On the other hand, as Schade (2013) points out, migration may not therefore always be an expression of vulnerability, but can also be a manifestation of 'capability': in Sen's terms, the ability to choose and live a life that a person values (Sen, 1997), and in this instance, the ability to choose whether to stay put or move. Migration is also a way through which individuals build social capital (through their engagement in social networks, their involvement with new labour markets and their exposure to other ways of life). However, the idea that migration reflects 'capability' needs to be investigated, and not assumed. This leads us away from a straightforward framing of migrants as 'adaptive agents' (where this implies they hold a responsibility to alter their behaviour) and towards what Ransan-Cooper et al. (2015) describe as a framing of migrants as 'political subjects'. Capabilities may be seen in terms of political and material control over one's environment – in other words, the freedoms needed to avoid risk and to influence those who govern and the broader political economic system (Ribot, 2014: 687).

The efficacy of migration in reducing vulnerability is strongly linked to intermediary factors, including the ties that households and individuals might have with other places, people and labour markets, and the formal and informal institutions that shape these (e.g. family and kinship reciprocal relationships, labour recruiters and so on). The social dynamics of migration, when understood in this way, also involve processes of exclusion: migrant networks are themselves power laden (through gender, generation and ethnicity), and the ability to invoke or actualise such networks may be unevenly distributed within social groups (Ribot and Peluso, 2003). As Kabeer et al. (2010: 2) put it, in developing a relational conceptualisation of vulnerability,

> not all forms of vulnerability can be conceptualised in terms of exposure to shock episodes or assessed in terms of fluctuations in income or consumption flows. Social relationships can give rise to forms of inequality in which some groups are positioned as subordinate to others through processes of economic exploitation, social exclusion and political marginalisation.

In some Southeast Asian contexts, social protection is available only through client relationships with more powerful individuals within communities. Kinship, gender, age, ethnicity and citizenship status thus take on a particular salience.

Furthermore, migration needs to be understood in relation to household and community assets, and therefore is a strategy that is unevenly available. This tempers some of the overly celebratory approaches to migration sometimes seen in development thinking. The ways in which migration may condition access to or exclusion from resources and rights, and can locate migrants within risky environments, point to a need to adopt conceptualisations of vulnerability that emphasise questions of social exclusion and 'flexible citizenship' (Hogan and Marandola, 2005).

Thus, a central approach to this book is to identify and analyse the types of vulnerabilities of people living in communities that experience flooding. Such vulnerabilities might be associated with the sociopolitical features of flood events, as well as with more general social and political vulnerabilities associated with poverty, precarity and marginalisation (e.g. a lack of access to secure forms of livelihood, exclusion from political processes). At the same time, we ask, what kinds of capacities and assets, resources and 'capitals' (to draw from Bebbington's, 1999 terminology) are available to households and communities in relation to flooding, and how might these shape their capacity to adapt and rebound – to be resilient – to environmental shocks and stresses?

Resilience

The search for a more holistic perspective has drawn some authors towards 'resilience thinking', where resilience is seen by some as dialectically related to vulnerability (Oliver-Smith, 2012). Within resilience thinking, the emphasis is on social-ecological systems and their ability to absorb or buffer disturbances and retain their core attributes, and on a system's capacity for learning and adaptation in the context of change (Miller et al., 2010).

A potential point of convergence between resilience thinking and livelihoods or entitlements versions of vulnerability analysis lies in the attention each pays to the role of governance and institutions, which are seen as holding the key to reducing social and environmental vulnerabilities by enhancing the resilience of social-ecological systems. This dimension of resilience thinking has been explored by Lebel et al. (2006), who find empirical support for improved resilience where social-ecological governance is through participatory, deliberative, multilayered and accessible institutions, and where there is recognition of the trade-offs made in relation to social and environmental priorities.

One stream of 'resilience thinking', however, has been derived from ecological economics, with an emphasis on rational choice theory and concepts such as social capital, and this has meant a tendency towards insufficient attention being paid to the analysis of interests, power and social identity (Turner, 2014). Resilience understood this way tends to align with neoliberal discourses of decreased state involvement and limited accountability, and increased individual and community self-reliance in relation to environmental challenges. Moreover, if 'resilience' is read as system stability, there is a risk that this may translate into the maintenance of a socially regressive social-ecological status quo, thus sidestepping issues of social and environmental justice (Cretney, 2014). In other words, critical elements of vulnerability analysis – processes leading to exclusion and marginalisation – may slip from view: an omission that is particularly problematic when analysing migration and migrant-based livelihoods.

In this book, whilst holding in play ideas about socioecological systems and relationships (Folke, 2006), we seek to contribute to an emerging critical perspective on resilience where we see resilience as socially uneven, multiscalar and politically embedded (Cote and Nightingale, 2012; Cretney, 2014). Our conceptual framework, therefore, places marginalisation and exclusion as central concerns in our analysis of how vulnerabilities are produced through the sociopolitical dynamics of human-environment interactions at various scales and mediated by relevant institutions.

A political ecology of floods

Whilst resilience thinking provides a useful starting point for considering social-ecological systems, we build on and extend this perspective through a political ecology approach that focuses attention on questions of power and politics in relation to environment-society relations. Political ecology is an umbrella term used to identify a broad and eclectic realm of scholarship and practice 'which seeks to understand the complex relations between nature and society through a careful analysis of forms of access and control over resources, and their implications for environmental health and sustainable livelihoods' (Watts, 2000: 257).

As Oliver-Smith (2012) has argued, understanding environmental change and its effects (including in relation to migration) requires a reframing of how environment-society relations are understood (also Greiner and Sakdapolrak, 2015). Social vulnerability to disasters, including flooding, brings to fore the economic system that lies at the crux of human-environment relations and consequent degradation and disaster. Instead of seeing each as separate and external to one another, environment and society should be seen as inseparable and mutually reinforcing, implicated in each other's vulnerability and resilience (Robbins, 2012: 59).

In contrast to much resilience thinking, political ecology emphasises the exercise of power in society and as a force that shapes material engagement with the biophysical world (Turner, 2014). A key concern is the role of political economy in producing particular environments (and, by extension, environmental vulnerabilities), and in underpinning the discourses and practices through which environments (and thus environmental vulnerabilities) are governed and managed (Felli and Castree, 2012). Political ecology focuses on the distribution and contestation of power and resources in relation to nature and socially produced environments, and in doing so, seeks to render visible and analyse the underlying institutions, incentives and interests that give these their shape. Moreover, most political ecology analyses are explicit in setting out their normative commitments to achieving social and environmental justice (Robbins, 2012).

Political ecologists also often draw attention to the linkages between scales, from the body (the links between bodies, nature and health) to community (mobilisation around questions of environmental justice), and outwards to the state and intrastate relations, including those associated with new forms of environmental governance (e.g. management of transboundary resources, multilateral regulation over climate change). From a political ecology perspective, therefore, the generation of vulnerability, rather than being an inherent property of an individual or social group, or something that "falls from the sky" (Ribot, 2009), is seen as being embedded in a combination of socioecological and political economic factors, both of which take shape through past and contemporary policy environments.

Floods (as a hazard) become 'risky' through their social production, where flood vulnerability is as much an outcome of political decisions and the power relations that surround them as it is the consequence of environmental change (Pelling, 2003: 258; Collins, 2009). The extent to which flooding may be called a 'natural' event is a topic of intense debate, especially when a flood is named as 'destructive' (Lebel and Sinh, 2009; Middleton, 2012). A flood, from the perspective of political ecology, can be viewed as social-natural assemblage that is constructed by the reflexive interaction of ecologies, political and economic power, social organisation and use of technology 'whose intricate geographies form tangled webs of different length, density and duration' (Braun, 2006; see also Robbins, 2012; Pelling, 2003). This contrasts with approaches that place a more singular emphasis on the biophysical properties of an environmental hazard. Thus, although the materiality of 'forces of nature' such as floods cannot be ignored, and indeed may be scaled in ways that exceed human control, political power and social organisation are critical for shaping the natural environment.

A flood-migration nexus

Recent debates on the links between migration and environmental change (especially climate change) have indicated the difficulties in identifying the environment as a singular driver of vulnerability and therefore of migration (Black et al., 2011). With regard to floods, as outlined previously, a political ecology approach links hydrological and related biophysical processes and their science to contested social processes including livelihoods, politics and history, providing an interdisciplinary approach to the analysis of risk, vulnerability and environmental justice.

In this section, we first bring migration and mobility into our political ecology conceptualisation by considering the complex and nuanced ways migration intersects with vulnerability, capacity and capability, resilience and social inequalities. We then outline a methodological strategy of 'progressive contextualization', which involves unpicking the social production of floods through a series of methodological steps, similar to those utilised in recent political ecology work on hazards (e.g. Collins, 2009), and specifically on flood hazards (e.g. Pelling, 2003). We add to these approaches an explicit analysis of the role of migration and migration-based livelihoods in shaping vulnerability and capacity, which has been given insufficient attention in progressive contextualisation approaches to date.

A mobile political ecology

Migration-based livelihoods, in which migration is 'managed' by households, may be an important means by which people avoid or mitigate the effects of environmental catastrophes, through diversifying income, spreading risk spatially and using migrant remittances earned in locations unaffected by the catastrophe. Migration is also a way through which individuals build social capital, including through their engagement in social networks, their involvement with new labour markets and their exposure to other ways of life. Social remittances of this kind may contribute to peoples' 'voice' or capacity to feel empowered sufficiently to make entitlement demands within governance structures when floods take place. Migration may also work as a substitute for the deprivation of *in situ* entitlements (i.e. the resources available to individuals on the basis of their own assets, reciprocal arrangements and relative claims within their society). Thus, there are multiple pathways through which migration may be an asset that contributes to household and individual capability and empowerment, reducing vulnerability and potentially building resilience to future shocks and stresses. It may be argued, therefore, 'to be mobile, whether practiced or not – is an expression of capability' (Schade, 2013: 239).

At the same time, processes associated with migration themselves can produce forms of social vulnerability where the freedom to move – that is, migration as an expression of capability – is tempered by the social and political exclusions in terms of access to rights, recognition and justice that this can bring as people find themselves 'out of place'. Migrants may end up in risky environments in flood-prone cities and thus face new vulnerabilities in place of old ones. Meanwhile, as multilocal livelihoods transcend the spatialities of social-ecological systems, migrants are potentially exposed to a variety of ecological risks beyond the forms of place-based vulnerability identified by Ribot (2014) and others. This form of simultaneous livelihood diversification means households can spread risk, but may also be required to deal simultaneously with different risks. For example, during the 1997 economic crisis in Southeast Asian, multilocal households comprising both rural and urban income sources were subject to a double squeeze, as urban incomes were impacted by layoffs from factories and rural incomes were blighted by drought-related crop failures (Silvey and Elmhirst, 2003). Moreover, some environmental risks (e.g. Typhoon Haiyan in 2013) may be scaled at a level that is beyond the scale of multilocal household coping strategies. A 'mobile political ecology' therefore requires an appreciation of the 'nested and teleconnected' nature of vulnerability in the context of geographical mobility (Adger et al., 2009), where a number of ecological and economic systems may be at work simultaneously in contributing to the vulnerability, capacity (assets and capitals) and resilience of households and individuals.

Importantly, the policy environment cuts across vulnerability, capacity and capability, as the institutional landscape shapes people's access to resources (i.e. assets and the capacity to realise the benefits from these assets), as well as people's capacity to challenge and shape policies. Policies shape the nature of floods (e.g. through the promotion of economic strategies that foster deforestation and urbanisation) and flood responses (as governments seek technical solutions to protect areas from inundation through infrastructure, or seek to relocate people from spaces deemed as risky). Development policies have indirectly given rise to particular forms of migration and multilocal livelihood as marketisation means agrarian livelihoods have given way to wage work and more urbanised forms of income generation, or have facilitated cross-border labour migration from low-wage to higher-wage countries and regions (Nevins and Peluso, 2008).

Tracing vulnerability in migration-flood contexts

Conceptualising vulnerability within different migration-flood contexts points to a methodological strategy of 'progressive contextualisation' (Ribot, 2014), which involves unpicking the *social production of floods* through a series of steps, outlined in this section. This approach, which has guided the analysis of the empirical chapters of this book, is augmented through an analysis of the generative dimensions of vulnerability and capacity that lie within the dynamics of migration and migration-based livelihoods. Rather than seeing vulnerability or capacity as innate characteristics of individuals, households and groups, progressive contextualisation helps identify the social and historical processes that produce these.

12 *Rebecca Elmhirst et al.*

Tracing the 'nature of nature'

In contextualising the linkages between flooding and migration, a first important methodological step in mapping out the generative dimensions of vulnerability is to characterise the type(s) of flooding evident in any particular case, and also to link its temporality to migration as the flood cycle moves from onset, to its peak, its recession and, finally, a return to normal conditions. Ecological or environmental sources of vulnerability can therefore be traced back to the 'nature' of the flood event (as a socially produced phenomenon), and how the characteristics of the ecosystem shape vulnerability. Lebel and Sinh (2009) describe a typology of flood regimes experienced in different places in Southeast Asian, including seasonal floodplain inundation, irregular riverbank overflow, flash floods in urban areas, landslides and flash floods in mountain areas and coastal floods. A political ecology approach also directs attention to the planned and informal 'engineering' of rural and urban landscapes and how they shape flood events, ranging from planned flood control infrastructures to unplanned settlement; these dimensions require exploration through further historical and contemporary contextual analysis as outlined next.

Developing a historical contextualisation of an evolving social context

As Oliver-Smith (2012) has put it, market logics and the structural constraints that these processes reflect are ultimately cultural products: the outcome of decisions and choices made in the past. Hence, consideration must be given to the role of neoliberalism, decentralization, marketization, urbanization and colonial or postcolonial histories and how these have produced particular flood environments in urban, rural and peri-urban landscapes.

Much of the unpredictable flooding currently experienced in rural areas in Southeast Asia could potentially be traced to human actions such as rapid deforestation of critical watersheds and large hydropower dam construction (as well as climate change), fuelled by global and national policies favouring resource exploitation and agricultural intensification, which are themselves reflective of colonial and postcolonial development strategies (Vandergeest and Peluso, 2006). Similarly, in some urban and peri-urban settings in the Southeast Asian region, a combination of rapid property development, industrial expansion and the creation of extensive middle-class housing zones work against and within local hydrological processes, sometimes with catastrophic outcomes (in terms of flooding), the impacts of which vary across social groups.

Moreover, past efforts to manage floods and subsequent disaster responses themselves form part of the wider socionatural context of floods, including urban or rural socionatures. Risk reduction for particular target populations (or spaces deemed worthy of protection) can result in risk redistribution, where nontarget populations find themselves at greater exposure to floodwaters, including migrants that frequently inhabit informal settlements in 'risky spaces', or where flood protection measures disrupt hydrological processes and agro-ecosystems, undermining resilience-building strategies of other groups (Lebel and Sinh, 2009).

Developing a contemporary analysis of power, patronage and unequal access

Following on from this historical contextualisation, the next step is to develop a more contemporary analysis of power, patronage and unequal access (to political, environmental, social and economic assets); the interaction of key political actors; and the role of local (in the context of higher-level) power structures in producing 'flood hazards'. As Robbins (2012: 74) writes,

> powerful actors and interests bend and funnel natural materials and forces into place in order to increase rents, develop properties, fuel growth and control citizens. At the same time, however, these objects and forces enact their own tendencies and interests in surprising ways, as rivers flood neighbourhoods ... and heat waves bake local residents, all with further implications for investment, social action and urban politics. . . . this means that these residents, material, and processes are always politicized in cities [and in rural areas also] and no technical solution or ecological analysis can free them from the struggle of interests that make up the life of a city.

This insight allows us also to explore the impact of flood responses in generating and reproducing vulnerability: the new 'natures' produced through highly technical (and thus power-asymmetrical) approaches that instigate changes to the physical environment by government, donor or corporate interests which without attention to social justice and governance issues may create vulnerabilities for some just as they mitigate the vulnerability of others. Moreover, as people themselves seek to manage floods, perhaps by moving to the city to spread risk in the face of rural flood vulnerabilities, and in turn modify the environment, they again produce new forms of hazard and risk.

Political ecology also highlights the institutional mechanisms through which society's most powerful are able to externalise risks in their pursuit of economic gain, as environmental risk – and the experience of risk – is relocated across scales (Collins, 2009). In respect to both of these dimensions, vulnerability is associated with inadequacies in local governance and inequalities in access to resources of various kinds, each in part reflecting the discipline of market logics that is deepening across the Southeast Asian region (Nevins and Peluso, 2008).

Considering vulnerability through social exclusion and 'flexible citizenship'

In developing a progressive contextualisation of the generative dimensions of vulnerability in migration-flood contexts, an important area for consideration is the vulnerability (and, by extension, capacity) associated with the social dimensions of migration itself. In other words, how does migration condition access to or exclusion from resources and rights? Questions of social exclusion and 'flexible' citizenship are key considerations in this regard (Hogan and Marandola, 2005).

Table 1.1 provides a summary of the elements that make up this part of the analysis of migration in relation to flooding. Migration has a paradoxical

14 *Rebecca Elmhirst et al.*

Table 1.1 Vulnerability and resilience through migration

Vulnerability	Threads of resilience
Household vulnerability • Break of physical family ties, fragmentation, desertion, divorce • Burdens on those left behind • Employment risks for migrants • Social, cultural and economic exclusion • Legitimacy and lack of rights • Vulnerability to displacement and resettlement • Lack of entitlement to social, political and economic resources • Conflict with existing population • Negative impacts of social networks (demands from family and others)	*Household capacity* • Reduction of place-based economic insecurity through remittances • Spreading of risks across different physical, social and economic environments • Impact of social remittances in terms of building human (i.e. knowledge) and social capital • Contribution of migration experience to developing political 'voice' • Capacity to draw on social networks • Elusiveness to authority (keeps open clandestine options for livelihood or further migration)
Community vulnerability • Loss of potential community leaders because of out-migration • Increased interhousehold inequality due to impact of remittances • Loss of community labour (forms of cooperation) because of out-migration • Brain drain (loss of community expertise) • Informal settlement of migrants in areas susceptible to flood hazards	*Community capacity* • Potential for adaptive strategies from remittance receipts • Increased capacity because of migration to manage and avoid environmental risks, including floods

relationship with vulnerability, compounding it in some instances, whilst being a strategy to mitigate its effects in others. As with ecological and social aspects of vulnerability, it is the generative dimensions of migration-based vulnerability that are key in the contextual analytical framework: political and institutional failings, coupled with uneven economic development and power asymmetries, underlie vulnerability.

Converging vulnerabilities: a flood-migration-vulnerability assemblage

Whilst the preceding section presented a step-by-step progressive contextualisation of vulnerability, in this section we consider how different forms of vulnerability (ecological, political, social and migration related) converge and compound one another within each case study of the book. We aim to move away from a simple causal analysis to instead look at the flood-migration-policy nexus as an assemblage of different elements that take shape in different ways in different geographical settings.

As Adamo (2010) notes, the interconnectedness of people and places that is so much a feature of Southeast Asian lives complicates the geography of place-based vulnerability and risk. In short, a 'mobile political ecology' analysis of flooding, migration and vulnerability takes us away from a simple flood-hazard response analysis, and involves instead a mapping out of the interlinkages between socially produced environments, vulnerability and different movements and mobilities (including displacement, commutes, long-term labour migrations, etc.) apparent in specific Southeast Asian contexts.

In Chapter 2, Carl Middleton and Borin Un examine fishing, farming and migration as livelihood strategies around Tonle Sap Lake, Cambodia. In this rural case study, they show how year-to-year differences in the seasonal flood cycle of the lake affect the viability of smallholder farming and family-scale fishing livelihoods differently, and discuss how this shapes decisions over family members migrating. Competition for land and wild-capture fisheries is intense around the lake, the natural resource base is under pressure and rights to access resources are contested. The chapter argues that amongst farming and fishing households, although relatively resilient to the seasonal flooding of Tonle Sap Lake, vulnerability is significant and growing, due to resource exclusion and degradation, and migration is a key strategy in response.

In Chapter 3, Maxime Boutry explores how migrants have sought out and settled land at risk of flooding at the peri-urban fringe of Hlaing Tha Yar township, Yangon, Myanmar, due to the affordable rent and the availability of factory work nearby. Boutry contextualises the chapter to Myanmar's rapidly shifting politics, and how these have produced waves of rural-urban migration and migration across Yangon itself. Life in the informal settlements at the peri-urban fringe offers both new opportunities and vulnerabilities. Relating the chapter to urban land-use planning, one particular vulnerability Boutry identifies is how the process of migrants settling in flooded areas ultimately leads to landlords' investment in improved flood management and towards the land's formalisation. As this process unfolds, rents increase, and the original migrant settlers, unable to afford them, must once again move on.

In Chapter 4, Albert Salamanca and coauthors present case studies of four rural villages in upland and lowland Laos where both flash floods and slow-onset floods occur. Salamanca and coauthors show how *in situ* vulnerabilities are contingent upon the governance of identities, spaces and natural resources. They find that the intersection of flooding and migration in the study sites is not straightforward. There was not a tendency for community members to respond to flooding through mobility. As livelihoods remain closely connected to land, instead of mobility, there was a common desire for secure land rights, improved infrastructure and the comfort of sustainable, fixed livelihoods. This, the authors argue, demonstrates that any person's decision to migrate is complex, and to understand how environmental change may (or may not) shape migration, appreciation of local context – including in rural Laos ethnicity, geography, agrarian transition and the implications of government plans for large-scale infrastructure – is important.

In Chapter 5, Naruemon Thabchumpon and Narumon Arunotai present empirical research on the impacts of the major flood in 2011 in Thailand on three urban, one semiurban and three rural communities. The chapter shows that whilst the rural communities are largely adapted to seasonal flooding, the 2011 flood increased vulnerability due to damage of property and livelihoods. In urban areas, communities were not well prepared and therefore were highly vulnerable. The chapter discusses the contentious politics of how vulnerability was exacerbated by government policy to protect core urban and industrial areas, leaving rural and suburban areas flooded. Thabchumpon and Arunotai find that in the case studies selected the relationship between flooding and mobility is subtle. For example, some, but not all, rural migrants living in urban areas returned to their rural family homes, where living with floods was more feasible.

In Chapter 6, Edsel Sajor and co-authors explore the migration experiences of poor urban migrants and their reasons for settling in flood-prone areas of Malabon City in the Philippines. Their findings show how the current causes of vulnerability must be examined in the context of the urban region and rural provinces from where migrants originate. They suggest that poverty, urban employment and inequitable access to land and housing means the adaptive capacity of migrants to flooding are not only multi-local and multi-level, but also emerge from actions and influences of government in other sectoral policy domains. The authors argue that a transformative approach to flood-risk adaptation requires an understanding of migration dynamics through a broader spatial analysis, and integration with policy domains that lie beyond disaster management and climate change concerns.

In Chapter 7, Nguyen Tuan Anh and Pham Quang Minh consider the linkages between migration, rapid urbanization and floods in Hanoi, Vietnam, in a context where government interventions have sought to 'manage migration' through policies designed to restrict entry to the city, and 'manage floods' by reengineering the city's infrastructure. The authors show how flooding is an integral part of Hanoi's migration dynamic, creating the conditions that make certain areas affordable for low-income migrants as a temporary residence while they build urban livelihoods. Those most vulnerable to flood disasters include migrants who have settled without registering in the city, and who lie outside circuits of government support. It is unlikely that improvements in the city's flood-prevention infrastructure and restrictions on population mobility will address the specific vulnerabilities of this group.

In Chapter 8, Rebecca Elmhirst and Ari Darmastuti investigate the intersection of historical migration, kin networks and clientelism at very localised scales in Bandar Lampung, Indonesia. In this city, a long history of migration continues to resonate in the ethnic networks that shape the political capital people are able to draw on at very localised scales and that enable them to gain access to support during and after flood events. Past migrations also remain significant in the complexities of urban land tenure and the ways in which low-income people 'make space' for themselves in areas close to employment opportunities whilst negotiating flood impacts. Ironically, household and community efforts to tackle floods have become a way of signalling a right to remain in places where formal tenure is unclear.

In Chapter 9, Mohammad Imam Hasan Reza, Er Ah Choy and Joy Jacqueline Pereira examine the impact of severe floods in Johor State, Malaysia, an area of the country which is a key destination for local and international migrants seeking factory employment in the state's industrial zones. Malaysia has recently signed the United Nations' Sendai Framework for Disaster Risk Reduction 2015–2030, which notes migrants as a key stakeholder group. In Malaysia, although there is no deliberate discrimination against migrants in flood risk management, this is a group that is relatively hidden: even in undertaking the research, authors found it difficult to locate migrants who had been affected by flooding, as they had already moved on. The authors show the importance of extending analyses of disasters to include migration and migrants, particularly where the latter have difficulties in accessing the support of the state.

The final chapter of the book turns to the policy implications of the case studies. In this chapter, Louis Lebel, Supang Chantavanich and Werasit Sittitrai synthesise the book's main findings, addressing how floods impact ongoing processes of migration, how floods impact the lives of migrants and why migrants end up in flood-prone places. They then propose a series of policy recommendations that would avoid simplistic assumptions of the relationships people have with floods, and thus that are supportive of migrants and their circumstances in the face of a range of different flood types.

Conclusion

In response to an urgent need to develop a more nuanced understanding of the connections between flooding and migration in the Southeast Asian region, this chapter has presented an analytical framework that seeks to clarify the connections between flooding, migration, vulnerability, resilience and social justice. In line with recent calls from migration scholars to investigate empirically the mutually reinforcing social, economic and environmental drivers of migration, the challenge has been to develop a workable conceptual framework that can be applied across diverse contexts in Southeast Asia.

One of the ironies of development policy in Southeast Asia is that neoliberalism and infrastructure development make mobility and migration increasingly important aspects of urban and rural livelihoods, as sustaining a livelihood in one place becomes difficult in the face of the restructuring of rural economies (Lund et al., 2013). In other words, the wider development trajectories of the Southeast Asian region are premised on the movement of people and material goods across space. Householding frequently involves different family members working in different localities, sharing resources and retaining footholds in several different places simultaneously. At the same time, governance is based on geographically defined and bounded territorial units, and is largely built on an assumption of households being attached to one place, in which livelihoods are derived and where people stay put: a kind of geographical fixity (Scott, 2009; see also Allen and Cochrane, 2010). Tensions between these two modes run through any analysis of the relationship between flooding, migration and policy, and through efforts to address socioecological vulnerability, as failures to grasp the mobile and multilocal character of most peoples' livelihoods compromise the success of development programmes that are designed to govern and deliver services to people by virtue of their membership in geographically defined communities of place (Li, 2007; Lund et al., 2013).

As Adger (2006) has noted, effective policy interventions to reduce vulnerability rest on identifying vulnerabilities within social-ecological systems along with the processes which produce vulnerability in the first place. Addressing marginality and exclusion is therefore a critical element in the design of good governance aimed at both tackling vulnerability and enhancing household and community capacities. The connectedness of migration to processes of marginality and exclusion make addressing the impacts of flooding in mobile populations a particularly complex governance endeavour. Our aim in producing this book is to sensitise policy to the complexities of migration and floods in an increasingly mobile region, in order to counter possible oversimplifications and sensationalising that too often becomes embedded in discourses of migration as a singular and catastrophic response to environmental change.

Notes

1 Rockenbauch and Sakdapolrak (2017) propose a comparable concept of 'translocality'.
2 Shocks are short-term, rapid changes that tend to return to their early state; stresses are gradual and enduring shifts in state.

References

Adamo, S.B. (2010). "Environmental migration and cities in the context of global environmental change." *Current Opinion in Environmental Sustainability* 2: 161–165.

ADB. (2011). *Climate change and migration in Asia and the Pacific*. Manila: Asian Development Bank (ADB).

Adger, W.N. (2006). "Vulnerability." *Global Environmental Change* 16: 268–281.

Adger, W.N., Arnell, N.W., Black, R., Dercon, S., Geddes, A., and Thomas, D.S. (2015). "Focus on environmental risks and migration: Causes and consequences." *Environmental Research Letters* 10(6): 060201.

Adger, W.N., Eakin, H., and Winkels, A. (2009). "Nested and teleconnected vulnerabilities to environmental change." *Frontiers in Ecology and the Environment* 7(3): 150–157.

Allen, J., and Cochrane, A. (2010). "Assemblages of state power: Topological shifts in the organization of government and politics." *Antipode* 42(5): 1071–1089.

Bardsley, D.K., and Hugo, G.J. (2010). "Migration and climate change: Examining thresholds of change to guide effective adaptation decision-making." *Population and Environment* 32: 238–262.

Bebbington, A.J. (1999). "Capitals and capabilities: A framework for analyzing peasant viability, rural livelihoods and poverty." *World Development* 27(12): 2021–2044.

Black, R., Adger, W.N., Arnell, N.W., Dercon, S., Geddes, A., and Thomas, D.S.G. (2011). "The effect of environmental change on human migration." *Global Environmental Change* 21S: S3–S11.

Braun, B. (2006). "Environmental issues: Global natures in the spaces of assemblage." *Progress in Human Geography* 30(5): 644–654.

Bulkeley, H., Schroeder, H., Janda, K., Zhoo, J., Armstrong, A., Chu, S.Y., and Ghosh, S. (2011). "The role of institutions, governance and urban planning for mitigation and adaptation." (pp. 125–160) in Hoornweg, D., Freire, M., Lee, M.J., Bhada-Tata, P., and Yuen, B. (eds.) *Cities and climate change: Responding to an urgent agenda*. Washington, DC: World Bank.

CNN. (2012). "Floods, heat, migration: How extreme weather will transform cities." *CNN*, 4 April 2012. www.edition.cnn.com/2011/12/23/world/asia/climate-change-impact-cities/index.html.

Collins, T.W. (2009). "The production of unequal risk in hazardscapes: An explanatory frame applied to disaster at the US-Mexico border." *Geoforum* 40: 589–601.

Cote, M., and Nightingale, A.J. (2012). "Resilience thinking meets social theory: Situating social change in socio-ecological systems (SES) research." *Progress in Human Geography* 36(4): 475–489.

Cretney, R. (2014). "Resilience for whom? Emerging critical geographies of socio-ecological resilience." *Geography Compass* 8(9): 627–640.

Cutter, S. (2003). "The vulnerability of science and the science of vulnerability." *Annals of the Association of American Geographers* 93(1): 1–12.

De Haas, H. (2012). "The migration and development pendulum: A critical view on research and policy." *International Migration* 50(3): 8–25.

di Floristella, A.P. (2015). "Dealing with natural disasters: Risk society and ASEAN: A new approach to disaster management." *The Pacific Review* 29(2): 1–23.

Dun, O. (2011). "Migration and displacement triggered by floods in the Mekong Delta." *International Migration* 49(S1): e200–e223.

Elmhirst, R. (2008). "Migration, multi-local livelihoods and natural resource governance in Indonesia." (pp. 67–86) in Elmhirst, R. and Resurreccion, B. (eds.) *Gender and natural resource management: Livelihoods, mobility and interventions*. Ottawa and London: Earthscan and IDRC.

Felli, R., and Castree, N. (2012). "Neoliberalising adaptation to environmental change: Foresight or foreclosure?" *Environment and Planning A* 44(1): 1–4.

Findlay, A.M. (2012). "Migration: Flooding and the scale of migration." *Nature Climate Change* 2: 401–402.

Folke, C. (2006). "Resilience: The emergence of a perspective for social – Ecological systems analyses." *Global Environmental Change* 16(3): 253–267.

Greiner, C., and Sakdapolrak, P. (2015). "Migration, environment and inequality: Perspectives of a political ecology of translocal relations." (pp. 151–166) in McLeman, R., Schade, J., and Faist, T. (eds.) *Environmental migration and social inequality*. Dordrecht: Springer.

Heikkilä, E. (2005) "Mobile vulnerabilities: Perspectives on the vulnerabilities of immigrants in the Finnish labour market." *Population, Space and Place* 11: 485–497.

Hogan, D.J., and Marandola, E. (2005). "Towards an interdisciplinary conceptualisation of vulnerability." *Population, Space and Place* 11: 455–471.

Hugo, G., and Bardsley, D.K. (2014). "Migration and environmental change in Asia." (pp. 21–48) in Piguet, E. and Laczko, F. (eds.) *People on the move in a changing climate*. Dordrecht: Springer.

Julca, A. (2011). "Multidimensional re-creation of vulnerabilities and potential for resilience in international migration." *International Migration* 49(S1): 31–49.

Kabeer, N., Mumtaz, K., and Sayeed, A. (2010). "Beyond risk management: Vulnerability, social protection and citizenship in Pakistan." *Journal of International Development* 22: 1–19.

Lebel, L., Anderies, J.M., Campbell, B., Folke, C., Hatfield-Dodds, S., Hughes, T.P., and Wilson, J. (2006). "Governance and the capacity to manage resilience in regional social-ecological systems." *Ecology and Society* 11(Article 19).

Lebel, L., Manuta, J.B., and Garden, P. (2011). "Institutional traps and vulnerability to changes in climate and flood regimes in Thailand." *Regional Environmental Change* 11: 45–58.

Lebel, L., and Sinh, B.T. (2009). "Risk reduction or redistribution? Flood management in the Mekong region." *Asian Journal of Environmental Disaster Management* 1: 23–39.

Li, T.M. (2007). *The will to improve: Governmentality, development and the practice of politics.* Durham, NC: Duke University Press.

Lund, R., Kusakabe, K., Panda, S.M., and Wang, Y. (eds.) (2013). *Gender, mobilities, and livelihood transformations: Comparing indigenous people in China, India, and Laos.* London: Routledge.

Marks, D. (2015). "The urban political ecology of the 2011 floods in Bangkok: The creation of uneven vulnerabilities." *Pacific Affairs* 88(3): 623–651.

McDowell, C., and de Haan, A. (1997). *Migration and sustainable livelihoods: A critical review of the literature.* IDS Working Paper 65. Institute of Development Studies (IDS): Brighton.

Middleton, C. (2012). "The 'Nature' of beneficial flooding of the Mekong river." *Journal of Social Science* 42(2): 180–208.

Miller, F., Osbahr, H., Boyd, E., Thomalla, F., Bharwani, S., Ziervogel, G., Walker, B., Birkmann, J., van der Leeuw, S., Rockström, J., Hinkel, J., Downing, T., Folke, C., and Nelson, D. (2010). "Resilience and vulnerability: Complementary or conflicting concepts?" *Ecology and Society* 15(3): 11–36.

Mosuela, C., and Matias, D.M. (2014). *The role of a priori cross-border migration after extreme climate events: The case of the Philippines after typhoon Haiyan.* COMCAD (Centre on Migration, Citizenship and Development) Working Paper No. 126. Universität Bielefeld: Bielefeld.

Myers, N. (2002). "Environmental refugees: A growing phenomenon of the 21st century." *Philosophical Transactions of the Royal Society* B357(1420): 609–613.

Nevins, J., and Peluso, N.L. (2008). *Taking Southeast Asia to market.* Ithaca and London: Cornell University Press.

Oliver-Smith, A. (2012). "Debating environmental migration: Society, nature and population displacement in climate change." *Journal of International Development* 24: 1058–1070.

Pelling, M. (2003). *The vulnerability of cities: Natural disasters and social resilience.* London: Earthscan.

Ransan-Cooper, H., Farbotko, C., McNamara, K.E., Thornton, F., and Chevalier, E. (2015). "Being(s) framed: The means and ends of framing environmental migrants." *Global Environmental Change* 35: 106–115.

Resurrección, B.P., and Sajor, E.E. (2015). "Gender, floods and mobile subjects: A post-disaster view." (pp. 207–304) in Lund, R., Doneys, P., and Resurrección, B.P. (eds.) *Gendered entanglements: Re-visiting gender in rapidly changing Asia.* Copenhagen: Nordic Institute of Asian Studies (NIAS) Press.

Ribot, J.C. (2009). "Vulnerability does not just fall from the sky: Toward multi-scale pro-poor climate policy." (pp. 47–74) in Mearns, R. and Norton, A. (eds.) *Social dimensions of climate change: Equity and vulnerability in a warming world*. Washington, DC: World Bank.

Ribot, J.C. (2014). "Cause and response: Vulnerability and climate in the Anthropocene." *The Journal of Peasant Studies* 41(5): 667–705.

Ribot, J.C., and Peluso, N.L. (2003). "A theory of access." *Rural Sociology* 68(2): 153–181.

Rigg, J. (2012). *Unplanned development: Tracking change in South-East Asia*. London: Zed Books.

Rigg, J., and Oven, K. (2015). "Building liberal resilience? A critical review from developing rural Asia." *Global Environmental Change* 32: 175–186.

Robbins, P. (2012). *Political ecology* (2nd edition). London: Wiley-Blackwell.

Rockefeller Foundation. (2016). *Global resilience partnership*. www.rockefellerfoundation.org/our-work/initiatives/global-resilience-partnership/.

Rockenbauch, T., and Sakdapolrak, P. (2017). "Social networks and the resilience of rural communities in the Global South: A critical review and conceptual reflections." *Ecology and Society* 22(1): 10.

Schade, J. (2013). "Entitlements, capabilities and human rights." (pp. 231–254) in Faist, T. and Schade, J. (ed.) *Disentangling migration and climate change: Methodologies, political discourses and human rights*. Dordrecht: Springer.

Scott, J.C. (2009). *The art of not being governed: An anarchist history of upland Southeast Asia*. New Haven, CT: Yale University Press.

Sen, A. (1997). "Editorial: Human capital and human capability." *World Development* 25(12): 1959–1961.

Silvey, R., and Elmhirst, R. (2003). "Engendering social capital: Women workers and rural – urban networks in Indonesia's crisis." *World Development* 31(5): 865–879.

Tacoli, C. (2009). "Crisis or adaptation? Migration and climate change in a context of high mobility." *Environment and Urbanization* 21(2): 513–525.

Turner, M.D. (2014). "Political ecology I: An alliance with resilience?" *Progress in Human Geography* 38(4): 616–623.

Vandergeest, P., and Peluso, N.L. (2006). "Empires of forestry in Southeast Asia. Part I." *Environment and History* 12(1): 31–64.

Warner, K., and Afifi, T. (2014). "Where the rain falls: Evidence from 8 countries on how vulnerable households use migration to manage the risk of rainfall variability and food insecurity." *Climate and Development* 6(1): 1–17.

Watts, M. (2000). "Political ecology." (pp. 257–274) in Sheppard, E. and Barnes, T. (eds.) *A companion to economic geography*. Oxford: Wiley-Blackwell.

Wisner, B. (2004). "Assessment of capability and vulnerability." (pp. 183–193) in Bankoff, G., Frerks, G., and Hilhorst, D. (eds.) *Mapping vulnerability: Disasters, development and people*. London: Earthscan.

Wisner, B., Blaikie, P., Cannon, T., and Davis, I. (1994). *At risk: Natural hazards, people's vulnerability and disasters*. London: Routledge.

Zhaung, J., Suphachalasai, S., and Samson, J.N. (2013). "The economics of climate change." (pp. 18–42) in Elliott, L. and Caballero-Anthony, M. (eds.) *Human security and climate change in Southeast Asia: Managing risk and resilience*. London: Routledge.

2 Living with the flood

A political ecology of fishing, farming, and migration around Tonle Sap Lake, Cambodia

Carl Middleton and Borin Un

Introduction

For over 1.7 million people within the floodplain of Tonle Sap Lake, Cambodia, living with floods is both a way of and a source of life (Keskinen et al., 2011). Tonle Sap Lake is the largest freshwater lake in Southeast Asia, located in Cambodia's central plains. It is connected to the Mekong River via the 120 kilometers long Tonle Sap River (Figure 2.1). In the rainy season water flows from the Mekong River into the lake, and during the dry season water flows back again. Colloquially referred to as the "heartbeat of Cambodia," the lake's surface area ranges between 15,000 square kilometers at its peak and 2,600 square kilometers at its lowest, varying from year to year (Arias et al., 2012).

Tonle Sap Lake is a "flood-pulse ecosystem," and the flood regime is intimately tied to the lake's ecological productivity (Lamberts, 2006). As the lake begins to expand, usually in May, fish migrations and fish eggs flow from the Mekong River into its flooded forest and grasslands that are ideal habitats for feeding and growth. Around November, as the Mekong River's water level drops and water flows out of the lake, large fish migrations are triggered from the lake to the Mekong River, and nutrient-rich sediments are deposited on the lake's floodplains. Water also remains behind in natural lakes within the floodplain; these lakes are habitats for fish then caught by fishers, as well as water for use by farmers.

Farmers and fishers thus benefit from the natural resources that the lake's flood regime sustains, albeit in different ways. Fishers benefit from flooding for productive capture fisheries; and farmers benefit from the fertile soils nourished by the floodwaters, and the availability of water for agriculture (Keskinen, 2006; Heinonen, 2006). Irregular flooding, however, can be detrimental or even disastrous: flooding that is too low or of too short a duration results in less productive fisheries, a shortage of water for agriculture, and a high pest incidence for dry-season rice farming; while flooding that is prolonged or arrives too early shortens the farming season and damages infrastructure, crops, and livestock, although it increases fish productivity (Middleton et al., 2013). Over the past 2 decades, irregular flooding or drought has become more commonplace; Parsons (2017: 147) observes, "Cambodia has suffered six of the worst ten natural disasters in its history during the previous two decades."

Living with the flood in Cambodia 23

While Tonle Sap Lake has sustained fishers and farmers for generations, life around the lake is changing. With the legacy of the country's tumultuous recent history shaping the present, contemporary postconflict Cambodia continues to be subject to significant and interconnected economic, environmental, social, and political transformations (Milne and Mahanty, 2015; Brickell and Springer, 2017). High national economic growth rates since the 1990s would suggest broad success, yet a far more complex story exists, in which, for the rural majority, contestation over access, use, and control of natural resources and land is a regular occurrence. Around Tonle Sap Lake, various processes of agrarian transformation are underway, restructuring the rural economy from a subsistence-based to an increasingly market-oriented one (Milne and Mahanty, 2015). Regarding fisheries, the expansion of the commercial fishing lot system since the 1990s, which had existed since the French colonial period and was a key source of revenue for the state, as well as patronage, increasingly marginalized smallholder fishers from access to fish resources (Sneddon, 2007). The unexpected, but welcome, release of the commercial fishing lots to communities partially in 2001 and wholly in 2010 holds the potential to increase the viability of small-scale fishing, yet the process has been complicated, largely unplanned, and fraught with contestation, with many smallholder fishers losing out to date (Dina and Sato, 2014; Chap et al., 2016).

There is a nascent but growing literature on environmental risk and migration in Cambodia. An early paper by Heinonen (2006), based on village surveys around Tonle Sap Lake in 2002, suggests that while many migration push factors are socioeconomic – including population growth, increasing landlessness, lack of work in rural areas, and wage differentials between rural and urban areas – environmental changes to a degree underlie these push factors, including changing environmental quality and flood regime. More recently, Bylander (2013), in a case study in an agricultural community in Siem Reap province, emphasizes how sequences of environmental shocks, rather than individual events alone, shape perceptions toward risks in agriculture and relative opportunity in migration. Meanwhile, Parsons (2017) explores the relationship between ecological risk, debt, migration, and wage dependency in Cambodia, arguing that ultimately these dynamics are reinforcing and widening inequality.

Building on this literature, this chapter presents empirical research on the mobile political ecologies of fishing and farming in two villages located in the Tonle Sap Lake's floodplains. It asks, what are the vulnerabilities of fishers and farmers, how are these produced, and in what ways are these vulnerabilities shaped by the lake's seasonal floods? Capacities to reduce vulnerability are identified, with particular attention paid to the role of migration. Drawing on the concepts of mobile political ecology, outlined in Chapter 1, this chapter seeks to explore the social dynamics and asymmetrical power relations that mediate between flooding, access to natural resources, and migration.

The chapter argues that among smallholder farming and family-scale fishing households, although they are relatively resilient to the seasonal flooding of Tonle Sap Lake, vulnerability is significant and growing. Small-scale fishers' vulnerability is heightened by inequitable access to a degrading wild-capture fishery.

For smallholder farmers, meanwhile, growing competition for access to land is a key challenge, together with the growing capital intensity of farming. While regular flooding brings benefits to fishers and farmers long adapted to it, shocks from irregular flood and drought are often the catalysts of indebtedness for households already challenged by high levels of vulnerability. Recent government policy on fisheries and agriculture has had limited impact to mitigate the vulnerabilities of smallholder fishers and farmers, and has oftentimes undermined them. The outcome is that nowadays many fishing and farming households are unable to maintain themselves through the resources and work available within the village alone. Thus, the chapter shows how the interaction of various types of seasonal flooding, associated ecological productivity, access to natural resources and land, and overarching processes of rural transformation in Cambodia produce the circumstances where households increasingly contain migrating family members as a strategy either to diversify livelihoods or, more often, to repay debts incurred from fishing and farming.

The chapter is structured as follows. In the next section, the research methodology is briefly summarized. This is followed by a brief overview of life in Prek Trob and Kampong Kor Krom villages. The subsequent two sections address the relationships between flooding, vulnerability, and fishing and farming, respectively, with a particular focus on the politics of resource access. Then, the chapter explores the conditions under which migration takes place and analyzes the key factors that shape the decision to migrate. The concluding section places fishing, farming, flooding, and migration in relationship to each other through a political ecology lens.

Method

Ethnographic fieldwork was undertaken in two villages located in the floodplain of Tonle Sap Lake: Prek Trob village in Aek Phnom district, Battambang province (June 2013), and Kampong Kor Krom village in Kampong Svay district, Kampong Thom province (April 2013) (Figure 2.1). The villages were selected as representative of "stand-stilt" communities within Tonle Sap Lake's floodplains,[1] which are seasonally flooded generally from early September to late October. The main livelihoods in the two villages studied are wild-capture fishing and rice farming, with migration increasingly a significant livelihood strategy. Both villages are located on major rivers and are connected to the commune centers via dirt-track roads.

Prek Trob village is located on the Sangke River and has a population of 1,577 people.[2] There is a primary school in the village, but no health center. Grid-connected electricity has been installed since 2012, although poorer fishing families are largely not connected. The water supply is principally from the Sangke River. One nongovernmental organization (NGO) called Krom Akpiwat Phum worked in the village until 2011, helping to establish a community fishery organization and savings group.

Kampong Kor Krom village is located on the Stung Sen River and has a population of 1,546 people. There is a health center and primary school in the village, but no grid-connected electricity. The water supply is principally from the Stung

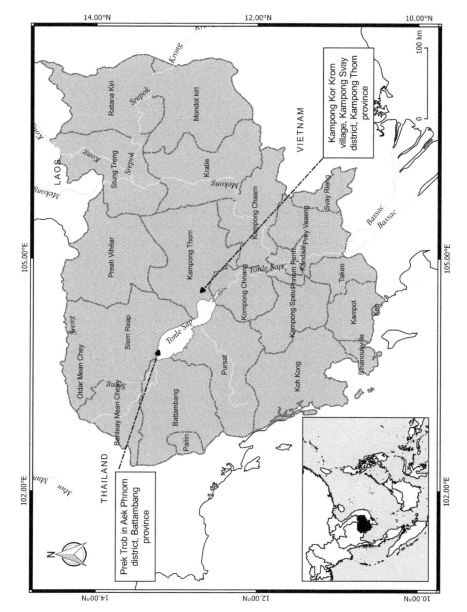

Figure 2.1 Location of Prek Trob and Kampong Kor Krom villages

Sen River and from ground water. There are three natural lakes in the commune, which were important for fishing but recently have become dried up during the dry season due to water extraction for irrigation.

In both villages, key informant interviews were made with the commune chief, village chief, and community fishery chief. A survey was administered with randomly selected households with closed and semiopen questions that assessed livelihoods, vulnerability, and impacts of flooding in the village (Prek Trob: n = 31 of 365 households; Kampong Kor Krom: n = 37 of 247 households). The proportion of fishers to farmers interviewed reflect the balance of principal livelihoods in the village. In each village, focus-group discussions and four in-depth interviews were made with selected small-scale fishing and farming households. Expert and in-depth interviews were coded, and data were triangulated with the semistructured interview data and a literature review.

Living with floods

Rice farming and fishing are the two principle livelihoods in Prek Trob and Kampong Kor Krom villages (Table 2.1), although many complementary activities are undertaken including the collection of wild plants and small animals such as snakes, birds, and insects – what Roberts (2015: 59, emphasis in original) calls a "flexible and diverse *productive bricolage*." Both villages have access to a similar range of natural resources including seasonally flooded land for agriculture; wild-capture fisheries; natural lakes, rivers, and streams; and flooded forest. Given the seasonal cycle of flooding, the land-waterscape of the villages is continually in flux and consists of many transitional spaces that Roberts (2015) refers to as "interstitial" and "ephemeral" environments,[3] including those in grasslands and flooded forest areas that are habitats for fish and a variety of collectable natural products, important to livelihoods.

Family-scale[4] fishing households fish in the open water of Tonle Sap Lake, as well as in the community's fishing area consisting of small natural lakes, flooded forest areas around them, and in the village's rivers and streams. Farming households, meanwhile, grow a crop of recessional rice, and some grow a second crop of dry-season rice depending on the availability of water; some grow other commercial cash crops, such as mung beans, and almost all grow vegetables for subsistence

Table 2.1 Self-identified primary and secondary household livelihoods

	Primary occupation (percent)			Secondary occupation (percent)			
	Farming	*Fishing*	*Other*	*Farming*	*Fishing*	*Other*	*None*
Prek Trob	65	16	19	3	68	13	16
Kampong Kor Krom	54	41	5	19	41	13	27

Source: Based on authors' household survey data (2013)

Table 2.2 Land ownership and primary livelihoods (percent)

	0 ha	<0.5 ha	0.5–1 ha	1–2 ha	2–3 ha	3–5 ha	5 ha
Prek Trob							
Farming (n = 20)	0	20	35	10	20	15	0
Fishing (n = 5)	100	0	0	0	0	0	0
Other (n = 6)	17	33	50	0	0	0	0
Kampong Kor Krom							
Farming (n = 20)	0	20	40	10	15	10	5
Fishing (n = 15)	60	40	0	0	0	0	0
Other (n = 2)	0	100	0	0	0	0	0

Source: Based on authors' household survey data (2013)

consumption. Most farmers are also family-scale fishers, fishing within the community fishing area. Most fishing households are landless, while many smallholder farming households are land poor (Table 2.2); exclusion from existing land, as well as the clearance of flooded forest for agriculture by well-connected families, which undermines the productivity of the fishery, is a key factor in fishing household vulnerability.

In both villages, processes of social differentiation and growing inequality in land ownership have been underway since the 1990s. Most farmers with smaller holdings of between 0.5 and 1.5 hectares of land gained their land when it was distributed by the government during 1980s, based on family size at the time. Since then, land has been sold by poorer farmers to wealthier farmers from within the village and from outside, such as the district centers, often as distress sales to meet accumulated debt obligations and due to failed farming. Parsons (2017) emphasizes that this process is occurring in many villages in Cambodia; he writes,

> although risk in Cambodia has never been a uniform process, the traditionally iniquitous exposure to hazards in the Kingdom is growing further and further apart as the smaller scale of risk faced by the better off allows them to consolidate an advantage in the long term, both in terms of assets and progressive risk reduction.
>
> (Parsons, 2017: 154)

Households have adapted to live with floods, literally translated "water rising" in the Khmer language. The villages are seasonally flooded between early September and late October as the lake expands. The surrounding farming lands and flooded forests are typically flooded earlier and longer compared to the homesteads.[5] Houses – of ranging quality – are built on stilts to prevent the rising water from inundating them. While during years of high floods water may reach the house floor, households tend not to move to a new house but rather to temporarily raise their sleeping area.

Within each village, some households are more exposed to flooding than others. Those who live closest to the river, while benefiting from easier access to water for domestic use, are also flooded first and experience greater risk, as the water flow is stronger and can damage houses and personal property. Those living close to the road, which is on higher ground, are normally flooded later but have to pay to pump water to their homes. In Prek Trob, generally fisher households live further away from the river and road, whereas wealthier farming households are closest to the road, where they have access to grid-connected electricity. In Kampong Kor Krom, both fishers and farmers settle along Stung Sen River.

During flooding, the dirt roads connecting the villages to the commune center are cut, and afterward left in poor repair. Village community infrastructure, such as the primary school, is also regularly flooded, interrupting children's schooling. For children studying at the secondary school or high school, which are located in the commune centers or provincial centers,[6] these schools often become inaccessible during flooding when the roads are cut. Hence, local mobility impeded by flooding contributes toward few children, especially girls, completing high school.

Similarly for health care, community members are vulnerable to health shocks during the flooded season. While Kampong Kor Krom has a basic health center, households in Prek Trob must travel 7 kilometers to a nearby village. Both village health centers, however, have limited medicine and medical staff. Thus, for any substantial treatment, including baby delivery, people must travel by boat, which is relatively slow and more expensive.

The governance of Tonle Sap Lake and its subbasin is exercised through multiscaled processes ranging from the local to the province to the national and the transboundary and involves the interests and actions of a diverse array of government agencies and politicians, civil society and community groups, development practitioners and academics (Sokhem and Sunada, 2006). The government institutions mandated to manage the Tonle Sap Lake's complex environment, water resources, agriculture, fisheries, and other social and political dimensions, including domestic and international migration, are sector focused and thus fragmented when it comes to linking the complex processes of society-nature interaction around the lake (Un, 2016). Moreover, as Roberts (2015: 57) observes, "Far from a level playing field, personal relationships, political connections and patronage networks are a particularly important factor in determining how institutions fit into an unstable network of hierarchies of power."

Regarding disaster response, in 1995 the Royal Government of Cambodia (RGC) established the National Committee for Disaster Management as the coordinating agency for disaster risk reduction, preparedness, response, and recovery. This national committee structure is replicated at the province and district level, and there are also coordinating committees at the commune and village levels. Since our fieldwork was conducted, Cambodia also adopted the Law on Disaster Management in 2015. However, this structure is documented as having limited effectiveness to date (Doch et al., 2015). On the ground, community members mostly learn about upcoming hazardous floods and droughts through television or radio, rather than via village authorities. During disastrous floods, aid packages and money is provided by the Cambodian Red Cross, the government, the World Food Programme, and NGOs and distributed by the local authorities. However, in some cases, this aid can become conflated with local patronage, in particular political party affiliations.

Fishing, floods, and vulnerability

Tonle Sap Lake is one of the most productive and intensively fished inland fisheries in the world (Baran et al., 2007a). Nowadays, however, there has been a shift from fishing to farming; approximately 10 percent and 50 percent of households in Prek Trob and Kampong Kor Krom, respectively, hold fishing as their main occupation. This shift was linked by some interviewees to the growing scarcity of fish. As discussed in the next section, however, households who have successfully transitioned to agriculture are generally more secure, and have more material assets, and thus the shift to agriculture may also reflect the capacity of some – but not all – to reduce their vulnerability, with access to land a principle factor.

In both villages, most fishing households are landless, or at best land poor (Table 2.2). In Kampong Kor Krom, where there are more fisher households, around 40 percent own less than 0.5 hectare, while the remainder are landless. In Prek Trob, all fishers are landless. Most landless fishing households had never owned land. For older fishers, they had not received land during Cambodia's post-Khmer Rouge land redistribution program during the 1980s, while the few who did had sold it. For younger fishing families, their parents were fishers and landless, and thus they did not have land to pass on, as is customary in Cambodia, revealing an intergenerational dimension to household vulnerability. According to interviews with fishing households, in the past, when fishery resources were more abundant, their lack of access to land was of little concern. However, their dependence on a resource in decline with limited alternatives has left them particularly vulnerable, in contrast to farming households who farm *and* complement their income with fishing.

Tonle Sap Lake's flood "pulse" is intimately tied to fishery productivity, recognized by fishers and scientists (e.g. Lamberts, 2006) alike. If the seasonal flood is high, and early or prolonged, more habitat is submerged and for longer, and thus the fish catch increases both in terms of fish size and number of fish. Conversely, if the flood is low and of a shorter duration, fish catch reduces. During low flood years, fishers struggle. During our interviews conducted in 2013, many fishers commented that 2011 was an exceptional flood, and the largest in a decade, which was beneficial to them, whereas in 2012, water was low and the fish catch was poor.

There is a widely held perception among fishers that the resource has been degrading since the 1990s, and more rapidly since the 2000s. A range of reasons has been linked to the degrading fisheries resource, including the construction of infrastructure around the lake, such as irrigation schemes and roads (Baran et al., 2007b); the construction of hydropower dams in the wider Mekong basin (Arias et al., 2012); and the unregulated and unmonitored conversion of flooded forest and grassland to agricultural land around the lake that reduces fish habitat (Keskinen et al., 2007; Packman et al., 2013). Widespread use of modern, illegal fishing gear by all fishers, but most destructively by medium- and large-scale commercial fishers, has contributed to resource decline (Sneddon, 2007; Mak, 2017). Family-scale fishers must expend more effort to catch less fish, with large, valuable fish less present in the catch composition. Without using more intensive – often illegal – gear, it is not feasible to catch enough fish for survival, creating deleterious feedback on the overall resource. Meanwhile, commercial medium- and (until 2010) large-scale fishers, with more capital investment, extract more fish, undermining the common pool resource for others. Given the centrality of Tonle Sap Lake's fishery to Cambodia's national food security, such fishing practices are of serious concern (Fisheries Administration, 2013, cited in Milne and Mahanty, 2015).

Cutting across these factors of fisheries' decline and the capability of family-scale fishers to catch fish, is inequitable access to resources. The governance of Tonle Sap Lake has transformed rapidly over the past 2 decades. It has been widely documented that commercial fishing lots were in conflict with local fishing communities, excluding small-scale fishers from access to the most productive fishing areas of the lake (e.g. Keskinen et al., 2007; Mak, 2011). Following a period of escalating conflict between commercial and family-scale fishers, in 2001, Prime Minister Hun Sen unexpectedly announced that 46 percent of the lake's 500,000 hectares of commercial fishing lots would be released for the creation of community fisheries (Mak, 2017), although initially a clear legal framework was not in place. By 2005, an area of over 412,000 hectares had been allocated to 175 community fishing lots, created by communities often with support from local and international NGOs, and with varied success (Mak, 2017).[7]

A second major reform was again unexpectedly initiated by Prime Minister Hun Sen in 2011, when two regulations were issued to crack down on illegal fishing (Regulation 01) and cancel the remaining commercial fishing lots (Regulation 02) (Un, 2016). Like the previous one, this reform was welcomed by local communities and NGOs, even if the motivation appeared more related to garnering votes in the general election and the redistribution of authority between government agencies (Dina and Sato, 2014). However, similar to the previous reform, clear mechanisms for implementation were not in place, and confusion was created in the revised mandate of government agencies (Kim et al., 2013).

While some community fishery organizations have become effective means for communities to co-manage their resources, others exist little more than on paper and have enabled illegal fishing activities (Kim et al., 2013; Chap et al., 2016). In Prek Trob and Kampong Kor Krom, both communities established a community fishery organization. However, to date, these organizations have not been able to protect each village's community fishing area from illegal fishing. The fishing reforms that led to the release of fishing lots near both villages resulted in complex outcomes. In Kampong Kor Krom, one community leader interviewee observed,

> The community fishery organization is unable to control the resources as they seem unable to challenge the illegal fishing activities in the commune. . . .

Moreover, the fishery resources in the area have become scarce after the release of the fishing lots during the last few years. Without fishing lots, illegal fishing activities have become disorganized. Only the wealthy and people with powerful connections can access to and control the fishing area.

In Prek Trob, the community fishing area was expanded from 1,224 hectares to 7,016 hectares following the cancellation of Battambang Fishing Lot 2 in 2012. While potentially of great benefit to family-scale fishers, at the time of the fieldwork (June 2013), no institutional, technical, or financial support had been extended to the community fishery organization to manage the significantly expanded area. One family-scale fisher from Prek Trob said,

> I see a lot of illegal fishing activities in or nearby the community fishing area.... A small-scale fishing family like mine sometimes can't go fishing in the community area, as the fishers with large boats and modern gears normally dominate the areas. We can only fish the areas that are less productive.

Another family-scale fisher from Kampong Kor Krom said,

> Wherever there are fishery officers, we have to pay because wherever we go to fish they claim it is the protected areas [since the release of the fishing lots in 2012]. I wonder, if it is a protected area why do I need to pay to do fishing in those areas? ... If it is a protected area, all fishing activities should be banned. However, when I am on the lake I see a lot of illegal fishing activities in the protected areas.

Tensions are also emerging between the interests of small-scale fishers and farmers. In Kampong Kor Krom, there are three natural lakes important for fishing. In the past, these were important dry-season fishing areas. However, over the past 5 years, nearby farmers have pumped water for irrigation from the lakes, drying them up, with severe impact for fishers' dry-season income.

The clearance of flooded forest and grassland, which are important fish habitats, is another tension between the interests of family-scale fishers and farmers. According to interviewees from Kampong Krom Kor, farmers from the village started clearing forest and grassland in the early 2000s, reflecting a wider trend around the lake (Packman et al., 2013). This land, however, has since been sold to wealthy people from outside the village and more recently to an agricultural company that invested there. These relatively small-scale – but numerous – illegal enclosures of common land, although garnering less media attention than the "land grabs" associated with large-scale economic land concessions for which Cambodia is increasingly infamous (Scurrah and Hirsch, 2015), reveal the range of inequitable access to resources that serve to marginalize fishing households and make them increasingly vulnerable (see also Diepart, 2010).

Thus, while surrounded by a productive but degrading fishery, present-day circumstances are increasing the vulnerability and reducing the viability of family-scale fisher livelihoods. Fishers face growing cycles of debt, due to their investment in modern fishing gear and the low returns from fishing. They often have only limited representation within local institutions and weak connections with local elites and thus struggle to represent their interests. Not having access to land, they are unable to diversify into farming, while the opportunity for agricultural laboring in the village has diminished due to the mechanization of farming. Thus, in particular since the late 2000s, in both villages, employment away from fishing through migration is increasingly significant as part of a household livelihood strategy.

Farming, floods, and vulnerability

Agriculture, and especially rice production, is central to the lives of the majority of the rural farming population of Cambodia. The Tonle Sap Lake's floodplains and wider basin are one of Cambodia's key rice production regions. Even as Cambodia's national economy transforms through processes of urbanization, industrialization, and globalization, with implications for rural and urban areas, it is predicted that smallholder farming will continue to grow in absolute terms, and thus will remain a key dynamic of the country's future development (Diepart, 2016).

The World Bank (2015) suggests that increasingly extensive areas of land turned to agriculture and growing productivity are key factors in Cambodia's recent agriculture growth, with land expansion the most significant factor to date. Growth in agriculture has been encouraged by the dual goals of the RGC's agriculture sector strategy, which are food security within Cambodia and for Cambodia to become a major rice exporter (Sok et al., 2011). In 2010, the government committed to export 1 million tons of milled rice by 2015, although the actual amount achieved was significantly lower, at 387,000 tons (Styllis, 2015). Overall, farming in Cambodia has become increasingly capital intensive, reflecting growing mechanization, increased chemical inputs, and the use of high-yielding seed varieties.[8]

Economic growth in agriculture has led to an estimated 4 million farmers moving above the poverty line between 2007 and 2012 (World Bank, 2015). While significant, the World Bank (2015) also highlights that most who moved above the poverty line still remain only marginally so, and are still vulnerable to economic and environment-related shocks. Furthermore, challenges loom as the rate of agricultural productivity growth is slowing (World Bank, 2015), while the closing land frontier will challenge the continued expansion of agricultural land (Diepart, 2016).

In Prek Trob and Kampong Kor Krom, over the past 15 years, rice farming has grown in importance relative to fishing as a primary source of livelihood (Table 2.1). Farmers principally grow recessional rice after flooding recedes, but some also grow dry-season rice and other seasonal crops. For households whose principle livelihood is farming, land holdings range from less than 1 hectare to up to 3 hectares, and occasionally more (Table 2.2). The World Bank (2015) notes that across Cambodia, vulnerability is greatest for farms of less than 1 hectare, and that "[i]n the last decade, there has been the trend in Cambodia for large farms (above 3 ha) to become larger and small farms (less than 1 ha) to become smaller" (2015: xv). This reflects a process of land differentiation linked most commonly to "distress sales" of poorer, more vulnerable farmers to wealthier ones (see the previous section, "Living with floods"; see also Diepart, 2016; Parsons, 2017). Access to land is a contested issue in Cambodia (Scurrah and Hirsch, 2015), and lack of access to land is a key factor in the migration of farmers from the Tonle Sap basin (Diepart, 2016).

Regarding flooding, farmers benefit principally from regular, predictable flooding and hence a regular farming season, which is neither too high, too early, nor too prolonged. If flooding is too early, it could destroy unharvested dry-season rice. When flooding is too high and prolonged, it extends the subsequent recession farming season such that farmers then face drought growing a dry-season crop. If the flood is too low, it increases the incidence of pests, creates a water shortage, and shortens the length of the farming season. There are many ecological traits farmers link to the type of flood; for example, if the seasonal flood is low, heavy grasses grow on the farming lands, which are difficult for farmers to clear, while if flooding is regular, the soil has good fertility and few grasses and weeds, which make farming much easier.

Illustrating the impact of flooding on farming, in 2011, the early arrival of floodwater destroyed much of the dry-season rice harvest, creating indebtedness among farmers. Some chose to migrate, while others remained to fish the more abundant available catch. Meanwhile, 2012 was a drought year, when farming failed again. In this year, as there were also few fish, many more people decided to migrate. Thus, similar to fishing households, paying back debt is a key push factor for migration. An indebt rice and mung bean farmer with 3 hectares of land from Prek Trob village said,

> Doing agriculture now needs a lot of money because we have to rent [machines] and buy chemicals for growing rice or other crops. When the rice or other crops can't provide income we lose a lot of money. Now my family have a loan . . . In my family, I sent one son and one daughter to work in the Thai Market [nearby the Poipet border]. As market sellers, they could earn some money to send back home and help to pay back the loan.

Many farmers interviewed indicated they faced debt from failed farming, with loans often from private microcredit institutions that are now commonplace in rural Cambodia (Bylander, 2015).

In Prek Trob and Kampong Kor Krom, there are no large-scale irrigation canals or large storage reservoirs. Thus, water availability is seen by farmers as a key risk associated with investing in agriculture (see also Bylander, 2013). Farmers depend upon the seasonal flooding as the main source of water for recessional rice production. For those located close to the river, they may pump water for irrigated agriculture in the dry season. Some wealthier farmers with sufficient land dig storage reservoirs on their farmlands, reducing their vulnerability to drought. In Prek Trob, just under one-third of agricultural land can farm two crops per year this way. In Kampong Kor Krom, farmers also pump water from the three natural lakes, as noted previously, placing their interests in conflict with fishers. Access to water is competitive between farmers; wealthier farmers who own their own irrigation pumps also can access water more readily than those who have to borrow them and thus take a larger share of the water. Thus, wealthier farmers to a degree can mitigate their drought-related risks, while poorer farmers are left vulnerable.

From our survey data, overall, farmers have greater material assets than fishers, are educated to a slightly higher level, and are generally more food secure from their production, although not necessarily for the full year. As farmers also fish part time, they also have a more diversified income than fishers. Yet, both smallholder farmers and family-scale fishing households have limited assets to manage shocks, including environmental shocks as a result of flooding or drought. We thus find that environment-related vulnerabilities link to the creation of debt for farmers and fishers, who then decide to send household members to migrate. Hence, while the flooding is central to viable livelihoods, irregular flood and drought and their linkages to the viability of fishing and farming, mediated by the politics of access to natural resources and land, is a key contemporary dynamic tying together rural and urban economies via migration and remittance flows (see also Bylander, 2013, 2015; Parsons, 2017).

Migration, local livelihood vulnerabilities, and flooding

In Cambodia, since the 1990s, migration has occurred between rural regions, and also from rural to urban areas (Diepart et al., 2014). A particularly significant rural-to-rural migration flow has been from lowland rice-based regions to upland regions, driven by people seeking land for agriculture or employment on economic land concessions. A key rural-to-urban movement has been toward Phnom Penh, following the establishment there of the garment-manufacturing industry in the mid-1990s (MoP and UNDP, 2007) and the growth of Cambodia's service and industrial sector more generally (Diepart et al., 2014). Regarding international migration, the main destination countries are Thailand, Malaysia, and South Korea, with Thailand the most common destination and informal migration being the most common mode (Diepart et al., 2014; Hing et al., 2011).

In both Prek Trob and Kampong Kor Krom, before the late 2000s, when the Tonle Sap Lake's fisheries and natural resources were more abundant, with greater (but far from complete) access, most fishers and farmers did not migrate for other work. Nowadays, however, the vast majority of households have at least one family member working as a migrant (Table 2.3). One male fisher from Kampong Kor Krom observed,

> About 10 years ago, it was shocking if local villagers migrated to work outside the village as a lot of fishing work was available. But now it is not strange anymore in the village.

Table 2.3 Primary occupation and percentage of households with at least one member migrating

Prek Trob	Farming (n = 20)	95%
	Fishing (n = 5)	80%
	Other (n = 6)	100%
Kampong Kor Krom	Farming (n = 20)	100%
	Fishing (n = 15)	93%
	Other (n = 2)	100%

Source: Based on authors' household survey data (2013)

A key push factor in the village has been a lack of availability of work. As discussed previously, in fishing, this has been due to declining fish stocks, barriers to access, and on occasion the impact of drought; and in farming, this is due to limited access to land, a number of recent destructive flood and drought events, and the mechanization of farming, reducing the demand for labor (see also Parsons, 2017).

Livelihood diversification – and thus risk diversification – is one incentive for migration. Under these circumstances, migration is often seasonal, patterned around when work is not available in the village. A household head in Kampong Kor Krom with less than half a hectare of land said,

> Farming has been just a complementary job for my family for many years, as we have a very small plot of land. The yield is not enough to feed our family the whole year. So, for my family fishing is more important. But when we can't catch enough fish we face a lot of difficulties. We are lucky that we have children who work in Thailand to send us some money to support our living, especially during the dry season.

Yet, more predominant in our interviews was the need to migrate to repay debts incurred from a livelihood shock – or series of shocks (see also Bylander, 2013). One farming household from Prek Trob said,

> If our family were not in debt, we would not allow our children to work in Thailand, as it is far away from the family. We got loans from Angka [a microcredit institution] for farming, but we could not get enough money from selling our rice to pay them back.

Not all families, however, consider migration as a viable strategy. For example, a fisher woman, aged 26, from Prek Trob said,

> In our family, no one migrates as there is only myself and my husband. We do not migrate because we are afraid of having problem. We can't read or write. We do not know many places. We do not have money to travel. We do not know anyone. So we can't migrate, and we do not know what to do as we know only fishing.

Furthermore, some of those remaining in the village lament the negative impact of migration on life in the community. For example, one fisher from Prek Trob commented,

> When there is a ceremony in the village there are hardly any young men or women. There are only old and young people.

Whether the incentive for migration is livelihood diversification or debt repayment, the character of the Tonle Sap's flood regime from year to year is significant. Yet it is not the physical presence or absence of water *per se* that is the key issue, but how it is generative of the viability of farming and fishing livelihoods. In particular, because the flood regime influences the productivity of fisheries (favorably during a high or prolonged flood, and unfavorably during a dry year) and farms (favorably during 'regular' floods, and unfavorably during high or prolonged floods and in drought), it also affects the availability of work in the village for fishers and farmers. Meanwhile, floods and droughts as hazards that can induce shock are a factor in creating debt, although as Parsons (2017) rightly observes, the production and response to debt is fundamentally a social phenomenon. It is also important to emphasize that access to water and its associated resources is determined by not only the flood regime but also power relations and practices in the village; for example, as discussed previously, in Kampong Kor Krom, the recent drying up of the natural lakes due to water extraction by farmers has affected the viability of fishing livelihoods in the dry season.

The means to migrate and to facilitate the return of remittance is now well established within the two villages. There are several preferred destinations: some migrate to work in Thailand, some work in the Cambodian border provinces with Thailand in agriculture,[9] and some work in Phnom Penh or Cambodia's provincial towns. To find employment, they will contract and follow relatives, friends, or neighbors, whether migrating domestically or internationally. For some, if they are traveling to Thailand, they may depend on brokers to arrange work for them, costing between US$100 and US$150. Migration within Cambodia is viewed as less risky, but less well paid compared to migration to Thailand. There are fairly regular reports on the exploitation of Cambodian workers in Thailand (Hing et al., 2011), for example in the fishing industry (Kijewski et al., 2017). Despite this, Chan (2009) concludes that the majority of Cambodian migrants are successful in their goal to earn money and send remittances home, although a significant few failed, resulting in greater debt. This finding was also echoed in our research.

In 2010, the RGC passed a labor migration policy supportive of migration's role in increasing employment and reducing poverty among the labor force (MLTV, 2010). This was accompanied by a series of subdecrees and *prakas* (regulations) regulating various aspects of Cambodian workers abroad, and strengthening intergovernmental collaboration, particularly with Thailand, Malaysia, and South Korea (ILO, 2009; Hing et al., 2011). Interviews with local authorities in Prek Trob and Kampong Kor Krom, however, revealed that at the village level there is little to no awareness of these policies and no systematic strategy, programs, or budget. It was a common sentiment among most of those working in local authorities that migration was not to be encouraged and should be managed or controlled in some way. One local commune-level official from Prek Trob village said,

> For villagers, they think migration is good as they can get more money to help the family. But, for the authorities, we do not want villagers to migrate. We want them to have work in the community. In fact, in the commune there are many jobs in farming, but people do not like to invest in their land as it is so risky for them. So many people find that it is better to migrate. We, as the authority, can't stop villagers from migrating as it is their right.

One local commune-level official responsible for Kampong Kor Krom village said,

> So far, we have cooperated with NGOs working in the commune to help to improve the villagers' lives. We hope that when the livelihoods of villagers become better, it can help to prevent people from migrating. However, so far, the projects by local NGOs seem unable to prevent migration.

Among the community, therefore, there is generally a low expectation of receiving support from the government and thus little demanded of it. Pushed on the role they take to support villagers intending to migrate, governmental officials said that they could provide informal advice on the risks. Thus, while many in the community adopt migration as part of their household livelihood strategy, there is limited institutional support to help mitigate risks and maximize any benefits.

Conclusion: fishing, farming, flooding, and migration through the lens of political ecology

Fishing and farming livelihoods in communities around the Tonle Sap Lake are in transition. Both family-scale fishers and smallholder farmers overall have few personal assets or savings and are vulnerable to shocks. Many family-scale fishers are marginalized from access to fishery resources, which are also increasingly degraded. For smallholder farmers, while agriculture is preferable to fishing as a primary livelihood, it too is perceived as risky. Hence, whether as a strategy for livelihood diversification or in response to debt, migration is increasingly important.

The pattern and type of flooding (or drought) of Tonle Sap Lake shapes the ecological productivity and hence the possibilities for fishing and farming practices, which in turn influence vulnerabilities and the decision to migrate. For family-scale fishers, during a year with high floods, there is more extensive fishing grounds and an increased fish stock, as well as a greater fish catch and bigger fish. Thus, there is a potentially higher income in fishing, a higher demand for labor, and less incentive to migrate. During a year with low floods, there is less fishing ground, less fish stock, and smaller fish. Thus, more effort and investment in fishing gear and fuel may only yield low returns, which is an incentive for households to consider migration of members to diversify income and reduce vulnerability.

For farmers, during regular seasonal flooding, farming can be practiced with relatively low risk and potentially can produce two crops per year if the farmer has access to water. Thus, with household labor in demand, there is less incentive for migration. However, during high floods, farming is less viable due to prolonged inundation of farmland, shortening the farming season, and during low floods farming is less viable due to water shortage and increased pest incidence. Under these circumstances, while noting that farmers also fish and therefore may benefit from high floods, there is also a greater incentive to diversify household income through migration.

While flooding and drought as hazards are important factors in producing vulnerability in rural livelihoods, also generative of vulnerability are the politics and contestations over access to and control over resources, including wild-capture fisheries and land. Access to natural resources is clearly differentiated by socioeconomic groups and their political influence. One reason why family-scale fishers and smallholder farmers are vulnerable to disastrous flooding and droughts is because they have less political power to influence who can or cannot access natural resources and land, as well as the resources of the state.

As highlighted in Chapter 1, state institutions and policies are generative structures and processes that enable or disable farmers' and fishers' capacities to make their living. Existing policies on fisheries' resources, agriculture, and land are producing vulnerability, as are illicit activities such as flooded forest-land conversions and illegal fishing, which continue unabated. Other ineffective policies and institutions, such as those around health care, heighten vulnerabilities in the communities. Meanwhile, regional-scale policies, such as those for large dam construction on the Mekong River, are also ultimately producing vulnerabilities in the localities of Tonle Sap Lake. In the everyday lives of the family-scale fishers and small-scale farmers, there is very little sense of state support, including when a household takes a decision to send members to migrate.

To reduce vulnerability, government policy and the formal institutions through which it is deployed need to become more sensitized to the relationship between environmental change, access to land and fisheries' resources, and migration as a livelihood strategy. Improving resource governance, while fraught with well-documented challenges, needs to be seriously addressed, including protecting fishing areas from illegal practices; maintaining flooded forest; strengthening community fishery organizations; and supporting more resilient farming practices through agricultural outreach. Yet, also important is a nuanced recognition of the risks and opportunities migration constitutes in relation to the contemporary and increasingly mobile livelihoods of family-scale fishers and smallholder farmers.

Notes

1 Houses are not moveable but are built on stilts for families to live above water during the flooding season (Mak, 2011).
2 For an excellent analysis of flood vulnerabilities in the wider Sangkae River basin, see Doch et al. (2015).
3 "Interstitial environments are places in the landscape characterized by a transition between vegetative communities and/or between production or land management systems. Ephemeral environments are highly seasonal and appear relatively briefly, most commonly associated with the rising and falling of the floods." (Roberts, 2015: 62-63)
4 As designated in the 2006 Fisheries Law, which permits fishers to use small-scale gear throughout the year.
5 From mid-August to November, or even as late as early December.
6 For Prek Trob, the secondary school is located in the commune center 7 kilometers away and the high school is located in the district center 13 kilometers away. For Kampong Kor Krom, the secondary school is located in the neighboring village 3 kilometers away, and the high school is in Kampong Thom provincial town 20 kilometers away.
7 Government legislation eventually caught up, with the Sub-degree on Community Fisheries Management (2005) and the new Law on Fisheries (2006), at which time the Fisheries Administration replaced the Department of Fisheries.
8 This contrasts with the period before the 1990s, when farming principally consisted of one paddy-rice crop per year, using traditional seeds and cattle as draft animals, which also produced natural fertilizer for the fields.
9 For example, one popular location for villagers from Kampong Kor Krom is an agriculture concession known as "Zone 99" in Preah Vihear province, where there is a guaranteed payment of 15,000 riel per day, and it is relatively easy and inexpensive to travel to.

References

Arias, M.E., Cochrane, T.A., Piman, T., Kummu, M., Caruso, B.S., and Killeen, T.J. (2012). "Quantifying changes in flooding and habitats in the Tonle Sap Lake (Cambodia) caused by water infrastructure development and climate change in the Mekong Basin." *Journal of Environmental Management* 112: 53–66.
Baran, E., Jantunen, T., and Kieok, C.C. (2007a). *Values of inland fisheries in the Mekong River Basin*. Phnom Penh: WorldFish Center.
Baran, E., Starr, P., and Kura, Y. (2007b). *Influence of built structures on Tonle Sap fisheries*. Phnom Penh: Cambodia National Mekong Committee and WorldFish Center.
Brickell, K., and Springer, S. (2017). "Introduction to contemporary Cambodia." (pp. 1–13) in Brickell, K. and Springer, S. (eds.) *The Handbook of contemporary Cambodia*. London and New York: Routledge.
Bylander, M. (2013). "Depending on the sky: Environmental distress, migration and coping in rural Cambodia." *International Migration* 53(5): 135–147.
Bylander, M. (2015). "Credit as coping: Rethinking microcredit in the Cambodian context." *Oxford Development Studies* 43(4): 533–553.
Chan, S. (2009). *Costs and benefits of cross-country labour migration in the GMS: Cambodia case study*. Phnom Penh: Cambodia Development Research Institute (CDRI).
Chap, S., Touch, P., and Diepart, J.C. (2016). *Fisheries reforms and right-based fisheries: Insights from community fisheries across Cambodia*. Phnom Penh: The Learning Institute.

Diepart, J.C. (2010). "Cambodian peasant's contribution to rural development: A perspective from Kampong Thom province." *Biotechnology Agronomie Society Environment* 14: 321–340.

Diepart, J.C. (2016). *They will need land! The current land tenure situation and future land allocation needs of smallholder farmers in Cambodia.* MRLG Thematic Study Series #1. Mekong Region Land Governance (MRLG): Vientiane.

Diepart, J.C., Pilgrim, J., and Dulioust, J. (2014). "Migrations (Chapter 10)." in Sandoval, R., and Nhiep, S. (eds.) *Atlas of Cambodia: Maps on socio-economic development and environment.* Phnom Penh: Save Cambodia's Wildlife.

Dina, T., and Sato, J. (2014). "Is greater fishery access better for the poor? Explaining de-territorialisation of the Tonle Sap, Cambodia." *The Journal of Development Studies* 50: 962–976.

Doch, S., Diepart, J.C., and Heng, C. (2015). "A multi-scale flood vulnerability assessment of agricultural production in the context of environmental change: The case of the Sangkae River watershed, Batambang province." in Diepart, J.C. (ed.) *Learning for resilience: Insights from Cambodia's rural communities.* Phnom Penh: The Learning Institute.

Fisheries Administration. (2013). "Key considerations: Food and nutrition security vulnerability to mainstream hydropower dam development in Cambodia." Policy brief from project by Inland Fisheries Research and Development Institute, Fisheries Administration, with support from DANIDA, Oxfam, and WWF.

Heinonen, U. (2006). "Environmental impact on migration in Cambodia: Water-related migration from the Tonle Sap lake region." *International Journal of Water Resources Development* 22(3): 449–462.

Hing, V., Lun, P., and Phann, D. (2011). *Irregular migration from Cambodia: Characteristics, challenges and regulatory approach.* PIDS Discussion Paper Series. Phnom Penh: Cambodia Development Research Institute (CDRI).

ILO. (2009). *Review of labour migration management, policies and legal framework in Cambodia.* Bangkok: International Labour Organization (ILO) Regional Office for Asia and the Pacific.

Keskinen, M. (2006). "The lake with floating villages: Socio-economic analysis of the Tonle Sap Lake." *International Journal of Water Resources Development* 22(3): 463–480.

Keskinen, M., Kummu, M., Salmivaara, A., Paradis, S., Lauri, H., de Moel, H., Ward, P., and Sokhem, P. (2011). *Baseline results from hydrological and livelihood analyses, exploring Tonle Sap futures study.* Helsinki: Aalto University and 100Gen Ltd.

Keskinen, M., Kakonen, M., Tola, P., and Varis, O. (2007). "The Tonle Sap Lake, Cambodia: Water-related conflicts with abundance of water." *The Economics of Peace and Security Journal* 2(2): 49–59.

Kijewski, L., Meta, K., and David, S. (2017). "Parents of trafficking victims testify in Thailand." *Phnom Penh Post*, 27 January 2017. http://m.phnompenhpost.com/national/parents-trafficking-victims-testify-thailand.

Kim, S., Mam, K., Oeur, I., So, S., and Blake, R. (2013). "Fishery reforms on the Tonle Sap Lake: Risks and opportunities for innovation." *Cambodia Development Review* 2: 1–4.

Lamberts, D. (2006). "The Tonle Sap Lake as a productive ecosystem." *International Journal of Water Resources Development* 22(3): 481–495.

Mak, S. (2011). *Political geographies of the Tonle Sap: Power, space and resources.* PhD dissertation: National University of Singapore.

Mak, S. (2017). "Cambodia: Territorialisation of natural resources and environmental management." (pp. 356–373) in Hirsch, P. (ed.) *Handbook of the environment in Southeast Asia.* London and New York: Routledge.

Middleton, C., Un, B., and Thabchumpon, N. (2013). "Human security, flooding and migration among fishing – farming communities around the Tonle Sap Lake, Cambodia." (pp. 95–122) in Chantavanich, S., Middleton, C., and Ito, M. (eds.) *On the move: Critical migration themes in Southeast Asia*. Bangkok: International Organization on Migration and the Asia Research Center on Migration, Chulalongkorn University.

Milne, S., and Mahanty, S. (2015). "The political ecology of Cambodia's transformation." (pp. 1–27) in Milne, S. and Mahanty, S. (eds.) *Conservation and development in Cambodia: Exploring frontiers of change in nature, state and society*. London and New York: Routledge.

MLVT (Ministry of Labour and Vocational Training). (2010). *Policy on labour migration for Cambodia*. Phnom Penh: Ministry of Labour and Vocational Training.

MoP and UNDP. (2007). *Cambodia human development report 2007: Expanding choices for rural people*. Phnom Penh: Ministry of Planning (MoP) and United Nations Development Program (UNDP).

Packman, C.E., Gray, T.N.E., Collar, N.J., Evans, T.D., Van Zalinge, R.N., Virak, S., Lovett, A.A., and Dolman, P.M. (2013). "Rapid loss of Cambodia's grasslands." *Conservation Biology* 27: 245–247.

Parsons, L. (2017). "Under pressure: Environmental risk and contemporary resilience strategies in rural Cambodia." (pp. 146–156) in Brickell, K. and Springer, S. (eds.) *The Handbook of contemporary Cambodia*. London and New York: Routledge.

Roberts, A.S. (2015). "Lost in transition: Landscape, ecological gradients, and legibility on the Tonle Sap floodplain." (pp. 53–74) in Milne, S. and Mahanty, S. (eds.) *Conservation and development in Cambodia: Exploring frontiers of change in nature, state and society*. London and New York: Routledge.

Scurrah, N., and Hirsch, P. (2015). *The political economy of land governance in Cambodia*. Vientiane: Mekong Region Land Governance.

Sneddon, C. (2007). "Nature's materiality and the circuitous paths of accumulation: Dispossession of freshwater fisheries in Cambodia." *Antipode* 39(1): 167–193.

Sok, S., Chap, S., and Chheang, V. (2011). *Cambodia's agriculture: Challenges and prospects*. CICP Working Paper No 37. Cambodian Institute for Peace and Cooperation (CIPC): Phnom Penh.

Sokhem, P., and Sunada, K. (2006). "The governance of the Tonle Sap Lake, Cambodia: Integration of local, national and international levels." *Water Resources Development* 22(3): 399–416.

Styllis, G. (2015). "Million-ton rice export goal remains elusive." *Cambodia Daily*, 19 January 2015. www.cambodiadaily.com/archives/million-ton-rice-export-goal-remains-elusive-76355/.

Un, B. (2016). "'Fishing-farming' communities around Tonle Sap Lake, Cambodia: Fisheries reform, natural resource management, and changing livelihood patterns." (pp. 209–238) in Blake, D.J.H. and Robins, L. (eds.) *Water governance dynamics in the Mekong region*. Petaling Jaya: Strategic Information and Research Development Center.

World Bank. (2015). *Cambodian agriculture in transition: Opportunities and risks*. Washington, DC: World Bank.

3 Migrants seeking out and living with floods
A case study of Mingalar Kwet Thet settlement, Yangon, Myanmar

Maxime Boutry

Introduction

Myanmar has witnessed drastic changes since the political shift from a military government to a quasi-civilian one in November 2010. However, the effects of the past 50 years under the rule first of the State Law and Order Restoration Council (SLORC) and then the State Peace and Development Council (SPDC) military governments continue to impact on Myanmar's population, who largely still struggle to secure their livelihoods. The decaying economy under the former governments drove many people from rural communities to migrate in search of paid labor to domestic urban areas in Mandalay and Yangon, abroad to Thailand and Malaysia, or to border areas working, for example, in gold and tin mining or on plantations. This rural population displacement was exacerbated by large-scale land confiscations by the military throughout the country (Global Witness, 2015). Natural disasters are another factor that have shaped migration patterns (Thiesmeyer, 2012).

This chapter focuses on domestic Burmese migrants living in a peri-urban area, in the Old 86th Gate Ward of Hlaing Tha Yar township, located on the western outskirts of Yangon city. This informal settlement, called Mingalar Kwet Thet (in Burmese, 'Auspicious New Ward') first emerged in 2012 but has since been continuously expanding. At the time of writing (2015), it was composed of more than 1,000 Burmese households, approximately 80 percent of whom have migrated from the Ayeyarwaddy Delta. The remainder comes from the inner parts of Yangon. It is one of many new informal settlements that can be found in Hlaing Tha Yar township now seeking to become formal ones.

Mingalar Kwat Thet is subject to annual seasonal flooding during the monsoon season, as it is located on low-lying land that until recently was rice fields. Yet it is precisely this characteristic, together with its informal status, that keeps rent prices affordable to the inhabitants. This chapter's case study, documented between 2012 and 2015, tells the story of migrants working at securing their livelihoods, in the process seeking out flooded peri-urban areas in response to fast-changing living conditions in the midst of Yangon's expansion, and living with floods as a consequence. It argues that the political shift in 2010 created new spaces of livelihood strategy for poor migrant households together with new challenges, in which exposure to floods becomes a tool manipulated by different actors (the local government, the state, the migrant communities) to fulfill their own objectives.

Methodology

The methodology applied in this study has been limited to qualitative research procedures because the issue of informal settlements is highly sensitive. Government decision makers don't yet have clear policy regarding the growing periurban population, who are regularly evicted by local authorities for 'squatting' or occupying farmland. Here, we must briefly discuss the use of the term 'squatter'. If defined as people living on others' land without the right to do so, there are in fact no 'squatters' in Mingalar Kwat Thet. Such squatters are found nearby in legalized settlements such as the 86th Gate Ward, with houses built on land belonging to the Yangon City Development Committee (YCDC), typically fringes of land left between factories, roads, and ponds – in other words, any public land left 'vacant' – or on others' private land without the owners' consent. By contrast, in Mingalar Kwat Thet, all houses are built by their owners on plots that have been purchased from farmers. Yet, since all land in Mingalar Kwet Thet settlement are still under farmland administration, these households are squatters from the state's point of view.

In addition to the sensitive nature of discussing informal settlements in periurban Yangon, the first national census since 1984 was about to take place in late March 2014 when the core fieldwork of this study was conducted (with regular follow-up visits until September 2015). Information has consequently been gathered through semistructured interviews with different types of households chosen in order to bring some representativeness of Hlaing Tha Yar's outskirts. A total of 24 households and 13 key informants were interviewed. Households were chosen randomly at first, then by relying on interviewees' networks within Mingalar Kwet Thet and the adjacent ward. Interviews covered the geographical trajectories of these households, their main livelihoods' opportunities and constraints at origin and in Mingalar Kwet Thet, the networks they rely on when facing economical stress, and on the impact of and strategies toward flooding events, together with the outcomes of these strategies. Interviews included households who moved within the last 2 years from Ayeyarwaddy region ($n = 5$), households who moved earlier to urban areas and later on to Mingalar Kwet Thet settlement ($n = 3$), squatter households in 86th Gate Ward ($n = 2$) with members having regular jobs in the factories ($n = 3$) or by contrast those relying only on unstable employment in daily labor ($n = 3$), and women-headed households ($n = 2$). The interviewees represented also a range of different exposures to flooding.

Among the key informants were house brokers ($n = 4$), a factory manager and employees, one police informant, the acting administrator of Mingalar Kwet Thet, and local authorities of the adjacent 86th Gate Ward (the ward administrator

44 Maxime Boutry

and one '100-households leader'). Informal discussions were also had with non-governmental and civil society organizations working in Hlaing Tha Yar.

Living in Mingalar Kwet Thet settlement: livelihoods in a flooded environment

Livelihoods

Mingalar Kwet Thet comprised in mid-2015 about 1,000 households. A more precise figure cannot be provided due to a lack of any official data and the fact that housing is constantly increasing. When the author first visited this area in 2013, there were only about 100 households, among which the first ones were settled in 2012.

The informal nature of this settlement, which is not yet recognized as a proper ward by the township administration and the YCDC, means that Mingalar Kwet Thet has almost no permanent infrastructure, such as concrete roads, a drainage system, waste management, electricity, schools or health centers. Thus, Mingalar Kwet Thet is in fact the frontline of peri-urban housing, which makes it both remote and 'urban' at the same time. Its 'remoteness' relates to the absence of services and infrastructures available in official wards: except for one section of concrete road built in May 2015, pathways leading to housing plots are mud, considerably hindering movements during the rainy season (between late May and September). Electricity is provided in some places by private generators at expensive rates: 100 Myanmar Kyat (MMK)[1] for one neon light per night. There is a shortage of drinking water in the dry season, which has to be purchased at around 300 MMK for a five-liter purified water bottle or 100 MMK for pond surface water. The 'urban' side of Mingalar Kwet Thet relates to its proximity to the factories of the Hlaing Tha Yar and Shwe Lin Ban industrial zones. Rapid housing densification is also turning Mingalar Kwet Thet into a residential area, although still with only few shops. Hence, most Mingalar Kwet Thet households' livelihood activities take place outside of the settlement.

Housing comprises a mix of small houses (10–18 feet wide and 30–50 feet long) and 'barracks' made of wood and bamboo with corrugated iron roofs. Barracks are long houses divided into five to six stalls of between 60 and 100 square feet, and are the cheapest rents available, ranging from 25,000 to 50,000 MMK per month. Small houses are partly inhabited by their owners and partly rented to tenants. Houses inhabited by their owners are more numerous in the peripheral part of the settlement, which can be explained by the fact that land is cheaper when farther from the access gate to the settlement adjacent to 86th Gate Ward (Figure 3.1). This reveals migrants' strategies to access housing ownership by settling on the very periphery of peri-urbanized areas. In exploring this strategy later in this chapter, I consider its sustainability in relation to migrants' livelihoods, flooding events, and government policies.

In the 'typical' poor household in Mingalar Kwet Thet settlement, women work in factories. Employment in the garment industry, which constitutes the bulk of factories in Hlaing Tha Yar, is 90 percent occupied by women (Thin Lei Win, 2014). It is common to have at least two generations of women in one household working in factories, though employment conditions are not the same for women above and below 30 years old. Below 30 years old, women can secure monthly based employment, with salaries ranging from 50,000 MMK to 80,000 MMK per month, depending on the position and the worker's skills. These salaries are often complemented with overtime, raising the total to between 100,000 MMK and 150,000 MMK per month.[2] Above 30 years old, women can only find daily wage employment, remunerated on a production basis. For example, in a cake factory, one woman was paid 285 MMK per 100 packed pieces of cake, representing between 2,000 and 4,000 MMK per day. While daily wages appear higher than monthly salaries, daily workers are mobilized only if there is work available. Other work performed mostly by women includes selling food items as mobile sellers (fruits, fish, and meat) in their ward and sometimes closer to downtown.

Men can work in factories as well, although employment is restricted to more physical tasks, such as carrying packs of garments. Management work is also by men but out of reach for unskilled laborers living in Mingalar Kwet Thet. Men are most often involved in daily work, for example, as carriers in the market in the adjacent 86th Gate Ward, trishaw drivers (yet most do not own their own trishaw), and construction workers across Yangon city. The average salary for an unskilled male laborer is around 3,000 MMK per day. Work in the construction sector is affected by the rainy season, during which time men may turn to other daily work as mentioned but also to fishing in the surrounding fields and creeks. A minority able to invest in motorcycles work as taxi drivers at the nearby 86th Gate Ward.

Flooding

Hlaing Tha Yar township is situated between the Hlaing and Pan Hlaing rivers, two tributaries of the Yangon River. The whole township has been built on former low-lying paddy fields (Figure 3.1). Hence most communities there experience seasonal flooding, the worst of which is during the rainy season between May and September. Furthermore, Mingalar Kwet Thet settlement is crossed by a small creek. Seasonal flooding is also exacerbated by river tides during new and full moon days. The apparent silting up of these rivers also reduces their flow capacity, worsening floods. Given the prevalence of flooding, farmers owning paddy fields in this area are keen to sell their land for conversion to urban settlement.

Inhabitants of Mingalar Kwet Thet have few options to cope with floods. About half of the people living in the settlement are tenants, rather than the owners of their dwellings. The owners build low-cost houses for tenants, and thus many are not high enough to avoid being flooded during flood peaks. Meanwhile, as mentioned previously, for those who are owners of their houses in Mingalar Kwet Thet, they are located in the outer areas that were previously regularly

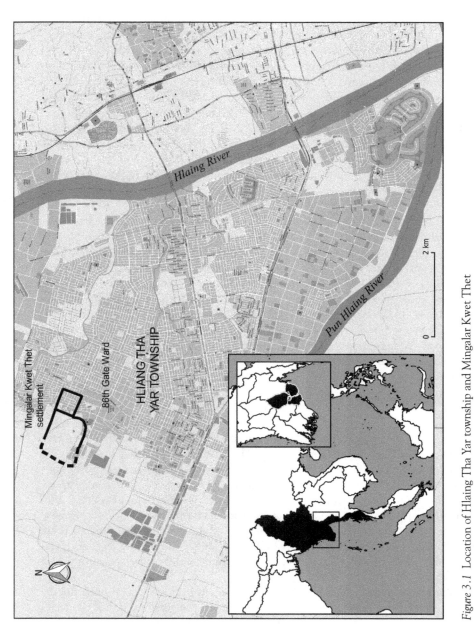

Figure 3.1 Location of Hlaing Tha Yar township and Mingalar Kwet Thet

Source: Adapted from OpenStreetMap and Digital Chart of the World

flooded paddy fields. During high flood events, as experienced during the 2015 monsoon season, even access to their homes becomes an issue. One interviewed family said they had to rent a barrack room because their own house became accessible only by boat. For others whose houses are accessible – yet only via deep, muddy tracks under water – if they can afford it, they may superimpose a bamboo floor to raise the room above the water. Others must go sleep elsewhere until the flooding subsides – for example, with family or friends or in the local monastery. Flooding causes many concerns; for example, parents carry their children on their backs to school for fear of leeches, as well as waterborne diseases, as stagnant floodwater is often covered with solid human waste and garbage thrown from behind each house.

Urban and rural migration to Mingalar Kwet Thet

Yangon city's expansion, industrialization, and domestic migrations

To understand the present situation of migrants in Mingalar Kwet Thet, it is necessary to contextualize Yangon's urban development pathway to its recent political history. The largest urban evictions in Yangon recently took place in 1989–1990, under the SLORC military government, in an urban 'squatter' resettlement program that moved 1.5 million people from inner-city areas countrywide. The program served the objective of relocating not only 'squatters' but also 'explosive crowds' (Lubeigt, 2007: 159). Those moved were largely relocated to peri-urban areas that until then had been paddy fields subject to flooding (Bosson, 2007). Within Yangon, as many as 500,000 people were relocated from central Yangon to South and North Dagon, Shwepyitha, and Hlaing Tha Yar (Bosson, 2007). This long-standing 'tradition' of eviction continued to be practiced under the quasi-civilian government of President Thein Sein (Myanmar Eleven, 2014), pushing populations to seek housing and new work opportunities in the most peripheral areas of Yangon.

Hlaing Tha Yar township is now a major industrial zone, and Mingalar Kwet Thet is developing on its fringes. Since the 1990s, thousands of migrant workers arrived in the township, leading to the integration of rural people into urban areas (Chaw Chaw, 2003). Besides, after 1990 the SLORC started to promote a more market-oriented economy in Myanmar in order to allocate resources according to market principles, to encourage private investment including foreign direct investment, and to promote exports (Yuen, 2011). Initially, most jobs were created in the newly emerging garments industry, which employed some 300,000 people at its high point, before the US-imposed sanctions of 2003 hit the industry and many workers were laid off (Moe Kyaw, 2001: 148).

The recent opening of the country to large-scale investments following its steps toward democratization is expected to foster rural emigration. The number of garment factories went down to 143 from around 400 in the peak period of the earlier market-oriented economy (before sanctions) in 2004. In 2011, it had slowly increased again to 180 factories, and in 2012 increased to 230 factories

(Moe Kyaw, 2013). Between 1998 and 2011, Hlaing Tha Yar township's average population growth rate reached 7.15 percent (against an average 2.6 percent for Yangon city) (JICA and YCDC, 2013: 2–20, 2–21).

In Myanmar's rural areas, conditions are difficult. In some village tracts in the Ayeyarwaddy Delta, as much as 70 percent of households are landless (Dapice et al., 2009). There are few economic opportunities other than in the farming sector, which itself faces great challenges. Thus, both landless and farming households often seek long-term – as opposed to seasonal – employment opportunities in urban settings. Cyclone Nargis, which struck the Ayeyarwaddy Delta in May 2008, severely impacted the area's economy and amplified migration from this region to Yangon, including to Hlaing Tha Yar (Thiesmeyer, 2012).

Migration patterns and trajectories

Approximately 80 percent of the population of Mingalar Kwet Thet are families who originate from the Ayeyarwaddy region and who migrated over the last 10 years. The remaining households originate from other regions, such as Bago and the Dry Zone, or from Yangon's inner townships or from other wards in Hlaing Tha Yar. While the reasons why these households moved to Mingalar Kwet Thet are diverse, one common characteristic is the quest for access to affordable housing in the midst of skyrocketing rents in Yangon since 2012 (AFP, 2013).

Rural to peri-urban migration

Detailed data on internal migration in Myanmar before the opening of the country in 2010 are available from three surveys conducted by the Department of Population of the Ministry of Immigration and Population with funding from the United Nations Population Fund[3] (UNFPA) (Nyi Nyi, 2013). The data detail that in absolute numbers of nonreturn migrants, the largest flow is from the Ayeyarwaddy region to Yangon with 14.8 percent of all nonreturn migrants. Over the 1991–2007 period, it is also indicated that married individuals occupy an increasing place in migration, representing more than half of recorded male and female migrants (Nyi Nyi, 2013). The only large-scale study measuring the pace of internal migrations in Myanmar under the new government, which is confined to formal sector workers reflecting only 2 percent of Myanmar's workforce, gives the proportion of migrants moving with all of their family at slightly over one-quarter of the total (Griffith and Kyaw Zaw Oo, 2015).

From our fieldwork in Mingalar Kwet Thet, we draw the following trends against information from the aforementioned studies. Mingalar Kwet Thet is made entirely of households who migrated fairly recently. Already-arrived families, furthermore, sometimes host relatives or others from their original village who are in search of employment in Yangon. As discussed previously, push factors to leave rural areas for a peri-urban one pertain to the few opportunities offered by the agricultural sector in the Ayeyarwaddy and Bago regions of lower Myanmar. Entire families or individuals from farmers' families without access to land are all potential candidates to migrate to urban centers (Boutry et al., 2017). Besides, interviews with young individuals living in Mingalar Kwet Thet underline the perceived undesirable nature of agricultural work, considering it 'tiring', 'dirty', and 'unstable', in contrast to urban salaried work in factories that could bring year-round income.

However, taking the cases of two families interviewed in Mingalar Kwet Thet reveals that being the household of a farmer or a landless laborer in the place of origin may shape a family's prospects at the destination. Daw Paing[4] and her husband used to cultivate 8 acres of paddy-rice land in their village in Hinthada township, Ayeyarwaddy Delta. They have four children, the youngest being the only boy. When they moved from their village to Hlaing Tha Yar 2 years ago, their eldest daughter was already married, and the second had just finished her diploma in the village's school. The two youngest are still at school. Daw Paing says it is the cost of education that drove them to Hlaing Tha Yar in order to seek regular urban work. They followed some villagers who had already moved into the 86th Gate Ward, adjacent to Mingalar Kwet Thet. They left all their children under the care of the eldest in the village. Daw Paing soon found some daily paid work in the 86th Gate Ward's cake factory. After living at their friends' house for half a month, they moved into a rental house in the nascent Mingalar Kwet Thet for 30,000 MMK per month in rent. After 1 year of renting, Daw Paing and her husband could buy a small plot in Mingalar Kwet Thet for 900,000 MMK. The money was raised from their own savings, plus some money that they borrowed from their eldest daughter who stayed to work the farm in the village. They then moved their two youngest children to put them at school in 86th Gate Ward.

In contrast, Daw Myi Gyi and her husband, who had no land at their village of origin, also in the Ayeyarwaddy Delta, moved to Hlaing Tha Yar in 2006 to seek a better living. At that time, they lived in a small bamboo house they rented in 86th Gate Ward, before it was a legalized settlement (see the section 'Land-use planning, urbanization, and migrants' linkages with flood' later in this chapter). At that time, their elder daughter, aged 16, worked with her mother in a cake factory, while their youngest was finishing her third year at school. The father only worked intermittently in physical wage labor, carrying packets at the market, for example, and rapidly became addicted to alcohol. Following multiple economic stresses, among which the husband's bad health was recurrent, they moved to a bamboo house they built themselves on land they occupied with the owner's consent and a bribe to the local authority, technically becoming squatters. In 2012, the eldest daughter married and moved to live with her husband, resulting in Daw Myi Gyi's household having one less income. Then the landowner planned to build and rent a house on their land, forcing Daw Myi Gyi, her husband, and the youngest daughter to move again. At that time, land in the several streets of 86th Gate Ward had just been formalized by the YCDC as proper housing lands. Hence, some absentee landowners returned to invest in the land or sell it, while those who had already built housing started raising the price of rent. With few resources, Daw Myi Gyi could not afford to rent land, so they built a house on YCDC land in a small space left between the road and the factory. Since then, the youngest daughter of Daw Myi Gyi dropped out of school and is now working in a garment factory, holding the only regular income of the family.

Intra-urban migration

Poor households, tenants, and squatters alike ended up in peri-urban areas following the military government's resettlement programs in the 1990s, described previously. The distance forcibly placed between these families and their previous urban work location resulted in increased transportation costs or simply cut them from their economic networks. Coupled with a peri-urban environment strange to them, which is actually closer to a rural setting but without the opportunity for agricultural activities, and with little or no access to government services, many families became indebted because of the forced relocation process (Boutry, 2015a). Under these conditions, many pawned their new peri-urban homes to invest in new jobs (trishaw, taxi rental, pig breeding) and eventually sold their property at low rates when they were unable to repay their debt.

The story of Daw Win follows such a trajectory. She is the elder of a household composed of her son's couple and their five children. They all live in a 100-square-foot barrack room. Daw Win moved from Mawbi township in the Ayeyarwaddy region to Yangon in the 1980s. After living in Thakketa township, southeast of Yangon, they managed to buy a small house in Kyi Mee Naing township in west Yangon. Yet, under the 'squatters resettlement program', they were resettled to Hlaing Tha Yar township, which at that time was the 'new fields' of Yangon (Skidmore, 2004: 150) and an area prone to cholera, dysentery, dengue, and malaria. There she began to sell vegetables at the market, while her son rode a trishaw. Far from her former social networks and from the town, debts started to rise, including those related to health, for food during the monsoon, for the marriage of her son, and for the delivery of her first grandson, until she had to sell her house. She repaid her debts and rented a house in another ward of Hlaing Tha Yar township. Her daughter-in-law was then working at a garment factory earning 80,000 MMK per month, and her son still rode a trishaw. However, when her daughter-in-law got sick and could not work for three days, she was fired. Then, with only her son's trishaw income of 3,000 MMK per day, they decided to buy a plot of land and build a house at the farthest boundary of Mingalar Kwet Thet from the 86th Gate Ward. Yet, as described previously, the inaccessibility of this area during the monsoon season made the house impracticable, and they ultimately decided to rent a more accessible barrack room, still in Mingalar Kwet Thet, but closer to the 86th Gate Ward. However, as discussed later in this chapter, their land ownership may still pay off in a few years.

A history of economic vulnerabilities: the pathway to living in flooded peri-urban areas

Despite the lack of quantitative data, our fieldwork shows without any doubt that the great majority of the households in Mingalar Kwet Thet can be considered to be living in poverty: a high birth rate (a mean of 5 members per household), low salaries (from 1,500 to 3,000 MMK per day, per household), and irregular incomes are largely shared traits within this community.

Economic vulnerability is a key pathway leading migrants from rural areas to peri-urban ones, with a perception that there is a greater range of job opportunities in urban areas, in contrast to unsecure livelihoods in their place of origin. An important change experienced by these populations is the transition from the cash-goods economy practiced in rural settings to a cash-only economy prevailing in urban areas (Boutry, 2015a). While cash availability is a limiting factor in rural areas, mutual aid based on exchanges of services, food, and other goods constitutes an important safety net. In urban settings, cash is almost exclusively required to access food and other services, while despite better salaries costs are also greater.

Debts contracted in an urban setting are not embedded in the traditional patron-client relationship found in rural areas (Boutry, 2015b). The vertical integration of different socioeconomic strata found in rural settings via patron-client relationships is limited or nonexistent in urban settings. Furthermore, the high mobility of many inhabitants of peri-urban marginal settlements such as Mingalar Kwet Thet leads to the dismantlement of any village-based migrants' communities that had once existed. The multiple origins of the migrants implies a very limited 'horizontal' integration on which they can rely, such as kinship and mutual aid among neighbors (Han Tin, 2008: 116). This lack of social capital leads households to rely on credit obtained at high rates, for example, through workmates in factories, or more often through their supervisors, at a 20–30 percent interest rate per month.

Thus, economic vulnerability in an urban setting cannot be dissociated from social vulnerability. Economic vulnerability implies a greater mobility for poor households, forced to move from one settlement to another according to job opportunities and housing prices. This mobility produces other forms of vulnerability. For example, given that migrants may not be registered in their new location of residence, it is also common that their children are unlikely to have a proper identity card (ID), although this is a condition to access jobs, in factories for example. Hence the practice of borrowing another's ID – used also to bypass the minimum legal age of 18 to work in industries – is widespread among factory workers, including in Mingalar Kwet Thet. Yet, the possibility of borrowing another's ID is linked to the individual's social networks, which are hindered by greater mobility. In this case, as we encountered in Mingalar Kwet Thet, individuals seeking work in factories have to rely on 'ID brokers' who are paid to link one job seeker to someone available to 'lend' his or her ID. In this regard, mobility is related to the production of 'flexible citizenship' (Hogan and Marandola, 2005) and its associated vulnerabilities, where migrants are not granted the same access to state services, such as IDs.

Ironically, for many, migration was undertaken in the first place as a strategy to cope with vulnerability in their place of origin. Urban employment, if gained, provides regular income in contrast to seasonal rural work, especially for

52 *Maxime Boutry*

farmlandless households, and can be observed in Mingalar Kwet Thet in the salaried employment in factories located nearby. Yet, this livelihood strategy directly links to the fact that to secure this work many migrants have only the choice of renting in peri-urban, informal settlements subject to flooding or squatting on public land given housing or rent costs.

In the following sections, I consider how migration intersects with flooding, and how this intersection shapes migrants' vulnerability in Mingalar Kwet Thet.

Land-use planning, urbanization, and migrants' linkages with flood

Flooding land as a source of low-cost housing for migrants

Since 2012, Mingalar Kwet Thet has grown rapidly as an informal settlement as land was sold by farmers to investors for building houses and for speculative purposes (Figure 3.2). The rising prices of land and housing in Yangon, even in peri-urban areas, coupled to the fact that these former paddy fields are low-lying land and thus prone to flooding, led many farmers to sell their lands. Speculators anticipate that what at first was established as an informal settlement will

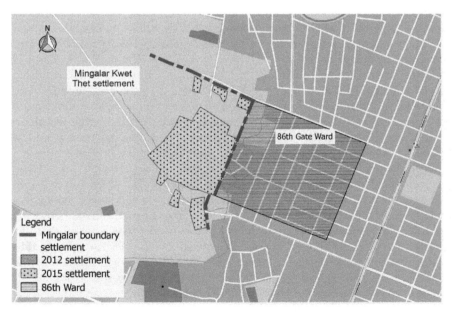

Figure 3.2 The location of Mingalar Kwet Thet settlement (86th Gate Ward, Hlaing Tha Yar township) in 2012 and 2015

Source: Adapted from OpenStreetMap and data from Google Maps

eventually become legally recognized as housing land, especially if they invest in drainage and flood management infrastructure. Even within 2012, land prices grew five times over their initial value. However, rent remains low enough that poor households can still afford it.

In 2015, Mingalar Kwet Thet settlement, while still not officially recognized as a ward under Hlaing Tar Yar township, is referred to as Mingalar Kwet Thet by the Hlaing Tha Yar authorities. In contrast, in 2012–2013, Mingalar Kwet Thet settlement was not yet 'named', meaning that although it is still informal, it is less so in 2015 than in 2012. Here, a reflection on the terminology related to the 'informal' nature of this settlement is necessary to understand the administrative context in which Mingalar Kwet Thet is evolving.

Mingalar Kwet Thet, like the whole township of Hlaing Tha Yar, has been built on former paddy fields. The differentiating factor between formal and informal settlements in Hlaing Tha Yar lies in land zoning and official recognition of land use by the concerned authorities: the Ministry of Agriculture and Irrigation (MoAI), regarding agricultural lands, and the YCDC, regarding housing land within Yangon district. Hence, what distinguishes Mingalar Kwet Thet from other inner Hlaing Tha Yar wards is that the land is not yet recognized as housing land and thus is still under the jurisdiction of the MoAI. For this reason, households in Mingalar Kwet Thet are under threat of being evicted at any time since the settlement does not fall under the official urban land-use planning strategy. Yet, the formalization process that is concretized by having proper registration as housing land (the 'LaYa' 30 form) is a progressive one. In the absence of proper land-use planning at the Yangon-region level, most current official wards – at least those created since the late 1990s – were once informal, and the formalization process would occur together with housing densification, the construction of new factories in the area, and unclear decisions made by the YCDC regarding Yangon's urban expansion.

In Mingalar Kwet Thet as of mid-2015, there are some signs that it may be formalized sooner rather than later. One interviewed household among those who settled in 2013 recalled that they were threatened by YCDC staff and the township administration when building their house at that time. A land broker interviewed suggested that, during Mingalar Kwet Thet's creation, the authorities were regularly threatening new households with eviction. Yet, he interpreted these acts as an attempt to generate income, rather than to enforce the law. As a matter of fact, none of Mingalar Kwet Thet's households have been evicted since 2012. Interviewed households confirmed that ward authorities and YCDC staff regularly visit under different pretexts to ask for money. For example, YCDC staff who visited at the beginning of 2015 asked for no less than 25,000 MMK for a Burmese boxing DVD as a compulsory purchase 'to support infrastructure' for the ward, providing no more details. Whether the purpose is really to improve the ward's infrastructure is difficult to know. Yet, the house broker interviewed, himself close to the 86th Gate Ward authorities, said that threats for houses to be evicted were now close to zero, due to the visit of a delegation from the YCDC and the

Ministry of Environmental Conservation and Forestry who found that Mingalar Kwet Thet was too polluted by the surrounding factories' waste to be suitable for paddy cultivation.

Flooding as a source of vulnerability

As described previously, Mingalar Kwet Thet experiences regular flooding during the rainy season. This has direct consequences on hygiene and environmental conditions. Given the poor state of sanitation (few houses are equipped with proper flush latrines), stagnant floodwater is a source of disease: chronic diarrhea, which affects children and old people especially; malaria and dengue, which have a high incidence; and tuberculosis (TB), which is a significant cause of death. Leeches are also abundant in surrounding waters. Exacerbating the impacts of the poor environmental conditions on the population's vulnerability are the lack of ready access to health services and the cost of accessing health services, which leads to higher death rates. In the absence of ward-based data, I draw on Hlaing Tha Yar township's statistics, which reveal the township as ranked seventh (among 33 monitored townships in Yangon Greater City) in terms of TB occurrence and second in terms of deaths due to TB, and third and second, respectively, for dysentery and malaria (YCDC, 2011).

Flooding also affects the livelihoods of Mingalar Kwet Thet's inhabitants. While the monsoon season marks generally fewer work opportunities, especially for daily labor working in construction, flooding sometimes even prevents people from reaching the main roads in order to go to work, or the children to school. This in turn creates economic vulnerability as, in the case of one interviewed household, the family has to find another temporary living place. This can be achieved by renting more expensive, less flooded rooms in inner wards during the highest flooding events. However, not all can afford such a move.

U Kyaw's household arrived in Mingalar Kwet Thet in early 2015. In his rural village, he used to drive power tillers to plow others' farmland, as well as do other casual labor. His wife used to work as a wage laborer in agriculture. They came together to Mingalar Kwet Thet at the request of one friend already living there who invited U Kyaw to work as a carpenter. They left their two children with the wife's mother. Their main motivation to leave their village was to quickly make enough money in order to repay debts contracted for various reasons, including the hospitalization of one of their children. In Mingalar Kwet Thet, they rent a barrack room for 25,000 MMK. Since he arrived, U Kyaw managed to save 200,000 MMK within 3 months, which is a substantial sum, especially for wage laborers in Myanmar. His wife, also looking for a job, did not find one, as employment in factories is difficult to obtain as she is over 30 years old. Despite the good start that they made in 2015, an extraordinary flooding event in August 2015 ended their employment, so they decided to return to their village instead of moving to more expensive housing.

Most interviewed households stated that they would like to move to wards with better facilities and a healthier environment, but they consider that they have few chances to do so. Rising prices of housing and land since the opening up of the country in 2010 constitute the greatest constraint to meeting basic needs when living in urban areas. Poor households are condemned to live in cheaper places – that is, new settlements that have little or no infrastructure since they are informal and hence do not receive government support (mainly from the YCDC) and basic urban services. Furthermore, the mobility induced by migrants' livelihood insecurity perpetually pushes them toward the fringes of urban development and its associated vulnerabilities.

As a last resort, families from rural areas may return to their village, if they didn't sell all of their belongings in their place of origin. Yet, according to my interviews, this rarely happens as most families, if they are willing to go back to their village, want to be in a 'successful' position when doing so. In other words, families are not willing to go back to their village if they have failed to improve their situation; they would rather go to another new settlement. Meanwhile, households who have moved from other urban areas generally have nowhere else to go. They cope, as best they can, potentially even turning to harmful coping strategies, including having children drop out of school in order to work,[5] including begging activities in markets, as well as commercial sex work for young girls (Boutry, 2015a).

Flood management as a source of vulnerability

Most landowners are seeking to improve the wards where they have bought land for their own habitation, as an investment, or for speculative purposes, and notably to improve it against vulnerability to flooding. Hence, in Mingalar Kwet Thet, wealthier investors started to improve basic transportation by building concrete roads or covering muddy pathways with sandbags. While it may profit the inhabitants living there in the short term, the landowners' actual objectives for such improvements are to be able to secure their land through formalization, and thus ultimately to raise the prices of their properties; the price of legal housing land is at least 10 times that of illegal land.

As this process proceeds, as it seems to be in Mingalar Kwet Thet, many poor households see their rents rise and are finally obliged to move to cheaper places. Hence, while push factors led households to migrate to peri-urban environments that flood, ultimately as flooding becomes managed, their economic vulnerability grows as rents increase and their likelihood of displacement grows as they are priced out of their tenancy. It can be understood as part of a 'risk redistribution' process (Lebel et al., 2011), where in this case managing floods results in pushing pioneer migrants away, most likely to other flood-prone areas.

While urban developments, mostly led under the former regime by the Union Solidarity Development Party (USDP)[6] and by the YCDC, helped reduce the impacts of flooding in many parts of Hlaing Tha Yar township, these developments have been unequally implemented. Among other reasons, the composition of the YCDC, as with other administrative bodies, is linked to administrative units such as the township, where allocated human resources are the same for all townships even as demographic characteristics differ (Kyi Pyar Chit Saw and Arnold, 2014).

As such, Hlaing Tha Yar is the township with the fewest staff per inhabitant given it is the most populated township within the Yangon region (Department of Population, 2015). Unofficial wards, such as Mingalar Kwet Thet, are thus left behind, and, as of mid-2015, it lacked intervention from the YCDC for flood management. Moreover, Mingalar Kwet Thet suffers from flood infrastructure built in formal wards, such as in the 86th Gate Ward, which discharges its sewage waters into the river nearby. On this, the constitution states that authorities (here, the YCDC)

> may cause all or any municipal drains to empty into the [Yangon], [Bago] or Hlaing rivers or any other place, whether within or without the City, and may dispose of the sewage at any place, whether within or without the City, and in any manner, which it shall deem suitable for such purpose.
> (Leckie and Simperingham, 2009: 402)

This leaves important urban-planning matters at the discretion of the authorities.

National policies

Since the political shift from the military to the semicivilian government in 2010, new policies have been created on an almost daily basis, with no proper planning and generally aimed at responding to immediate needs.

Policies on urban flood management

Regarding policies directly related to flooding, the MoAI has been implementing a National Flood Protection Plan since late 2011, based on lessons learned from recent disasters, including Cyclone Nargis, and flash floods in Pakkoku, Bago, Pathein, and Kachin regions. Yet, these policies are principally for responding to disasters rather than flood management in rural and urban areas, which are yet to be systematically planned.

The Dutch government supported a *Strategic Study for Integrated Water Resources Management (IWRM) in Myanmar*, which, of significance to Hlaing Tha Yar township, led to the dredging of the Pan Hlaing River and the installation of additional sluice gates to manage floods in the north of Yangon (van Meel et al., 2015; Myanmar News Agency, 2015). Yet, most of the issues regarding flood management in peri-urban environments relate to the ambiguousness of such areas. As an example, in the aforementioned strategic study (van Meel et al., 2015), there is no mention of 'peri-urban' areas, and only a little about urban growth with particular concern for potential increases in demand for energy and fresh water, and with no particular propositions for preventing flooding in urban areas. The Myanmar government focuses mainly on rural development and even the Pan Hlaing River Project is mainly aimed at fostering agriculture in northern Yangon rather than managing floods in peri-urban areas (Myanmar News

Agency, 2015: 3). The government's prioritization of water management regarding the Pan Hlaing River Project is well summarized by the Dutch study:

> Originally purely designed for agriculture, mainly low-value paddy, the integration with new developments must be aimed at a higher added value for the restoration of this river: drainage for new urban and industrial areas, potential water supply and navigation for industrial developments, serving developments for crop diversification and aquaculture.
> (van Meel et al., 2015: 122)

Foreign organizations involved in water management, such as the World Bank, the Asian Development Bank, the Japan International Cooperation Agency (JICA), and others, are pushing for IWRM (van Meel et al., 2015: 53). However, the main problem for tackling water management issues in peri-urban areas relates to the poor state of land-use planning and urbanization policies, as well as governance issues. Interministry collaboration is also a problem in many sectors, including land use, and this is especially so regarding peri-urban areas. For example,

> The Ministry of Health is responsible for drinking water quality standards, the Ministry of Environmental Conservation & Forestry is responsible for standards of industrial waste water and its impact on the environment, and the actual monitoring of water quality is done by municipal entities [like the YCDC]. But none of these parties have the standards, the equipment, the models or the laboratories to actually monitor water quality. So licensing is weak, or none existent, there are more illegal than legal tube wells in the Yangon area, and integrated, transparent decision making is not possible at the moment.
> (van Meel et al., 2015: 73)

Land-use planning and urbanization policies

The impacts of flood- and environment-related policies, land-use planning, and urbanization policies (or the lack thereof) are core determinants in understanding peri-urban migrant households' vulnerability. Yangon's expansion started to be planned in the wake of the country's open-door policy adopted in 1988, followed by the creation in 1995 of the Myanmar Industrial Development Committee (Lubeigt, 2007). But the creation of industrial zones in Hlaing Tha Yar, Dagon, and Shwe Pyi Thar townships was also linked to the forced resettlement of so-called squatters and small private industries from residential areas. Since that time, land-use planning in peri-urban Yangon has been chaotic, with the perpetual transformation of rural lands into urban ones, as discussed previously. Meanwhile, in the absence of proper land-use planning, the government is challenged by peri-urban growth sustained by increasing foreign investments in the industrial sector. The semicivilian government of President Thein Sein viewed squatters and informal settlements in terms of law enforcement and order rather than in terms of vulnerability and poverty alleviation (Irrawaddy Magazine, 2014). In other words, squatters are seen as illegal occupants rather than people who migrated to cope with economic and environmental vulnerability. Following squatter evictions in Hlaing Tha Yar township in March 2014, Ye Htut, the presidential spokesman, admitted that 'for eviction cases, the government system seems to be broken down. There is no law enforcement in some areas, even in Naypyidaw' (Irrawaddy Magazine, 2014).

The drafting of a *Strategic Urban Development Plan of the Greater Yangon* with the support of JICA (JICA and YCDC, 2013), set over a 40-year period, far from ascertaining control over urbanization and land-use change in peri-urban areas, created a wave of speculation in locations foreseen to be included in the project (Ye Mon and Myat Nyein Aye, 2015). As discussed previously, this speculation process is directly affecting migrants and creating exclusion for the poorest households who cannot afford the increasing rent prices. Migrant households are caught in the middle of contradictory forces: on the one hand, industrialization calls for more workers (often originating from rural areas), and on the other hand, land speculation tends to push migrants farther from formal urbanized wards and these work opportunities. The Myanmar government is however trying to solve this issue through the expansion of low-cost housing units, built both by the YCDC and in contract with private companies. For the fiscal year 2015–2016 alone, the government had planned to launch seven new projects in Yangon of around 13,000 housing units in total, yet Hlaing Tha Yar Township was not included (Myat Nyein Aye and Tin Yadandar Htun, 2015). Besides, despite being termed 'low cost', each unit still costs around 30 million MMK, an amount that low-income households can definitely not afford.

Ways forward to reduce vulnerability

In order to address the vulnerability of migrant households living in peri-urban, informal, and flooded settlements, a better conceptualization of the peri-urban areas, a hinge between urban and rural settings, is necessary. The government prioritizes agriculture and rural development as drivers of growth and broad-based development (ADB, 2012) rather than addressing urban forms of poverty, despite the fact that economic incentives for urban migration are likely to remain and even grow. Up to now, urban growth is mostly market driven, leading to a chaotic urban sprawl where land-use planning remains weak. Land-use planning taking into account housing needs in relation to industrial growth should be an important policy priority, intersecting with other policies, including flood management.

Flood management

Major flood management projects, for instance the Pan Hlaing River dredging project – despite being rural development oriented – will benefit Hlaing Tha Yar Township as a whole, including Mingalar Kwet Thet. Nevertheless, more localized flood management projects such as drainage and wastewater management remain necessary. Here, however, land-use planning and a longer-term vision of Yangon city's expansion is necessary. By managing urbanization within short time frames, or even reactively, informal settlements where poor migrant households are confined are poorly considered. This is well illustrated by the waste 'management' in Mingalar Kwet Thet, where brokers had to collectively ask the YCDC to cease uncontrolled dumping, the waste of which came in great part from housing in 86th Gate Ward.

Land-use planning and urbanization policies

Land-use planning could help to secure migrants' ownership. However, as discussed previously, the formalization of land from agriculture to housing land under YCDC's jurisdiction sees an increase in land prices due to speculative, market-driven development, pricing migrants out. Meanwhile, government-led low-cost housing projects require better support from banks, such as the Construction and Housing Development Bank, including lower interest rates than currently practiced, which hinder the efforts to decrease housing prices (Myat Nyein Aye and Tin Yadandar Htun, 2015).

A peri-urban growth-centered approach?

Government policy must take into account the connection between industrial growth and increasing demand for factory workers in relation to housing and land. Here, the land market's regulation, subsidized housing projects, and monitoring of peri-urban growth is strongly recommended. These objectives have to be considered in the long term, having in mind the relationship between rural livelihoods' (in)security and migration to peri-urban areas. While rural development has to be welcomed, it should not conceal the growing need for urban development and the implications for poor migrant households that constitute the bulk of factory workers.

Conclusion

Intersecting sets of government policies on rural land tenure, urban planning, and economic development, accompanied by – and tied to – the very rapid rise of housing prices since 2012, have shaped migration patterns to peri-urban areas. In this context, many vulnerable migrants are found in unplanned and illegal settlements because these are characterized by cheaper housing (and are even 'free' for squatters). These settlements, however, are more likely to be flooded because of the lack of public policies and services that apply there.

In Hlaing Tha Yar township, migrants have deliberately settled in areas prone to flooding since these are far cheaper than officially recognized and managed settlements. Hence, flood, while being a driver of economic vulnerability, may be considered at the same time an opportunity for providing the 'squatters' a space in the development of Yangon's outskirts. Most of the migrants don't own the land on which they live but can rent it at cheap prices, since these are illegally constructed lands. They thus also face risks of eviction while, at the same time, landowners fight this threat upon their property by elevating roads and digging water drainage systems to show their role in the development of this new settlement and possibly gain official recognition by the authorities. We can anticipate that Mingalar Kwet Thet settlement will become an official settlement in the near future. Consequently, this would lead to the departure of the former migrants, as land price and rents will rise. For migrants moving to pioneer areas such as the Mingalar Kwet Thet settlement, the lack of 'social glue' characterizing these contexts is a factor producing vulnerability; the lack of social networks results in less means to access resources and to cope with vulnerability, especially in unhealthy environments to which regular flooding greatly contribute.

The ongoing shift in governance at the national level in Myanmar tends to also reveal its weakness, especially in fast-growing townships such as Hlaing Tha Yar where authorities have much difficulty monitoring changes, including the transformation of farmlands to housing areas, population growth and related demands (in health services, education, and the drinking water supply), and constraints (waste management, flood-prone settlements). Yet, urban population growth is inevitable, hence the necessity for the government to address at an early stage the different issues faced by new settlers in urban settings. The intersection of flooding and migration issues reveals much about the governance transition of Myanmar. These dynamics are torn between economic development and human/citizen empowerment, which represent at the same time both threats and opportunities for communities experiencing floods, and especially migrant ones.

Notes

1 US$1 is approximately 1,200 Myanmar Kyat (MMK) in March 2015.
2 The Myanmar government officially set its first minimum wage at 3,600 MMK (US$2.80) per day on 29 August 2015 for all sectors and businesses employing more than 15 people. Since then, many factories cancelled overtime work to compensate the increase in salaries (Khin Wine Phyu Phyu, 2015).
3 The 1991 Population Changes and Fertility Survey, the 2001 Fertility and Reproductive Health Survey, and the 2007 Fertility and Reproductive Health Survey.
4 For the purpose of confidentiality, names in this chapter are pseudonyms.
5 Many workers in factories start at 16 years old despite the 18-year minimum age threshold.
6 The party of the ruling junta under the SDPC.

References

ADB. (2012). *Myanmar in transition: Opportunities and challenges*. Mandaluyong: Asian Development Bank (ADB).
AFP. (2013). "Soaring land prices push Myanmar's poor into streets." *The Star Online*, 11 September 2013. www.thestar.com.my/News/Regional/2013/09/11/Homeless-due-to-rent-hikes-Soaring-land-prices-push-Myanmars-poor-into-streets.aspx.

Bosson, A. (2007). *Forced migration/internal displacement in Burma with an emphasis on government- controlled areas*. Geneva: Internal Displacement Monitoring Center and Norwegian Refugee Council.

Boutry, M. (2015a). *Urban poverty in Yangon greater city: A qualitative study of urban poverty, its causes and consequences*. Yangon: WFP, UNICEF and UN-HABITAT.

Boutry, M. (2015b). *Trajectoires littorales de l'hégémonie birmane (Irrawaddy, Tenasserim, Sud Thaïlande)*. Paris: Les Indes savantes-Irasec.

Boutry, M., Allaverdian, C., Mellac, M., Huard, S., San Thein, Tin Myo Win, Khin Pyae Sone (2017). *Land tenure in rural lowland Myanmar: From historical perspectives to contemporary realities in the Dry zone and the Delta*. Of lives and land Myanmar research series. Yangon: Groupe de Recherche et d'Echanges Technologiques (GRET).

Chaw, C. (2003). "Rural women migrating to urban garment factories in Myanmar." (pp. 203–224) in Kaosaard, M. and Dore, J. (eds.) *Social challenges for the Mekong region*. Chiang Mai: Social Research Institute, Chiang Mai University.

Dapice, D., Vallely, T., and Wilkinson, B. (2009). *Assessment of the Myanmar agricultural economy*. Cambridge, MA: Harvard Kennedy School, Asia Program for International Development Enterprises.

Department of Population. (2015). *The 2014 Myanmar population and housing census, Yangon Region census report, Volume 3 – L*. Nay Pyi Taw: Ministry of Immigration and Population.

Global Witness. (2015). *Guns, cronies and crops: How military, political and business cronies conspired to grab land in Myanmar*. London: Global Witness.

Griffith, M.P., and Zaw Oo, K. (2015). *Formal sector internal migration in Myanmar: Results from 2013–2014 formal sector survey*. Yangon: Social Policy and Poverty Research Group/LIFT.

Hogan, J., and Marandola, E. (2005). "Towards an interdisciplinary conceptualisation of vulnerability." *Population, Space and Place* 11: 455–471.

Irrawaddy Magazine. (2014). "Burma needs policy for squatters: Ye Htut." *The Irrawaddy Magazine*, 14 March 2014. www.irrawaddy.org/burma/burma-needs-policy-squatters-ye-htut.html.

JICA and YCDC. (2013). *The project for the strategic urban development plan of the greater Yangon*. Yangon: Japan International Cooperation Agency (JICA) and Yangon City Development Committee (YCDC).

Khin Wine Phyu Phyu. (2015). "New minimum wage sees workers sacked and struggling." *Myanmar Times*, 31 August 2015. www.mmtimes.com/index.php/national-news/yangon/16221-new-minimum-wage-sees-workers-sacked-and-struggling.html.

Kyaw, M. (2001). "Textile and garment industry: Emerging export industry." (pp. 143–173) in Kudo, T. (ed.) *Industrial development in Myanmar: Prospects and challenges*. Chiba: Institute of Developing Economies, Japan External Trade Organization.

Lebel, L., Manuta, J.B., and Garden, P. (2011). "Institutional traps and vulnerability to changes in climate and flood regimes in Thailand." *Regional Environmental Change* 11: 45–58.

Leckie, S., and Simperingham, E. (2009). *Housing, land and property rights in Burma: The current legal framework*. Geneva: Displacement Solutions and The HLP Institute.

Lei Win, T. (2014). "Myanmar's garment workers join forces amid lure of city jobs." *Reuters.com*, 1 December 2014. www.reuters.com/article/2014/12/01/us-women-cities-myanmar-idUSKCN0JF2FS20141201.

Lubeigt, G. (2007). "Industrial zones in Burma and Burmese labour in Thailand." (pp. 159–188) in Skidmore, M. and Wilson, T. (eds.) *Myanmar: The state, community and the environment*. Canberra: Australian National University Press.

Moe Kyaw. (2013). *Textile and garment, presentation by the federation of chambers of commerce and industry*. www.centroestero.org/FTP/FocusMyanmar_FederChambersCommerce_MYANMAR.pdf.

Mon, Y., and Nyein Aye, M. (2015). "Sparse starting point for first new city." *Myanmar Times Online*, 22 June 2015. www.mmtimes.com/index.php/business/property-news/15133-sparse-starting-point-for-first-new-city.html.

Myanmar Eleven. (2014). "Evictions in Yangon strand thousands." *Myanmar Eleven Journal* 18(February): 1.

Myanmar News Agency. (2015). "Pan Hlaing river conservation project will benefit 20,833 households." *Global New Light of Myanmar* (15 March): 1.

Nyein Aye, M., and Yadandar Htun, T. (2015). "Yangon urgently needs low cost housing." *Myanmar Times Online*, 9 June 2015. www.mmtimes.com/index.php/business/property-news/14938-yangon-urgently-needs-low-cost-housing.html.

Nyi, N. (2013). *Levels, trends and patterns of internal migration in Myanmar*. Nay Pyi Taw: Department of Population Ministry of Immigration and Population.

Saw, K.P.C., and Arnold, M. (2014). *Administering the state in Myanmar: An overview of the General Administration Department*. Subnational Governance in Myanmar Discussion Paper Series. Yangon: Asia Foundation and Myanmar Development Research Institute.

Skidmore, M. (2004). *Karaoke fascism: Burma and the politics of fear*. Philadelphia: University of Pennsylvania Press.

Thiesmeyer, L. (2012). *Responding rural communities and environmental degradation in the Mekong River Basin*. Fujisawa: Keio Research Institute.

Tin, H. (2008). "Myanmar education: Challenges, prospects and options." (pp. 113–126) in Skidmore, M. and Wilson, T. (eds.) *Dictatorship, disorder and decline in Myanmar*. Canberra: Australian National University Press.

van Meel., P., Leewis, M., Tonneijck, M., and Leushuis, M. (2015). *Myanmar IWRM strategic study: Research and analysis, strategies and measures*. The Netherlands: Consortium Royal Haskoning DHV, Arcadis, Rebel Group, UNESCO-IHE, Dutch Water Authorities, and Tygron.

YCDC. (2011). *Unpublished survey on health indicators in Yangon greater city*. Yangon: Yangon City Development Committee (YCDC).

Yuen, L. (2011). "Prospects for economic development in Burma using the neoclassical model." *Indian Journal of Economics & Business* 10(2): 221–248.

4 Risky spaces, vulnerable households, and mobile lives in Laos

Quo vadis flooding and migration?

Albert Salamanca, Outhai Soukkhy, Joshua Rigg and Jacqueline Ernerot

Introduction

The Lao People's Democratic Republic (Lao PDR or Laos) is a landlocked country in mainland Southeast Asia. Many areas of Laos regularly experience various types of flooding affecting rural livelihoods. Depending on the location, the causes of flooding can range from those caused by large infrastructure developments such as hydropower dams to those that are linked with (extreme) climate variability, and probably climate change (ICEM, 2013). Some 97 percent of Laos's population lives within the Mekong basin (Mekong River Commission, 2011), making monsoonal flooding an annual reality that the population has adapted to, and takes advantage of. On the lowlands and in communities along riverbanks, the yearly pattern of livelihoods such as fishing, farming, and stock raising occurs alongside seasonal flooding. In rural upland areas, there is dependence on swidden agriculture and the gathering of nontimber forest products to meet needs (Yokoyama, 2014).

In Laos, we see flooding as not only a natural phenomenon but also one created by societal conditions, politics, policies, and decisions so that vulnerability is dynamic and context specific. This chapter details how different sources of vulnerability underpin flooding and migration in Laos, based on field research in areas where sudden-onset and long-duration floods occur. We then highlight how the intersection of flooding and migration is far from straightforward. The decision to migrate may be shaped by a number of considerations including *in situ* vulnerability factors, assets available to households, and the overall livelihood strategies of the household. In turn, we see vulnerability (and its obverse, capacity) as contingent on ethnicities and historical and current policies pertaining to infrastructure and upland development. In other words, the governance of identities, spaces, and natural resources impinge on the vulnerability of households to flooding such that the decision to migrate lies within a nexus of factors that impinge and are played out in different, often unique ways according to the assets and priorities of each household and the individual potential migrant.

Episodes of flooding are increasing in Laos (author collated data from EM-DAT). The Kammuri flooding and Typhoon Kesana in August 2008 and

August 2009, respectively, caused considerable damage (IDA and IFC, 2012). The European Union's (EU's) Index for Risk Management (INFORM) for 2015 showed an index of 9.8,[1] of which physical exposure to floods is a major source of risk. By comparison, earthquakes and drought have indices of only 3.7 and 1.42, respectively.

In the following sections, we describe our case study sites and why they were chosen. We also highlight the tools and approaches we used. Then we address the key question that underlines this volume: the relationship between flooding and migration. This leads into a discussion of the complex nature of vulnerability among the households we studied, and the dynamics of their livelihood strategies, before turning to illuminate the nexus between flooding, migration, and the creation of vulnerable households in the study sites.

Methodology

Morrow (1999: 2) points out that 'most people experience and respond to storms as members of households . . . most households are comprised of families, implying some degree of resource sharing. In the disaster context, this includes marshalling the necessary resources to respond to a hazard'. Taking the household as an organizing context then necessitates looking at the multiple dimensions, hierarchies, and relationships that sustain householding and generate the diverse livelihood portfolios that are so often a feature of households in the global South. Informed by a process of 'progressive contextualization' (after Vayda, 1983), correlates of vulnerability and capacity are explored, guided by some of the components of Mustafa et al.'s (2011) 'vulnerability and capacity index' (VCI). Households enter and exit out of conditions of vulnerability due to periodic hazards and the nature of existing stocks of assets. When numerous short and recurring situations of vulnerability become a crucible for the household, then mobility and migration as well-being enhancing steps may be pursued.

In the case of flooding and migration in Laos, four villages in two provinces at different altitudes were studied to explore how vulnerability manifests and is constructed in Laos by communities and households in different resource and environmental contexts. These villages represent areas where sudden (flash) and slow-onset floods occur and have had, historically and more recently, damaging impacts. The villages in northern Laos (Luang Prabang) experienced flash flooding while the villages in southern Laos (Savannakhet) more usually faced the challenge of slow-onset floods. We assumed that, by studying four sites representing different types of flooding, altitude, and topography informed by our understanding of migration in Laos, we would be better able to unpack and understand how flooding and migration intersect.[2]

We surveyed nearly all of the household members of each village covering, in total, 157 households: 37 households from Pha Vieng, 43 from Huay Man, 47 from Dong Yang, and 31 from Ban Lao (Table 4.1; Figure 4.1). The surveys were conducted between October and November 2012. From these households, we selected at least three households per village for in-depth qualitative interviews

Table 4.1 Selected characteristics of surveyed households (HHs)

Village	District	Province	Key ethnic characteristics	No. of HHs/Total HHs in the village	Average HH size (no. per HH)	Average number of HH members with productive full-time occupation	No. (percent) of HHs with labor migrants
Pha Vieng	Luang Prabang	Luang Prabang	A mixed village with a Khamu majority (Hmong accounts for 14 percent)	37/43	4.7	1.81	0
Huay Man	Phonexay	Luang Prabang	A mixed village with a Khamu majority (Hmong accounts for 12 percent)	43/44	5.4	1.63	4 (9.3%)
Dong Yang	Savannakhet	Savannakhet	Lao Loum	46/47	5.4	3.62	3 (6.5%)
Ban Lao	Savannakhet	Savannakhet	A mixed village with Phu Tai majority (Lao Loum accounts for 29 percent)	31/33	6.7	5.06	1 (3.2%)
Total				157			

Source: Authors' survey

Figure 4.1 Location of the village case studies

to understand the impacts of flooding on these households and their coping strategies. Resource maps, seasonal calendars, and historical time lines of each village were also produced with the participation of village members through participatory group exercises.

Case study sites

The sites in this study cover upland areas represented by Pha Vieng and Huay Man in Luang Prabang province in northern Laos, and lowland areas represented by Ban Lao and Dong Yang in Savannakhet province in the central portion of the country. All of the villages had access to electricity but none to an all-weather road, and they generally lacked easy access to medical facilities.

Luang Prabang province

Luang Prabang province, located north of Vientiane, has a tropical, wet-dry monsoon climate. The province has an average annual rainfall of 1,400 mm, and more than 90 percent of this falls between April and October (Lestrelin and Giordano, 2007). Northern Laos largely consists of steep mountains, and swidden agriculture producing upland rice and an assortment of other crops is a dominant occupation (Ingxay et al., 2015). It is the fourth-most populous province in Laos based on the 2005 census (Lao Statistics Bureau, 2005).

Pha Vieng village

Pha Vieng village, Luang Prabang district, is a linear settlement at the bottom of a forested valley inhabited largely by Khmu households and a handful of Hmong who pursue farming as their main livelihood. There are 43 households in the village. The surveyed households had an average household size of 4.7 members (Table 4.1). The village, which experienced flash flooding, is named after the prominent cliff that overlooks the village. Many of the households are resettled ethnic minorities, part of national resettlement programs initiated by the Lao government in the 1980s and 1990s. The first 16 households were moved to the village in 1988 and, in 1996, a further 21 households were resettled on the site. Following resettlement, the government provided plots for houses (10 by 50 meters), but no land for agriculture.

The Nam Pha River runs behind the village; tomato gardens and rice fields separate the village from the river. After harvesting, the rice fields are used for grazing. There is no bridge across this river, and the villagers must wade across to reach their fields.

The most basic houses in this village are unraised single rooms, thatch with bamboo sidings, often with a simple wooden bench outside. The houses of the slightly better-off consist of sturdier structures on sturdy wooden stilts set into concrete foundations.

Huay Man village

Huay Man village, Phonexay district, sits just off the only road that traverses the district and is located next to Pha Vieng. The majority of the houses are different from Pha Vieng and are made of teak or bamboo, most have corrugated roofs, and are of a better quality. It is also a mixed village with a Khmu majority and some Hmong.

Huay Man is also located beside the Nam Pha River and has experienced flash flooding, with steep-sided banks down to the channel, and fields are located both upstream and downstream. The village consists of 44 households and the surveyed households had an average of 5.4 members (Table 4.1). A school was established in 1988. Following an EU grant in 1997, the school was improved and expanded, although this school was damaged by a massive flooding in 2014. The surrounding environment is even more dramatic than that in the vicinity of Pha Vieng, with higher and steeper forested valley sides.

Like Pha Vieng, Huay Man was originally populated by 'voluntary' migrants from the uplands in the 1980s.

Savannakhet province

In contrast to the mountainous terrain of Luang Prabang province, Savannakhet province, at least close to the Mekong, is flat. Wide expanses of dry paddy fields are dotted with field shelters and wiry trees. Both study villages were located on the Xe Bang Fai River, where it acts as a border between Savannakhet and Khammouane provinces. The overall house quality is better than in Luang Prabang, with the majority of houses on stilts and elevated from the ground by up to 20 feet. The more recent constructions sit on concrete stilts, teak walls have been fashioned by professional carpenters, and official blue address signs sit above the doors showing the houses in the villages that have been enumerated by governmental officials. Based on the 2005 census, Savannakhet is the most populous province in Laos (Lao Statistics Bureau, 2005).

Dong Yang village

Don Yang village, Savannakhet district, consists of 47 ethnic Lao households with an average household size of surveyed households of 5.4 members (Table 4.1). Rice fields surround the village. Rice, vegetables, pumpkin, watermelon, corn, chili, papaya, sugar cane, and bananas are grown here. The farmers also multicrop with sesame, morning glory, and lemons.

In 1997, an irrigation system was constructed, enabling double cropping of wet rice. Rainwater is collected in nearby artificial ponds and channels are dug connecting the ponds and the Xe Bang Fai River. The villagers see the irrigation system and the construction of ponds as the main cause of flooding due to the increase in the volume of water during the rainy season and its slow discharge. For example, in 2011, all households except for three were flooded.

Ban Lao village

Located in Savannakhet district, Ban Lao village is split into a 'new' and 'old' village with about 70 meters of road through paddy fields separating the two hamlets. The 'new' village was established around 80 years ago and was the result of a shortage of space around the old village as the population increased. The status of the road, whose maintenance was funded by the monetary contribution of each household, is poor and it floods every year. There are 33 households in the village with a mix of ethnic Lao and Phu Thai, who are the majority, and an average household size of surveyed households of 6.7 members (Table 4.1).

Approximately 8 years ago, the first eucalyptus company came to the village. After harvesting their first rice crop, many men work for the company, leaving women and children to work in the fields and garden plots. The village has a simple school at the primary level only. When cropping is finished, the women go to the forests to collect mushrooms and bamboo shoots for their own consumption. They also make handicrafts (mats, sticky-rice baskets, and fabrics) to sell at the market; Many households, however, lost their equipment and materials during flooding in 2011.

These villages can be further characterized in terms of their access to basic infrastructure, ethnicity, and the characteristics of their household members.

Ethnicity

As already detailed, three of our four field sites were also characterized by their mixed ethnic composition. The largest ethnic group in the study villagers were the Khmu, with 43.3 percent, followed by ethnic Lao, at 36.9 percent. Other groups represented were Phu Thai (13.4 percent) and Hmong (6.4 percent). Of all the villages in the study, only Dong Yang was composed solely of one ethic group, namely ethnic Lao (Table 4.2).

Before 1991, the government of Laos classified its population into three broad categories based on altitude: the *Lao Loum*, *Lao Theung*, and *Lao Soung*, or 'lowland', 'midland', and 'highland' (or 'upland') Lao (Rigg, 2009; Baird, 2015). These classifications, however, are no longer used officially, although they are still widely used by the media, in everyday conversations, and in development circles to refer to different groups of Lao (see also Rigg, 2009). The Khmu belong to the *Lao Theung* category, the Hmong to the *Lao Soung*, and the Phu Thai to the *Lao Loum*, together with the ethnic Lao. These groups are ethnolinguistically distinct. The Lao and Phu Thai belong to the Tai group, Khmu to the Austroasiatic group, and Hmong to the Meo-Yao group in ethnolinguistic terms (Chazee, 1999). As Table 4.2 shows, the original altitudinal distribution of ethnic groups (implicit in the terms *Lao Loum*, *Lao Theung*, and *Lao Soung*) is no longer followed in the study sites where Hmong, Lao, and Khmu are collocated along the same altitude due to the relocation and resettlement policies of the government, livelihood-related reasons, and mobility (see also Roberts, 2015).

70 Albert Salamanca et al.

Table 4.2 Ethnicity of surveyed households

Villages	Ethnicity (%)				
	Hmong	Lao	Khmu	Phu Thai	Total
Pha Vieng, Luang Prabang (n = 37)	13.51	2.70	83.78	–	100.00
Huay Man, Phonexay (n = 43)	11.63	4.65	83.72	–	100.00
Dong Yang, Savannakhet (n = 46)	–	100.00	–	–	100.00
Ban Lao, Savannakhet (n = 31)	–	29.03	3.23	67.74	100.00

Source: Authors' survey

Occupations of household members

Some 62 percent (539) of 873 household members were considered working (but not necessarily earning a wage), and hence productive. Of these productive household members, 94 percent of their occupations were related to agriculture, forestry, and fisheries, of which farming was the dominant form of livelihood (86 percent). Others were raising livestock (9 percent), working in forestry (4 percent), and collecting non-timber forest products (NTFPs) (1 percent). The large majority – 84 percent – of these 'agriculturalists' worked full time, the remainder working seasonally (10 percent) or part time (1 percent). Of the 157 households, only 5 had a single productive household member (or breadwinner); the remainder had more than one working householder.

Education of household members

Household members had very low levels of education. Of the 873 total household members, 75 percent (659) were aged 6 years old and above. Of these, 16 percent had no formal education, while a small number (3 percent) had received only a temple (monastery) education. At most, the remaining 'educated' household members only had primary- (37 percent) or lower secondary-level (31 percent) education. A very small number had attended vocational (5 percent) college or university (1 percent). On average, female household members had spent slightly longer in school than their male counterparts (6.7 vs. 6.2 years, respectively).

Nature of floods and flooding

In this study, the hazard considered is flooding, of which there are two types: flash floods and river floods. In the two upland villages in this study, we learned from communities that the onset of flooding in 2012 was sudden due to unusually high precipitation levels in the mountainous areas of the catchment, coupled with denuded hillsides, resulting in flash flooding (Figure 4.2).

In the two lowland villages, Ban Lao and Dong Yang, river flooding occurred due to the inundation of the Xe Bang Fai (XBF) River. This was attributed by villagers to the construction of the Nam Theun 2 Dam (NT2), commissioned in 2010. Before NT2, flooding only occurred for a few days respondent households told us; now, it lingers for 2–3 months due to the release of water from the NT2. The situation became critical during the rainy season when water levels in the Nam Kong River, another tributary of the Mekong, were also high, pushing water further back up in its tributaries.

The issue of flooding has been regularly raised by various civil society organizations as among the key downstream impacts of NT2's operation to the World Bank and Asian Development Bank (ADB), who were key project financiers and backers. These concerns have been discounted by the World Bank and ADB (The World Bank Group, 2012). Baird et al. (2015: 1091) have argued that, although the physical role of NT2 in the severe flooding of villages in the XBF basin in 2011 is not clear-cut, NT2 has significantly added to the villagers' perceptions of flood risk. Villagers they have met from Gnommalath down into Nong Bok and Xaibouli districts reported 'increased levels of flooding since 2011. . . during the first full year of NT2 operation'.

Prolonged flooding episodes in the lowland villages of Dong Yang and Ban Lao occurred in 2011 (Figure 4.2). This could explain why 80 percent of lowland households described their experience of flooding as 'exceptional'. For 80 percent

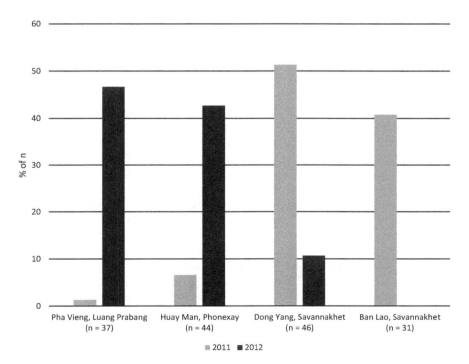

Figure 4.2 Years when flooding affect households in upland and lowland study sites

Source: Authors' survey

of the upland households, the flooding they experienced was described as 'seasonal'. Such differences could be due to how the question was posed, but it could also imply something experiential. For lowland villages, flooding of that intensity had been rare; although they are located on a floodplain and have experienced flooding in the past – and have built their houses in the light of such seasonal flood events – the 2011 experience was out of the ordinary. For upland villages, they considered the 2012 flash flood as 'normal'.[3]

During the flooding event immediately prior to our survey, 84 percent, 98 percent, and 74 percent of households in Pha Vieng, Dong Yang, and Ban Lao were, respectively, affected and badly impacted. In Huay Man, 84 percent of households were affected but only 59 percent badly impacted. The reasons given by the six households who were not affected in this village is that they neither owned farmland nor farmed so the flood had little impact on them. In both Pha Vieng and Huay Man, the flooding affected farmlands but not houses because they are located at higher elevations. In contrast, flooding in lowland villages of Ban Lao and Dong Yang affected both houses and farmlands.

Flooding, clearly, is a problem in all four villages, and one that is growing in intensity and severity. The questions explored next are how flooding and migration intersect in these four settlements, how households' different vulnerability signatures shape adaptation and response, and what capacities they have to embrace strategies of mobility in general and migration in particular to deal with such challenges.

Status of migration in Laos

As migration is the backdrop of this study, this section will offer a short profile of migration in Laos. In the 2005 census, Thailand is an important destination for Lao migrants. Southichack (2014) reported that expert estimates of Lao migrant workers in Thailand placed the total number at around 300,000 in any given year, including legal and illegal, long-term and seasonal workers combined. This was about 4.4 percent of Laos's population in 2013 of 6,770,000. Thailand is a magnet for migrants from Laos due to its proximity and cultural and linguistic similarities, as well as abundant employment opportunities (SERC, 2008; Baker, 2015). Laos's young population (in fact, the youngest population in the Mekong subregion), consumption of Thai media, and unmet demand for workers in the Thai economy drive migration to Thailand (Baker, 2015). Based on interviews of returnees in Savannakhet province and Mukdahan (Thailand) by the Social Environmental Research Consultant (SERC) in 2008, several reasons were cited as to why migrants come to Thailand, including food insecurity, lack of farmland, lack of job opportunities, and economic problems in the household. Migration was also made easier by the presence of personal or family networks in Thailand and the existence of brokers.

In 2011, the four main types of work that registered migrants from Laos were doing in Thailand included household domestic work (19 percent), agriculture (16 percent), food sales (12 percent), and construction (11 percent) (Huguet et al., 2011).[4] Lao migrants are largely unskilled, attracted by wage differentials and originating from poor rural households (Southichack, 2014; Baker, 2015). Remittances benefit sending households in terms of increased household income to fund daily needs and new skills (Southichack, 2014).

Substantial internal migration has also occurred through resettlement, which some authors have described as a form of internal displacement (High et al., 2009), due to government policies on shifting cultivation (Petit, 2008) and infrastructure development (Baird et al., 2015). Historically, war (Sisouphanthong and Taillard, 2000) and security concerns (Evrard and Goudineau, 2004) were also causes of internal migration. Some internal labor migration occurs toward key cities such as Vientiane (the capital city), Luang Prabang (a UNESCO World Heritage Site), and other areas where there are large commercial establishments such as resorts and casinos. Luang Prabang attracts labor from surrounding provinces, such as Xayaboury, Luang Namtha, Phongsaly, and Oudomxay, to work in its tourism industries (Southiseng and Walsh, 2011).

Having discussed the dynamics of flooding and migration in Laos, we now turn to look at the key objective of this chapter: exploring the intersection of flooding and migration.

Flooding and migration: how did they intersect?

The intersection between flooding and migration in the study sites is not straightforward. Some 73 percent of respondents did not think there was a relationship between flooding and migration (Table 4.3), which is significant because only 4 percent of households were not negatively affected by flooding during 2009–2012. Of those who saw a relationship (27 percent), the key reason given, especially in Pha Vieng and Huay Man, was that flooding had negative impacts on the village and the livelihoods and health of households.

The lack of a widespread appreciation of a connection between flooding and migration might also be due to the fact that livelihoods are not multilocal (i.e. households do not have 'mobile' livelihoods in which multiple places support them). Though there are some movements to other localities to work, this is very minimal, as discussed later in this chapter.

Domicile status

Our survey shows that around 95 percent of 873 household members lived (domiciled) in their place of residence during the 6 months preceding the survey (late 2012). This means that only around 5 percent (40) lived elsewhere during this time, but are still part of the household. Table 4.4 shows their village and occupations or reasons for being away.

If we remove those absent for non-work-related reasons, then there are just 17 individuals who were nondomiciled due to work-related reasons. Two of them were living in the same village, but in another homestead. This could have been in another house owned by the household, which might be a farm shelter away

Table 4.3 Relationship between flooding and migration

Villages	Relationship between flooding and migration (percent)		Types of relationships (percent within 'yes')		
	None	Yes	Flooding has negative impacts on the village, livelihoods, health, and households.	People are afraid of coming to the village because of the danger of flooding.	Did not know the relationship
Pha Vieng, Luang Prabang (n = 37)	56.8	43.2	75.0	–	25.0
Huay Man, Phonexay (n = 43)	58.1	41.9	77.8	11.1	11.1
Dong Yang, Savannakhet (n = 46)	89.1	13.0	66.7	16.7	16.7
Ban Lao, Savannakhet (n = 31)	90.3	9.7	66.7	–	33.3

Source: Authors' survey

Table 4.4 Nondomiciled household members and reasons for being away

Reasons	Pha Vieng	Huay Man	Dong Yang	Ban Lao
Non-work related				
Other reasons (none employment related)	1	6	5	–
Study	4	–	–	1
Disability	–	3	3	–
Work related (types of work)				
Community party officials of all levels (career)	–	–	4	–
Professionals	–	2	–	–
Farmers	–	–	1	1
Collectors of non-timber forest products (NTFP, e.g. honey, bamboo, herbs, vines, etc.)	–	1	–	–
Skilled construction workers	–	2	–	–
Drivers and operators of motorized equipment (transportation vehicles, agricultural machinery, etc.)	–	–	1	–
Other simple services on the street not elsewhere specified (e.g. shoeshine)	–	–	2	–
Unskilled workers in agriculture, forestry, or fisheries	–	–	2	1
Total (n = 40)	5	14	18	3

Source: Authors' survey

from the residence, or in another house possibly belonging to a relative. Those who were located a distance away from their residence, who might be interpreted as labor migrants, were distributed as follows: one in a different town in the same province, one in another province, three cross-border,[5] and five in other countries.[6] In other words, only 10, or 1 percent, were labor migrants, of which five came from Huay Man, four from Dong Yang, one from Ban Lao, and none from Huay Man.

Insights from coping strategies

Further insights on why many respondents did not see an intersection between flooding and migration can be gleaned from the coping strategies households deployed during disasters. Coping strategies during disasters and the learning that accompanies them are the components of long-term adaptation. They also illuminate existing adaptive capacities. The ability of a household to withstand future hazards may be gauged from its ability to cope during previous hazard episodes.

Table 4.5 lists a sample of coping strategies deployed by households during the floods. None of these strategies involves migration. Except for Dong Yang, a significant number of households in Pha Vieng, Huay Man, and Ban Lao did nothing and let time handle the flooding. Propinquity of life in the village seemed to be the most effective coping strategy; solidarity and kinship were the collective safety net that prevented singular tragedy. During interviews, we heard stories of borrowing equipment, farming other's land, help with construction, staying with relatives during flooding, and general gratitude for family and social ties. The importance of 'social capital' in negotiating hardship was clear.

Indeed, among the Hmong, their traditional nomadic livelihood put great importance on retaining clan ties so that 'support between its members can be maintained' (Lee, 2005: 22). For example, in Huay Man, Mr. Bounxong had moved to the village due to marriage. He described how during flooding he had helped his wife's relatives move equipment to higher grounds, and when the waters had subsided he had helped clear the fields. These acts of communality were not limited to periods of environmental danger. Mr. Bounxong also explained how he was receiving help from relatives who were both donating materials and helping with the construction of his new concrete house. Such embedded and ongoing norms of mutual help during normal times provide the context and the covenant for help during crisis episodes.

In Dong Yang, quick reactions such as moving self, materials, belongings, and livelihood implements away from harm were important steps undertaken to cope with the flood. This reaction among Dong Yang residents was expected as they were located 5 meters lower than nearby Ban Lao. Their temporary evacuation was assisted by the state (a school was used as a temporary flood shelter) and social capital (many of the villagers stayed with relatives). On one occasion in 2010, the evacuation of Dong Yang residents to the nearby village of Mak Nao lasted 15 days, and animals were left in Mak Nao for 1 month. Villagers took tools, animals, and food with them, and made handicrafts.

76 Albert Salamanca et al.

Table 4.5 Various coping strategies of households during the previous flooding (percent within village)

Types of strategies	Pha Vieng (n = 31)	Huay Man (n = 22)	Dong Yang (n = 46)	Ban Lao (n = 23)
Used flotsams (floating debris) to build fence or dyke to protect the house	3.2	13.6	–	–
Planted trees around the house to protect it	12.9	–	–	–
Moved self and/or materials, belongings, animals, plants, furniture, and other household items to higher grounds	16.1	9.1	78.3	–
Dug trenches to drain water out of flooded areas	16.1	–	–	–
Developed a planting system to replant flooded areas	3.2	–	–	–
Stabilized lowland areas with trees and grass	3.2	9.1	–	–
Allowed floodwater to naturally drain out through evaporation and absorption of the soil	6.5	4.5	2.2	21.7
Went to bed when it flooded; didn't believe it was worth rebuilding irrigation channels	6.5	13.6	–	4.3
Stocked food and supplies during the dry season in preparation for flooding	–	–	4.3	4.3
Collected non-timber forest products	3.2	–	–	–
Replanted destroyed crops, vegetables, and so forth	–	–	2.2	4.3
Built or bought a boat	–	–	8.7	4.3
Worked together; cooperated	–	–	–	4.3
Made sandbags	–	–	2.2	4.3
Prepared medicine for people and animals	–	–	–	4.3
Didn't do anything	29.0	50.0	2.2	47.8
Total	100.00	100.00	100.00	100.00

Source: Authors' survey

Dynamics of migration, livelihood strategies, and flooding

Clearly neither migration in particular nor mobility in general are defining characteristics of the villages studied. We were unable to find migrants in our case study villages moving into exposed locations (although we may have been looking in the wrong places) or leaving flood-prone areas. Rather, we found in Luang Prabang flooding intersecting with the historical vestiges of government policies on swidden agriculture and sedentarization leading to social and economic marginalisation, and in Savannakhet a story of people who have not been historically moved but were now affected by modern infrastructure – in particular NT2 – which was meant to bring economic development to the immediate locale and the wider country.

As shown previously, we have found in our study sites that social networks are heavily embedded within the village, and livelihoods remain intimately connected to land. Instead of mobility, the respondents in our survey wanted secure land rights; improved infrastructure; and the comfort of sustainable, fixed livelihoods in order to cope with annual and seasonal vicissitudes. Houses – the home – were particularly important; even during flooding men remained with the house and when asked whether they would think of leaving the village one respondent stated, 'this is where I live, this is my house and my land. I am a farmer. Why should I move?'

So, *quo vadis* flooding and migration? Flooding produces a variety of migratory responses, from permanent international migration, to local transitory displacement. A risk-hazard perspective would examine the multiple 'impacts' of an exogenous biophysical pressure (sea-level rise, erosion, flooding) and, assuming a dualism between society and nature, restrict analysis to the outcomes over certain temporal and spatial scales. However, the landscape is a 'substantive reality, a place lived, a world produced and transformed, a commingling of nature and society that is struggled over and in' (Mitchell, 2003: 792). Thus, the evolving flooding-migration nexus must be understood as complex, multidimensional, dynamic, and power laden. Cutter (2002) uses the term 'hazardscape' to conceptualize the multiple material processes, social actors, and discourses that make up the social construction of disaster.

Moreover, any person's decision to migrate is complex, driven by the intricate interactions between agency and structure so that such intersection is underpinned by the nature of the hazards, vulnerability, mobility, exclusion, and accumulation (see Chapter 1). Borrowing from Rigg (2007: 173), context is important as it influences the 'likely causes, patterns and impacts of migration'. In the case of villages in the study, we see the following as potential context-setting processes that will define mobility decisions in the future: migration networks, household livelihood strategies, and other proximate factors. Over time, these contexts will become the components of what Rigg et al. (2013) term the 'textures' and 'movements' of livelihoods in the *longue durée*.

Household livelihood strategy, vulnerabilities, and capacities

Our goal in this chapter is to elucidate how flooding and migration intersect. In other words, we want to find out whether migration is a livelihood strategy in villages that experienced flooding. Thailand is considered the destination of choice for migrants from southern Laos (Southichack, 2014; Baker, 2015), while for northern Laos, it is Luang Prabang (Rigg, 2007; Southiseng and Walsh, 2011). But our findings, discussed previously, showed that this has not been the case, at least for our four sites, and point toward other explanations within the ambit of a household's livelihood strategy and the role of income diversification within that.

To get an insight into the potential livelihood trajectories of the households, we need to look to at least three aspects that will determine household livelihood strategies: income, educational attainment, and social networks. Their dependence on agriculture now means that access to land is important to them. Existing educational attainment also determines what work opportunities will be

78 Albert Salamanca et al.

available to them. Access to social networks also determines the information and opportunities they could rely on to build their livelihoods.

Income source

Our survey showed that the villages, whether in the uplands or lowlands, were dependent on agriculture, forestry, and fishery sectors. As shown in Table 4.6, 63 percent of total household members considered themselves in full-time work of which a sizeable majority was in these sectors, which in turn accounted for 88–97 percent of occupations in the four villages. Although they were involved in agriculture, they were not earning wages, so they might be appropriately classified as subsistence farmers. Heavy reliance on agriculture increases susceptibility to the vagaries of the weather and heightens the risk of flooding, as reflected in the 2011 and 2012 flooding episodes (Figure 4.2).

In addition, vulnerability or capacity changes with the number of productive members in the household. Here, productivity means having an occupation but not necessarily earning a wage. As shown in Table 4.1, Pha Vieng had the smallest total number of members per household while Ban Lao had the largest. It follows, in Table 4.1 again, that Ban Lao households have more members with productive full-time occupation at about five household members generating a consistent stream of production for the household. These occupations could range from different forms of agricultural activities, nonfarm work, and skilled and unskilled work. Ban Lao, therefore, and Dong Yang, to a certain extent, were better off due to the number of members bringing produce to the household. The differences among the villages appear also to follow national trends wherein Luang Prabang has a higher dependency ratio[7] than Savannakhet at 83 versus 77 dependents per 100 persons of working ages, and the latter has more economically active persons than the former (Lao Statistics Bureau, 2005). A study in northern Laos showed that households with more labor available cope better than those with less (Ingxay et al., 2015).

Educational attainment

The average number of years of schooling between the upland and lowland villages in the survey are similar (6.5 vs. 6.4 years). This shows that the majority of individuals in the survey were poorly educated but not necessarily illiterate, although the literacy rate may be low. In general terms, the level of education[8] in Laos is very low.

Social networks

Social networks could play an important role in providing emergency support in the aftermath of a disaster. They could also play a role in the diffusion of technologies and technical insights. In general, membership in organizations (rotating savings and credit association [ROSCA], Farmer Field School, Lao Women's

Table 4.6 Occupational characteristics of household members who are working full time

Village		Type of work						
		Agriculture, forestry, and fishery	Community/ party officials of all levels	Unskilled workers	Assemblers and machine operators	Personal services, protection, and sales	Professionals	Skilled manual workers	Grand Total
Ban Lao, Savannakhet	%	96.58%	2.74%	0.68%	–	–	–	–	100%
	Count	141	4	1	–	–	–	–	146
Dong Yang, Savannakhet	%	91.67%	4.17%	3.13%	0.52%	–	–	0.52%	100%
	Count	176	8	6	1	–	–	–	191
Huay Man, Phonexay	%	88.70%	0.87%	0.87%	–	1.74%	1.74%	6.09%	100%
	Count	102	1	1	–	2	2	7	115
Pha Vieng, Luang Prabang	%	89.11%	0.99%	2.97%	0.99%	–	–	5.94%	100%
	Count	90	1	3	1	–	–	6	101

Source: Authors' survey

80 Albert Salamanca et al.

Union, Lao Youth Union, the Lao Revolutionary Front, temple associations, farmers associations, and, the Laos People's Revolutionary Party) is very low in Pha Vieng and Huay Man with only 12 percent each, while it is 28 percent and 21 percent for Dong Yang and Ban Lao villages (Figure 4.3). This might be an artifact of the historical development of the Lao political system that favors lowland ethnic Lao rather than other ethnic groups, although there is an expanding political space for the Hmong in particular (Stuart-Fox, 2006). Of the organizations listed in Figure 4.3, the Lao People's Revolutionary Party (LPRP) is an important one. Martin Stuart-Fox (Stuart-Fox, 2006: 64–65) described it as 'not only the avenue of political (and social) advancement, but it is the principal one'. He adds that 'the Party permeates and controls four key institutions in the country: the government, the bureaucracy, mass organisations, and the military'.[9] Leadership work in the party or community seems to be more prominent in the lowland villages of Ban Lao and Dong Yang with 2.7 percent and 4.2 percent, respectively, of household members describing their full-time occupations as such (Table 4.6).

Of the organizations listed in the survey, local farmer's associations were the most prominent. In Dong Yang and Ban Lao, 77 percent and 81 percent, respectively, of household heads were members of these organizations, while the figures for Pha Vieng and Huay Man were 35 percent and 34 percent, respectively (Figure 4.3).

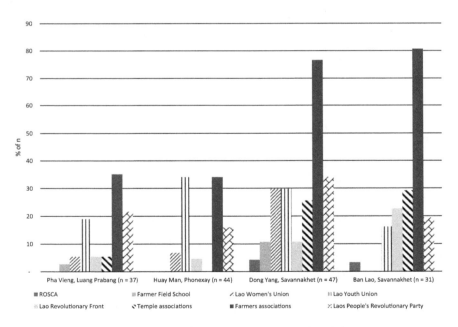

Figure 4.3 Membership of household heads to organisations (% of n)
Source: Authors' survey

Overall, lowland village households were members of more organizations than upland villages (Figure 4.3). It also follows, and this is supported by the survey, that both Dong Yang and Ban Lao villages received more assistance during disasters than Pha Vieng and Huay Man villages due to their access to more organizations. In fact, during the 2011 floods (see Figure 4.2) every household in Dong Yang and Ban Lao received assistance from the organizations they are members of compared to only 38 percent and 45 percent in Pha Vieng and Huay Man, respectively. This assistance included food, some cash, water, seeds, and household items. In view of this, lowland villages were better networked and had wider access to political capital than upland villages. Whether this was tied to issues of ethnicity, education status, income, organization membership or connection and access, or to a complex amalgam of these could not be ascertained.

Vulnerability, capacity, and opportunity

For now, the narrative of 'migration as adaptation' or 'migration for adaptation' is not yet clear in the villages studied. Whether such a trajectory will materialize will be determined by how the household engages with the drivers of its vulnerability and capacity and the opportunities that prevail. Taking a cue from the findings of Barney's (2012a) work in lowland Laos, land and agrarian issues in the home villages of the migrants leading to 'resource displacements and economic coercions' could underpin future migration processes. We find resonance in Barney's findings in the context of our case studies, so that we see the possibility that migration could be driven by resource capture, particularly in the context of rising large-scale land concessions and continuing government policies that are limiting swidden agriculture, as well as tightening the resource frontier, resulting in land fragmentation.

Government policies on infrastructure and ethnicities

Information on income, livelihood dependence, and occupational characteristics highlighted previously point to the fact that agriculture is an important activity among the households, hence reprising a reality in Laos where agriculture is a predominant source of income and subsistence, and a major activity of a large segment of the population (Sisouphanthong and Taillard, 2000; Lao Statistics Bureau, 2005). Migration will therefore interact with these agricultural households within the context of livelihood strategies aided by government policies.

Barney (2012b) has shown a connection between the government's infrastructure policy and youth migration in a village in Champasak province. Government policies could be held responsible for the creation of landscapes, risky or otherwise, that will enable and drive migration. The resettlement and sedentarization policies of the Lao government on upland Lao have far more devastating impacts that continue to resonate today than any other policies (Evrard and Goudineau, 2004; Baird and Shoemaker, 2007; Rigg, 2005). For instance, the location of Pha Vieng and Huay Man along a river and their current levels of human development are a function of those policies. Yet lowland Laos is not necessarily in a better position; government policies on infrastructure development are creating new forms of vulnerabilities, prolonging or creating flooding in this instance. It would seem that Dong Yang is better off compared to other villages by virtue of its greater sense of empowerment but this is just a veneer that needs to be unpicked. The NT2 caused flooding in Dong Yang and other downstream villages (Baird et al., 2015). This means that future vulnerabilities in Dong Yang and Ban Lao will continue to be associated with major infrastructure development, which is not the case among upland villages. Instead, key sources of their vulnerability lie in their location; the growing prevalence of watershed flooding due to changing climatic conditions; their poverty; and their social, economic, and political marginalization.

Migration networks

As shown in Table 4.1, there are only eight households (5 percent) with members who may be classed as labor migrants. Over time, and when household livelihood strategies require, these household members will lay the foundations for future labor migration, particular irregular migration. Based on Baker's (2015) survey of deportees, he found that 79 percent of his respondents knew someone in Thailand before migrating there. He reckoned that 'knowing and hence being able to ask someone who had already migrated to Thailand about their experiences there might be a protective factor against ending up in exploitative working conditions' (2015: 15). The decision to migrate could be informed in large part by the knowledge that a friend or a relative is already there at the destination enabling ease of settlement. They could also provide information on where the job opportunities are and the prevailing salaries, as well as be a source of comfort in a foreign land.

Village transnationalization

Rigg (2009: 23) has demonstrated that there is a process of village transnationalization going on in rural Laos. He showed that 'the notion of village transnationalism focuses on the way that labor migration to Thailand and contact between Lao and Thai lives and lifestyles infiltrates Lao village spaces'. He proffered two reasons for this. First, the young Lao migrants in Thailand repatriate not only money but also cultural tastes and influences. Second, Thai media influences have become widespread in Laos. These processes, therefore, had an impact in shaping aspirations.

Televisions and mobile phones were ubiquitous; some respondents had children completing further education in nearby towns; and, at one dinner in Pha Vieng during the fieldwork, the desire to learn English, and to understand and interact with a wider sphere, was powerfully evident. As a female respondent in Huay Man said, 'without an education my children face a tough life as a farmer, a life of hard work and poverty' (interview, 18 November 2012). However, the geography of resettlement prevents this. Without an all-weather road or the provision of social services, aspirations went largely unrealized. The fluorescent glow of Thai television programs and the sound of Hmong pop music at first seemed incongruous – at odds with the reality of subsistence livelihoods. Modern amenities may be limited, but the omnipresent satellite dish allows for the consumption of, and engagement with, modern sound, imagery, and representation. It propagates the conception of the village as 'backward' and the urban as 'modern'. We would assume that this lays the foundations for future material and social demands that could facilitate future migration and mobility.

Whither migration?

Whether the aforementioned factors will initiate migration is another matter. Baird and Fox (2015) found that ethnic minorities are less likely to move away from their original lands compared to lowland Lao. Furthermore, upland ethnic Lao are less likely to choose to become illegal workers in Thailand than those lowland Lao residing close to the border with Thailand. The processes outlined previously are much more likely to underpin migration among the majority lowland Lao but will have less mobility implications – unless forced, coerced, or displaced – for the upland ethnic Lao. Instead, 'chain migration' could be initiated among already resettled upland ethnic groups in lowland areas where further migration might be taken to other places in the lowlands but not returning to their origin. This has been reported in Laos due to the failure of earlier resettlements (Evrard and Goudineau, 2004). Or, due to changing aspirations and exploiting opportunities, migration for commercial sex work could also happen, especially in areas where entertainment complexes such as casinos abound and places where there are large-scale investments and mobile men (Lyttleton and Vorabouth, 2011).

The government's policies on ethnicity, therefore, will underscore vulnerabilities (e.g. resettlement) of upland ethnic groups and will continue to play a role in the well-being of these households. According to Rehbein (2007), the ethnic Lao dominates the symbolic universe of Laos through its national language, emblems, and the media such that other ethnic groups have had to adapt. In fact, other ethnic groups have to learn the Lao language and customs to achieve any form of higher education. This suggests that being an ethnic Lao provides access to more social and political assets, which can be used to sustain a household's well-being, than those households belonging to other ethnic groups. In other words, being an ethnic Lao commands wider options than other ethnic groups. This reprises earlier findings that 'poverty and underdevelopment are concentrated among the *Lao Theung* and *Lao Soung*' (Jerndal and Rigg, 1998) to which broad groups the Hmong and Khmu belong. Our survey has showed that only Dong Yang is purely composed of ethnic Lao; the other villages were mixed Khmu and Hmong (Pha Vieng and Huay Man) or Phu Thai and ethnic Lao (Ban Lao).

84 Albert Salamanca et al.

The Hmong, usually found in the highlands, have achieved a certain level of notoriety in Laos because they were used as accessories during the Vietnam War by the Americans, who mounted a clandestine war of interdiction along the Ho Chi Minh Trail, which snakes into Laos. Their participation in that war and their relationship with the Americans did not sit well with the now reigning Pathet Lao. Even today the Hmong are still seen in many places in Laos as a security threat (Baird, 2010). The Khmu are found mostly in northern Laos and are considered the largest minority group in Laos (Évrard, 2010) but Evrard (2010: 79) described them as 'twice marginalized', in conceptual and economic terms. The Phu Thais are found in southern Laos, especially in the provinces of Khammouan, Savannakhet, and Saravan. They are non-Buddhist Tai (Evans, 2002).

While in these ways we can read off ethnicity among the key factors that underpin vulnerability, it is not straightforward, especially in the present context. Ethnicity in Laos, according to Michaud (2011), is a complicated issue due to interethnic-group political and social dynamics. Neither is it benign and neutral. Alongside culture and agency, it plays a central role in livelihood decision making as deployed within the ambit of local politics and configured by history (Michaud, 2011). Certain ethnic groups do better, at least in economic terms, than others. Moreover, within the context of flooding as a hazard, the distinction between upland and lowland in terms of shaping vulnerabilities and capacities fell short. Both locations are made riskier by extreme events, of which intense rainfall is a manifestation, and the government's infrastructure development policy, of which the impacts of NT2, is an example.

Conclusion

In the case of our four research sites, flooding did not initiate individual migration despite overall poverty. Felli and Castree's (2012) critique of vulnerability and migration as an adaptation rings true. Assuming individuals have control over a 'rational', and feasible, assortment of adaptation possibilities fails to acknowledge the broader processes that shape village life. If the residents of villages use migration as a 'transformational and strategic approach to adaptation' (UK Government Office for Science, 2011: 200), village conditions become the individuals' choice rather than the result of the political, social, and environmental context of Laos. This creates a neoliberal paradox, whereby an emphasis on abstract individual agency hides the idiosyncrasies of reality.

We do not deny that migration as a result of environmental change may be happening, but that focus must be on the uneven nature of this process, giving attention to those who don't move, either due to choice or circumstance. It may be a frequently made point, but sensitivity to local conditions is paramount. Climate hazards and extreme events have the tendency to produce work on a grand scale. But they are just one of numerous dynamics. In Laos, processes such as the transition from subsistence to cash crops, the resettlement of ethnic minorities, and the government's infrastructure projects that aim to 'develop' Laos and intervene in nature overlap with, obscure, and are interrelated with the intersection of flooding, and the possibility of migration. This makes the initiation of migration complex and one that is likely to be deployed to serve overall household well-being or to enable *in situ* resilience. Strategies for the latter could include mobility, short-term moves, or enabling some members of the household to seek livelihoods beyond the confines of the village. Migration, therefore, could serve either 'as adaptation' or 'for adaptation' depending on the household context, which is socially constructed, historically embedded, and geographically shaped.

Among the study villages, topography and ethnicity have something to say. Villagers in lowland Laos, especially those close to the border with Thailand, are much more likely to migrate due to a number of predisposing factors around their vicinity, including networks already present in Thailand, their cultural propensity to migrate, transnational cultural influences and connections, and their location near an international border (cf. Rigg, 2009; Rigg, 2005; Rigg, 2007; Barney, 2012b; Southichack, 2014; Baker, 2015). Among upland villages, except for transnational influences, such predisposition is absent (cf. Baird and Fox, 2015), but some forms of mobility are already noted due to new road networks, new towns, and new occupational opportunities arising from, or associated with, large-scale infrastructure (cf. Lyttleton and Vorabouth, 2011). These could pave the way for future long-term labor migration.

Acknowledgment

We would like to thank the enumerators who helped us collect the data: Somphong, Bounmee, Sengsong, Nouyang, Loun, Vongsouvanh, Chammpha, Keovongkoth, and Chengmalang. Thanks also to the Northern Agriculture and Forestry College for hosting and providing us with logistical support. Our gratitude also goes to Ajarn Supang Chantavanich and Carl Middleton for leading the Flood and Migration Project. Thanks also to the editors for their critical comments and for Jonathan Rigg for providing advice on how to sharpen the write-up. Despite their guidance, any remaining shortcomings are solely the responsibility of the authors. The work in Laos was supported by the Sida Programme Support to SEI.

Notes

1 www.inform-index.org/Portals/0/Inform/2015/country_profiles/LAO.pdf
2 We adapted the dichotomy of upland/lowland as a useful device to topographically select representative sites while acknowledging that they are politically loaded terms and we do not impute the distinction of 'modern lowlands' and 'backward uplands' (cf. Rigg, 2009; Lund, 2011).
3 Among upland villages, flooding badly affected more households in 2012. However, flooding had already started to affect households from 2006 and the number of households affected has increased since then. This could be due to a number of factors such as river realignment and heavy rainfall, which villagers perceived to be the cause of the flooding. Serious flooding was also reported in Luang Prabang in 2013.
4 These proportions could change if undocumented migrants are included.
5 This refers to temporary departure for work but not for settlement.

6 There are two responses with reasons not provided.
7 The dependency ratio has been used as an indicator of vulnerability in a number of studies (e.g. Below et al., 2012).
8 Laos's education system is composed of 3 years of creche, 3 years of kindergarten, 5 years of primary, 3 years of lower secondary school, and 3 years of upper secondary school, followed by postsecondary education with a duration of 1–6 years. Formal education starts at 7 years old when children go to primary school.
9 The only mass organisations permitted in the country are the Lao Front for National Construction, the Federation of Lao Trade Unions, the Lao Women's Union, and the Revolutionary Youth Union. Martin Stuart-Fox (Stuart-Fox, 2006: 65) considers the Lao Women's Union as 'probably the most active mass organization in the country' while the youth union provides a pool of recruits for the party.

References

Baird, I., and Fox, J. (2015). "How land concessions affect places elsewhere: Telecoupling, political ecology, and large-scale plantations in Southern Laos and Northeastern Cambodia." *Land* 4(2): 436–453.

Baird, I.G. (2010). "The Hmong come to Southern Laos: Local responses and the creation of racialized boundaries." *Hmong Studies Journal* 11: 1–38.

Baird, I.G. (2015). "Translocal assemblages and the circulation of the concept of indigenous peoples in Laos." *Political Geography* 46: 54–64.

Baird, I.G., and Shoemaker, B.P. (2007). "Unsettling experiences: Internal resettlement and international aid agencies in Laos." *Development and Change* 38(5): 865–888.

Baird, I.G., Shoemaker, B.P., and Manorom, K. (2015). "The people and their river, the World Bank and its dam: Revisiting the Xe Bang Fai River in Laos." *Development and Change* 46(5): 1080–1105.

Baker, S. (2015). *Migration experiences of Lao workers deported from Thailand in 2013: Human trafficking trends in Asia*. Bangkok: United Nations Action for Cooperation against Trafficking in Persons.

Barney, K. (2012a). "Locating 'green neoliberalism,' and other forms of environmental governance in Southeast Asia." *Newsletter: Center for Southeast Asian Studies, Kyoto University* 66(Autumn): 25–28.

Barney, K. (2012b). "Land, livelihoods and remittances: A political ecology of youth out-migration across the Lao-Thai Mekong border." *Critical Asian Studies* 44(1): 57–83.

Below, T.B., Mutabazi, K.D., Kirschke, D., Franke, C., Sieber, S., Siebert, R., and Tscherning, K. (2012). "Can farmers adaptation to climate change be explained by socio-economic household-level variables?" *Global Environmental Change* 22(1): 223–235.

Chazee, L. (1999). *The peoples of Laos: Rural and ethnic diversities with an ethno-linguistic map*. Bangkok: White Lotus Press.

Cutter, S.L. (2002). "The changing nature of risks and hazards." (pp. 1–12) in Cutter, S.L. (ed.) *American hazardscapes: The regionalization of hazards and disasters*. Washington, DC: Joseph Henry Press.

Evans, G. (2002). *A short history of Laos: The land in between*. Chiang Mai: Silkworm Books.

Évrard, O.J. (2010). "Oral histories of livelihoods and migration under socialism and post-socialism among the Khmu of Northern Laos." (pp. 76–99) in Michaud, J. and Forsyth, T. (eds.) *Moving mountains: Ethnicity and livelihoods in highland China, Vietnam, and Laos*. Vancouver: University of British Columbia Press.

Évrard, O.J., and Goudineau, Y. (2004). "Planned resettlement, unexpected migrations and cultural trauma in Laos." *Development and Change* 35(5): 937–962.
Felli, R., and Castree, N. (2012). "Neoliberalising adaptation to environmental change: Foresight or foreclosure?" *Environment and Planning A* 44(1): 1–4.
High, H., Baird, I.G., Barney, K., Vandergeest, P., and Shoemaker, B. (2009). "Internal resettlement in Laos' Reading too much into aspirations: More explorations of the space between coerced and voluntary resettlement in Laos." *Critical Asian Studies* 41(4): 605–620.
Huguet, J.W., Chamratrithirong, A., and Richter, K. (2011). "Thailand migration profile." (pp. 7–16) in Huguet, J.W. and Chamratrithirong, A. (eds.) *Thailand migration report 2011*. Bangkok: International Organization of Migration.
ICEM. (2013). *USAID Mekong ARCC climate change impact and adaptation study: Main report*. Prepared for the United States Agency for International Development by ICEM. International Centre for Environmental Management (ICEM): Bangkok.
IDA and IFC. (2012). *Country partnership strategy for Lao People's Democratic Republic FY12–FY16*. Lao PDR Country Management Unit East Asia and Pacific Region. Washington, DC: The International Finance Corporation (IFC) East Asia and Pacific Region.
Ingxay, P., Yokoyama, S., and Hirota, I. (2015). "Livelihood factors and household strategies for an unexpected climate event in upland northern Laos." *Journal of Mountain Science* 12(2): 483–500.
Jerndal, R., and Rigg, J. (1998). "Making space in Laos: Constructing a national identity in a forgotten country." *Political Geography* 17(7): 809–831.
Lao Statistics Bureau. (2005). *Laos population update 2005*. Vientiane: Lao Statistics Bureau.
Lee, G.Y. (2005). "The shaping of traditions: Agriculture and Hmong society." *Hmong Studies Journal* 6: 1–33.
Lestrelin, G., and Giordano, M. (2007). "Upland development policy, livelihood change and land degradation: Interactions from a Laotian village." *Land Degradation & Development* 19: 55–76.
Lund, C. (2011). "Fragmented sovereignty: Land reform and dispossession in Laos." *Journal of Peasant Studies* 38(4): 885–905.
Lyttleton, C., and Vorabouth, S. (2011). "Trade circles: Aspirations and ethnicity in commercial sex in Laos." *Culture Health and Sexuality* 13(Suppl 2): S263–S277.
Mekong River Commission. (2011). *Integrated water resources management-based basin development strategy*. Vientiane: Mekong River Commission.
Michaud, J. (2011). "Conclusion: Lessons for the future." (pp. 215–227) in Michaud, J. and Forsyth, T. (eds.) *Moving mountains: Ethnicity and livelihoods in highland China, Vietnam, and Laos*. Vancouver: University of British Columbia Press.
Mitchell, D. (2003). "Cultural landscapes: Just landscapes or landscapes of justice?" *Progress in Human Geography* 27(6): 787–796.
Morrow, B.H. (1999). "Identifying and mapping community vulnerability." *Disasters* 23(1): 1–18.
Mustafa, D., Ahmed, S., Saroch, E., and Bell, H. (2011). "Pinning down vulnerability: From narratives to numbers." *Disasters* 35(1): 62–86.
Petit, P. (2008). "Rethinking internal migrations in Lao PDR: The resettlement process under micro-analysis." *Anthropological Forum* 18(2): 117–138.
Rehbein, B. (2007). *Globalization, culture and society in Laos*. London and New York: Routledge.

Rigg, J. (2005). *Living with transition in Laos: Market integration in Southeast Asia*. London and New York: Routledge.

Rigg, J. (2007). "Moving lives: Migration and livelihoods in the Lao PDR." *Population Space Place* 13(3): 163–178.

Rigg, J. (2009). "A particular place? Laos and its incorporation into the development mainstream." *Environment and Planning A* 41(3): 703–721.

Rigg, J., Nguyen, T.A., and Luong, T.T.H. (2013). "The texture of livelihoods: Migration and making a living in Hanoi." *The Journal of Development Studies* 50(3): 368–382.

Roberts, M.S. (2015). "Understanding farmer decision making in Northern Lao PDR." *Culture, Agriculture, Food and Environment* 37(1): 14–27.

SERC. (2008). *A comparative picture of migration in Laos, Myanmar, Cambodia, Vietnam and Thailand: Summary*. Social Environmental Research Consultant (SERC). http://www.burmalibrary.org/docs08/A_Comparative_Study_of_Migration-SERC.pdf.

Sisouphanthong, B., and Taillard, C. (2000). *Atlas of Laos: The spatial structures of economic and social development of the Lao people's democratic republic*. New York: St. Martin's Press.

Southichack, M. (2014). *Lao labor migration and remittance: Trends and economic and livelihood implications*. Vientiane: Swiss Agency for Development and Cooperation (Laos Program).

Southiseng, N., and Walsh, J. (2011). "Study of tourism and labour in Luang Prabang province." *Journal of Lao Studies* 2(1): 45–65.

Stuart-Fox, M. (2006). "The political culture of corruption in the Lao PDR." *Asian Studies Review* 30(1): 59–75.

UK Government Office for Science. (2011). *Foresight international dimensions of climate change*. London: Government Office for Science.

Vayda, A.P. (1983). "Progressive contextualization: Methods for research in human ecology." *Human Ecology* 11(3): 265–281.

World Bank Group. (2012). *Letters and responses August 2003 – June 2012: Nam Theun 2 multipurpose development project*. Washington, DC: World Bank.

Yokoyama, S. (2014). "Laos in transition: The runner in front, leading the race or lagging a lap behind?" (pp. 3–28) in Yokoyama, S., Okamoto, K., Takenaka, C., and Hirota, I. (eds.) *Integrated studies of social and natural environmental transition in Laos*. Advances in Asian Human-Environmental Research series. Tokyo: Springer.

5 Living with and against floods in Bangkok and Thailand's central plain

Naruemon Thabchumpon and Narumon Arunotai

Introduction

Thailand's central plain, located in the Chao Phraya basin, has long been a major agricultural area or 'rice cradle.' Its fertile soils are due to the accumulated sediment deposits from several rivers, including the Chao Phraya, Pasak and Tha Chin Rivers. Given the monsoonal climate and major rivers in the basin, seasonal flooding is very common, which farming communities are largely adapted to. Yet, since the 1960s and more rapidly since the 1980s, the central plains have also witnessed a remarkable and rapid transformation. Signaled by the first national development plan in 1962, Thailand accelerated its agricultural exports and reoriented the economy toward one that has become heavily industrialized with a large services sector. With the growth of Bangkok and other major urban and industrial areas such as Ayutthaya, this has significantly changed the rural and urban landscape and water regime in the process (Marks, 2015). Agricultural areas have been increasingly tied to the industrial and urban areas, including physically via roads and also via markets (Middleton and Krawanchid, 2014). Thai peoples' livelihood strategies have also transformed, with large movements of people migrating either seasonally or permanently from rural to urban areas for work. Thailand has also attracted a large migrant population from neighboring countries, in particular Myanmar, Cambodia and Laos (UNESCAP, 2015).

In 2011, 66 of Thailand's 77 provinces faced the most severe flooding in living memory, lasting 6 months from July 2011 to January 2012. The areas most affected were the central plain provinces including Bangkok, Ayutthaya, Nakhon Sawan, Pathum Thani and Samut Sakhon, which include many of the country's major industrial and manufacturing locations. According to the World Bank (2012), the disaster resulted in 815 deaths, and caused US$46.5 billion of economic damage with 13.6 million people affected and over 20,000 square kilometers of farmland damaged. According to the World Bank, the flood ranked as the world's fourth-costliest disaster, following the 2011 earthquake and tsunami in Japan, the 1995 Kobe earthquake and Hurricane Katrina in 2005.

The 2011 flood also bought to the fore long-standing challenges in Thailand's water management and disaster relief response. While the government at the time claimed the flood was a natural disaster and also linked to climate change, others have highlighted how historical policy decisions related to Thailand's development pathway were also key factors in the extent and severity of the flooding (Marks, 2015). This includes Thailand's extensive infrastructure development, together with policy decisions emerging from Thailand's water management regime. One particularly contentious issue was how the government tried to protect central Bangkok, leaving surrounding rural and peri-urban areas flooded and more vulnerable.

According to Pongsudhirak (2011), politics behind the flood in Thailand could be seen from the mismanagement of the country's upstream dams to accommodate the monsoons, problems related to unreliable information and a lack of policy coordination among governmental agencies,[1] which created more problems during the crisis (see also Boonyabancha and Archer, 2011; Marks, 2015). Overall, while rainfall was particularly heavy that year between June and October 2011, certainly Thailand's sociopolitical circumstances contributed to the worsening of the effect of the floods.

This chapter presents empirical research on the impacts of the 2011 flood in three urban, one semi-urban and three rural communities located in the suburbs of Bangkok, and Ayutthaya, Saraburi and Nakhon Pathom provinces, Thailand. While there is now a significant literature on Thailand's 2011 flooding, including from economic, engineering, water management, social and political perspectives, little of this literature has considered the role of mobility during the flood period within the affected areas, and also how impacts relate to the circumstances of recent and long-term migrants within the affected communities. The chapter is thus framed by the idea of mobile political ecology presented in Chapter 1, including the concepts of vulnerability, capability and adaptability. We find that while rural communities are accustomed and largely adapted to seasonal flooding, the 2011 flood inflicted severe damage on property and livelihoods, which were exacerbated by the government's policy to protect urban and industrial areas, leaving rural areas flooded. Meanwhile, urban areas were not well prepared, and in the case of Bangkok, suburban communities were left frustrated at how inner areas were protected, which increased their own difficulties as floodwater could not drain. All of our case studies revealed the importance of communities organizing to seek state-distributed resources, and to shape policies that were impacting them, including regarding flood management, recovery and compensation.

Overall, we find that the role played by migration and mobility in relation to flooding is subtle. During the 2011 flood, some, but not all, migrants to urban areas returned to their rural family homes, where living with floods was more possible. More broadly, rural areas have proceeded through various processes of agrarian transition, establishing households with multilocal livelihood strategies in the process; in particular, there are changing labor practices in agriculture as many working adults move away from farming into factories and other waged income in urban areas. These trends reflect Thailand's development policies that have encouraged urbanization, industrialization and associated migration, but that have also produced contradictions as new economic risks and vulnerabilities have been created as revealed in the 2011 flood.

The chapter is structured as follows. In the next section, the research method is briefly introduced. This is followed by a brief description of the rural case study locations (Bang Chanee village, Ayutthaya province; Don Phud municipality, Saraburi province; and Lan Takfa village, Nakhon Pathom province), and how communities there have adapted to regular seasonal flooding. We then discuss the impacts of the 2011 flooding, first in the rural locations, followed by three urban locations in Bangkok (Poonsup community, U-Chareon community and Tung Songhong housing estate) and one semiurban/industrial location (Khanham community, Ayutthaya province, near the Rojana industrial estate). In each section, we relate the experience of flooding to patterns of mobility and migration. The final section brings the rural, urban and semiurban/industrial case studies into relationship with one another, and some conclusions are offered.

Methodology and study area

Field research was undertaken in 2013 in seven communities flooded in 2011. Three case studies are located in rural communities, three in urban areas and one in a semiurban area (Figure 5.1). Approximately 35 semistructured questionnaires were administered in each of the communities using a random sampling technique (n = 236; Table 5.1). These questionnaires were guided by the vulnerabilities and capabilities framework of Mustafa et al. (2011). In addition to basic socioeconomic data, information was gathered on migration history, flood-risk exposure and socioeconomic impact from the 2011 flood, assistance received and coping strategies and decision making within the community including in relation to the 2011 flood. Between three and seven in-depth interviews were

Table 5.1 Number of household questionnaires and in-depth interviews

	Type	Number of questionnaires (households)	Number of in-depth interviews
Bang Chanee village, Bang Ban district, Ayutthaya province	Rural	22	3
Don Phud municipality, Don Phud district, Saraburi province	Rural	45	4
Lan Takfa village, Nakhon Chai Si district, Nakhon Pathom province	Rural	45	3
Poonsup community, Sai Mai district, Bangkok	Urban	42	5
U-Chareon community, Don Mueang district, Bangkok	Urban	27	5
Tung Songhong housing estate, Laksi district, Bangkok	Urban	32	5
Khanham community, Uthai district, Ayutthaya province	Semiurban/industrial	23	7
Total		236	32

Source: Authors' survey

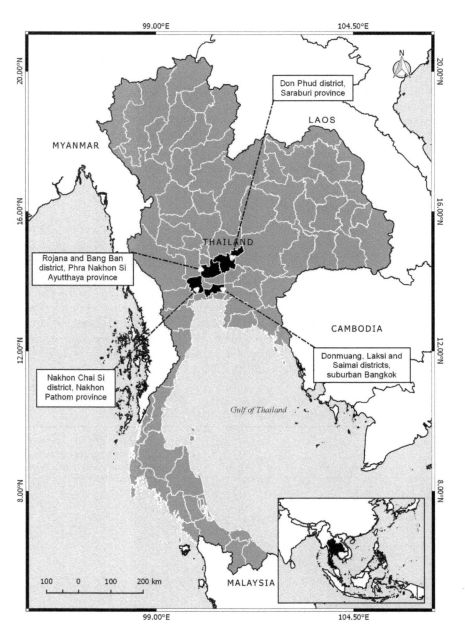

Figure 5.1 Map of study sites

also conducted per community with community leaders and local government officials.

The experience of seasonal flooding in rural Thailand

Three rural farming communities were visited to understand the relationship between flooding, livelihoods and migration.

Bang Chanee village in Bang Ban district, Ayutthaya province, is a farming community located on a canal connected to the Chao Phraya River. The main occupations are rice farming and tending fruit and vegetable gardens, with some households engaged in making incense sticks and house bricks. Others work in factories nearby the village. People in Bang Chanee experience seasonal flooding every year. In 2011, however, this area was designated by the government as a water retardation area and consequently experienced prolonged flooding.

Don Phud municipality of Don Phud district is a rice- farming area located in the west of Saraburi province, adjacent to the Pasak River. Two factories in the district also employ people from the village. Don Phud is seasonally flooded by between 1 and 3 meters of water for almost a month, which overflows from the canals that connect to the Pasak River. While the residential areas are on elevated ground and thus generally resilient to flooding, in the 2011 flood even these houses were inundated.

Lan Takfa village in Nakhon Chai Si district of Nakhon Pathom province is a rural area in the vicinity of Bangkok and one of the pioneer sites for commercial rice farming for export since the time of King Rama IV in 1860. It is located on the Tha Chin River and within the Western Chao Phraya Plain Irrigation Project. Housing estates are being built for commuters working in Bangkok, such that the village is partially transformed into an urban space. The area has also attracted internal migrants to work in factories nearby. Among the longer-established households, people's main occupations are fruit gardening (pomelo, rose apple and coconut) and rice farming, together with factory work. While Lan Takfa village used to be seasonally flooded, water management associated with increasing urbanization has reduced the extent of flooding. Yet, some areas still regularly flood from canal overflow that connects to the Tha Chin River.

Reliable irrigation in each community means that farmers can produce two to three rice crops per year. The majority of households in these communities own farming land, while a minority rent land for rice farming. Most interviewed had completed elementary school education, and almost all have their names in house registration. While most of the families in the village identify their primary livelihoods as rice farming, younger people in particular have been drawn to waged employment in Bangkok and Ayutthaya. As migrants, they then send remittances that are invested in homesteads, farming and day-to-day expenses and have reduced some forms of material vulnerability in rural Thailand. Young people also migrate for education opportunities in urban areas. Overall, households in the village practice multiple strategies for their livelihood with diverse occupations, starting from farming and with various supplementary occupations including wage labor, factory work, salaried work, home crafts and petty trade. Most of the work – including farm work – is not full time.

Rural areas regularly experience seasonal flooding in Thailand and consider it normal. The areas' flooding is recognized by the farmers to be beneficial to fertilize their soil. They have adapted their lifestyles according to the flooding, for example, by owning boats for transportation. Residential areas of the villages are vulnerable to flooding, but are designed to be resilient to this. For example, many houses are built on stilts, and depending on the wealth of the family, some may be quite high off the ground. Furthermore, local administrative offices are located on elevated grounds so that they can still function even during periods of seasonal flooding.

The experience of the 2011 flood in rural Thailand

Bang Chanee village, Don Phud municipality and Lan Takfa village were all badly affected by the 2011 flood. All three areas were designated as water-retainment areas. Bang Chanee village received water diverted from the Chao Praya in a bid to protect Ayutthaya's town and industrial areas, as well as Bangkok further downstream. Meanwhile, Don Phud and Lan Takfa received water from the Pasak River and Tha Chin River, respectively, to protect Bangkok. Among the three locations, Don Phud was particularly heavily flooded, with the water level in some areas as high as 3 to 4 meters and remaining in some places for more than 2 months.

According to interviews, households faced five main problems: decreased income, difficulty in transportation, damage to houses and other property including crop products, limited access to amenities and various illnesses and general discomfort caused by the flood. During the flood, most people continued to live in their own houses, especially those that live in traditional stilted houses. Some made scaffold planks so that the living areas were raised, as the water entered the house beneath them. Houses in lowland areas, however, were submerged and temporarily evacuated (in particular, in Bang Chanee), and the residents stayed in temporary shelters on higher ground. In Lan Takfa village, the long-term farming residents who are more adapted to living with seasonal floods managed better, due to their stilted house design, compared to the more recent arrivals in the housing estates with buildings at ground level.

Agriculture in all three villages was severely affected. To the extent possible, farmers adjusted their rice-farming cycle, and planted their fruit and vegetable according to time lines suggested by the Departments of Irrigation or Disaster Prevention and Mitigation, derived from the government's flood management policies. Bang Chanee village's rice farming was not as badly damaged compared to the other two villages because the government issued more information about the flood and warned against planting off-season rice. In many cases, farmers also decided to do short-crop planting to mitigate their risks.

The government provided compensation packages, mainly because these areas were flood-retention areas protecting urban areas. The compensation list included the following:

- Rice paddies at 2,222 Thai baht (THB) per *rai*[2] (about 55 percent of production costs)
- Cash crops (e.g. sugar cane, cassava and maize) at 3,150 THB per *rai*
- Gardens and plantations (e.g. flowers, vegetables, herbs, perennials and rubber plantations) at 5,098 THB per *rai*

Grouping diverse agricultural products together was problematic for some, however, because the investment in terms of time and money varies greatly, for example, between fruit tree production and ornamental plants. However, the higher-value-crop growers had more capacity to organize themselves into associations, and they were able to request extra support from the government in the long term. For house repair, compensation was based on the cost of housing material. Some expenditure spent during the flood, however, remained uncompensated, including costs for sandbag purchase, water pumps to remove water from residential areas and costs for raising the floors of houses.

Regarding social structure, the farming community is based on kin-based relations; therefore, there was generally a strong sense of solidarity and mutual support within the family and between families during the flooding. However, our semistructured surveys also revealed that within the community some households could link more effectively with social or political networks, and thus had more capability to access economic and political resources for temporary shelter, flood relief schemes and postflood recovery funds.

Ability to cope with the flood differed between communities depending on their capability to network beyond the village. The community of Lan Takfa, in particular, had gained past experience of networking and engaging the government through their long-term campaign for a community land title, and their established relationship with a wider Tha Chin River basin group network. Through these networks, they were able to arrange for the installation of water pumps to drain out their plain early in 2012 (Pintobtang, 2012). They also tried to develop a database to discuss with the government water management on the basis of river basin ecological conservation, which can be seen as the community's attempt to promote public participation in decision making in a very centralized national process (Meesang, 2013). In contrast, Bang Chanee village and Don Phud municipality had little choice but to allow their paddy fields to be water retainment areas, and adapt as best they could by adjusting their rice-farming cycle. They received assistance and compensation, although it was delayed and did not cover all losses incurred.

Considering the 2011 flooding through the lens of mobility, the flooding affected peoples' local mobility, which was challenging in particular for households who had members working in local factories. However, many of these factories were also shut down and during the postflood period even had to lay off part of their workforce, which affected in particular Ban Chanee village. At Lan Takfa, where a significant number of residents, in particular the newer ones, are commuters who work in Bangkok or other locations outside the village, their mobility and therefore livelihoods were also undermined by the flood.

Regarding migration, household members who had left the village to work outside and send remittances back, and who were temporarily laid off due to the flood, often came back to stay in the village, as it was still possible to live there with the flood compared to their urban residences. For these households, the rural households served as a social safety net.

In our interviews, we did not find anyone who had migrated or sold their land in the postflood period as a result of their experience of the 2011 flood. This was the case even though government policy was perceived as transferring risks of extreme flooding to rural agricultural areas, and it is likely that rural areas will be flooded again to protect urban areas in the future. One reason was that the government agreed to pay compensation if land is used for future floodwater storage, as well as to provide support for short-time crop cycles. Another reason is that there is a general trend of rising land prices in these areas due to their vicinity to Bangkok.

The experience of the 2011 flood in urban Thailand

For urban areas, flooding is seen as an exceptional condition, as various flood defenses and water management systems usually protect them. In this section, urban case studies are presented of when flood defenses fail, as in the case of Poonsup community, or when flood defenses protect some urban areas at the expense of others, as in the case of U-Chareon community and Tung Songhong housing estate. Houses in urban areas are concrete and most have two stories, with the first story at ground level. Therefore, they are not resilient to flooding in the same way that stilted houses in rural areas are. Instead, some people have to move out when the floodwater level is too high, while others struggle in the floodwater to protect their property or because they have limited options.

Poonsup community in Sai Mai district of northern Bangkok is an urban-poor community consisting of 170 households of second- and third-generation migrants from rural areas who used to live rough along a canal under bridges. Following a policy of the Bangkok Metropolitan Administration (BMA) on flood protection, intended to keep the canal routes free of obstacles, they were evicted 20 years ago. However, with the backing of a strong social movement called the Urban Poor Network, they negotiated with the government to be resettled in Sai Mai district. While the land belongs to the government rather than private owners in the community, the community received a guarantee for cheap rent for a 30-year period. In the process of establishing their community, reflecting their solidarity as a group and drawing on support from the Urban Poor Network, they adopted a participatory process to design the community's housing plan, which included public areas, a sports field, a nursery and a playground. The main livelihoods in Poonsup community are street vending and other petty trade and labor-based work within the city.

In 2011, Poonsup community was flooded with water from the Klong Thanon Canal that connects to the Chao Praya River to the north of Bangkok. The flood came following the collapse of a sandbag wall that had been built to prevent water from entering Bangkok. The Poonsup community ultimately faced flooding of up to 1.5 meters for 2 months, as once the flood defense had failed the BMA did not try to recover and reprotect the area. The flooding was especially severe along a 3-kilometer stretch of road used for commuting in to the city, and this reduced mobility, affecting resident's livelihoods and income. While the impact of the flood created hardship for the community, building on their community solidarity and also their connections with the Urban Poor Network, they were able to negotiate with the BMA to arrange for shelter for the elderly, as well as the distribution of flood relief items.

Despite the severity of the flooding, the community does not plan to leave the area. As a community of historical migrants, their current capabilities and vulnerabilities are reflected in their life histories. They have moved from a riskier location alongside the canal, where they were considered illegal settlers, to a relatively more secure one in Poonsup community. While they do not have land ownership, they do have access to basic services, such as water and electricity, which were unavailable alongside the canal, and they also have recognized legal household registration. They cannot return to rural areas as they have no land, and they cannot move into the city as it is too expensive. Therefore, they anticipate that they will be able to negotiate their continued residence beyond the 30-year low-rent period in their current location. Thus, while their choices appear limited and the current situation is far from perfect, their community solidarity and networks with social movements have enabled them to negotiate relatively favorable outcomes with the government both during the 2011 flooding and more broadly over the past two decades.

Turning to our second urban example, U-Chareon community of Don Mueang district and Tung Songhong housing project of Laksi district are two communities located in the northern area of Bangkok, nearby Don Mueang International Airport and Air Force Base. The U-Chareon community was established under the Sixth National Economic and Social Development Plan in 1991 aiming for urban development in BMA's suburb area, while Tung Songhong housing project was built by the National Housing Authority of Thailand (NHA) in 1984 as a resettlement site during Thailand's rapid expansion. The communities are adjacent to each other, with middle-income families living in U-Chareon community and lower middle-income families living in Tung Songhong housing project. Most commute to work in Bangkok or work at the nearby airport and air force base.

During the 2011 flooding, at first Don Mueang Airport hosted the headquarters for the Flood Relief Operations Centre (FROC), which was the key governmental decision-making entity managing the response to the flooding. However, as the flood advanced toward the city and it became apparent that Don Mueang Airport would be inundated, FROC was relocated. As flood defenses were prepared to protect the inner-city area, U-Chareon community and Tung Songhong housing project were designated as the sites for the construction of a 'big-bag' sandbag dike 2 meters high, while lying outside of the flood defense themselves. As a result, both communities experienced flooding of between 1.5 and 2.5 meters for almost 2 months. They faced severe difficulties as they did not have experience with flooding and had limited time to prepare. In the end, some used the elevated Don Mueang Tollway as their temporary shelter, while others whose work was still open in Bangkok used it to commute into the city while reaching the tollway by boat.

Viewing their communities' flooding as unjust, given the high water level and prolonged period of flooding, people from U-Chareon community and Tung Songhong housing estate began to organize protests. They also blocked the road to the tollway and destroyed one of the sandbag barriers, which allowed floodwaters to rapidly flow into inner Bangkok, flooding several areas near the barrier before it was repaired. In response, the government sent a representative to talk and discuss the flood relief project with the people. At the same time, the government continuously sought to repair and reinforce the sandbag floodwalls to prevent water from entering inner Bangkok.

Initially, the government proposed to temporarily evacuate the residents (i.e. mobility as a solution), but people did not agree due to their concern over the security of their households' properties. Communities instead drew on support from local politicians, related to their voting in the Bangkok governor's election and parliamentary by-elections, to negotiate for flood relief projects and support for those who decide to stay in the flooded area, under a model titled the 'U-Charoen Model for Living With Floods.' Thus, in contrast to a mobility solution to flooding, people in U-Chareon used self-mobilization to further their resilience at the community level. Their model involves five practices, three processes, and three coordinating centers. The five practices are monitoring information; operating an alert system; assessing the flood-containment situation; preparing materials, funding and personnel; and supporting each other physically and psychologically. The three processes were of evaluation, analysis and resolution. They also organized three centers: an information center on the level of flooding; a self-help support center, which was a community shelter for elderly and vulnerable people; and lastly a coordination center, enabling coordination between government staff, private companies and civil society organizations. Under this model, people in the area sought to continue their daily lives while living with a 2.5-meter-high flood for more than 2 months.

The conflict at U-Chareon community and Tung Songhong housing project over the big-bag floodwall came to represent the resentment held more widely by the affected people who questioned the government's policy of unconditionally protecting inner Bangkok at all costs above the city's surrounding areas (Rojanaphruk, 2011). For them, the policy was not only perceived as unjust but also affirmed the problems of centralization of power and wealth in the hands of a small group in Thailand. Since FROCs flood management policy was top down, without consultation and without fair compensation being offered, some affected people took matters into their own hands by dismantling the flood protections that were flooding them, and demanded the authorities come up with a better approach.

The experience of the 2011 flood in a semiurban/industrial area

Khanham community of Uthai district, Ayutthaya province, is located near the 2,400-hectare Rojana Industrial Park, which is one of five industrial sites in Ayutthaya province. In the industrial park are located many transnational and domestic businesses in manufacturing. The number of households registered in Khankham community is 1,402 with a population of 6,077 persons,[3] yet the actual total number of residents working in 236 factories in Rojana Industrial Park, including internal and transnational migrants, is as many as 99,751 workers.[4] They work within the industrial estate in the factories, or in related businesses nearby, either as temporary or permanent workers. Some factories provide a daily shuttle from the community to the factories.

During the 2011 flood, the Pasak River flooded its bank and inundated the area with over 2 meters of water. Despite investment in significant flood defense, including a 3.5-meter-high earthen dyke around much of the industrial estate, and reassurances from the government that the flood was manageable, the industrial estate's defenses were eventually overwhelmed on 9 October 2011 when water moved up the Kao-Mao Canal. Even as the industrial estate at first stayed dry, the surrounding resident and migrant communities in Khankham community were flooded. However, according to our in-depth interviews, most people living around the industrial estate agreed with the protection of factories, given that they depend upon the industry for their livelihoods.[5]

Given the composition of the population in Khanham community, many of the people flooded in this area were migrants. During and following the flooding, all factories in the Rojana industrial estate were closed, and due to the slow process of insurance claims, reopening took 4 months (from October 2011 to February 2012) to reach full capacity. Most factories laid off part of their workforce, often providing only partial salaries to a skeleton staff.

For the local Thai population living in the area, right after the flood on 7 October 2011, many moved to temporary shelters organized by the Ayutthaya local government located opposite the provincial administration office. Others relocated to the Asian Highway nearby and built shelters themselves, as well as parked their cars and movable belongings there while regularly visiting their flooded houses (Thairath Online, 2011). After 2 weeks passed, most local Thais became more accustomed to the flood, and started to take turns visiting their houses and going to work locally, except those who worked at the factories, some of whom had to seek work in other provinces.

Regarding the Thai domestic migrants working at the Rojana industrial estate, given that both the factories and their dormitories were inundated up to 2 meters, many returned to their hometowns during the flood without payment and came back once the factories began operating again. Some, however, migrated to provinces around Thailand's eastern seaboard, such as Chonburi, Prajinburi and Srakeaw provinces, which also have industrial estates but without the risk of flooding. A few, meanwhile, stayed behind to keep the factories secure.

For informal international migrants, however, there is little official information available. However, a recent study by the nongovernmental organization International Centre for Migration Policy Development (ICMPD) found that informal foreign migrants from Myanmar, Cambodia and Laos had limited access to information about the flooding and so could not plan accordingly, especially if they could not speak Thai. These migrants mostly did not to return to their home country, due to difficulties in transportation, as well as concerns over arrest and consequent deportation if they were to try to travel home (Hendow et al., 2016). They also feared losing their job, and salaries yet to be paid also made them not leave their place of residence.

In terms of access to support from local governments and civil society organizations, according to ICMPD, local Thai and domestic migrants could access various resources (Hendow et al., 2016). International migrants, however, received less support and became more vulnerable during the flood. They did receive some donation from flood relief organizations as immediate relief, and in principle they could also access government resources including government shelters. However, in practice, they were concerned about their legal situation and did not draw on these resources. Furthermore, because of the limited official data about the numbers and locations of these informal international migrants, they were invisible for emergency planning and difficult to reach with an outreach program. Thailand's existing disaster risk reduction (DRR) policies and practices still do not include international migrants or have particular provisions for irregular migrants.

For postflood operation, several factories took months to reopen due to the slow insurance claims process. Some companies decided to move their plants to neighboring countries, such as China and Malaysia. When the factories reopened, young adults were able to get jobs in the factories, but middle-aged workers who previously received higher salaries seemed to have less chance to find new jobs as the factories intended to employ younger staff due to cost. For international migrants, due to the high demand for unskilled labor in the area, many came back to work, especially those who migrate under the government's Memorandum of Understandings with neighboring countries, or who have a legal status to work in Thailand.

In 2012, one year following the flood, Rojana industrial park built a 6-meter concrete wall around the industrial park to provide more comprehensive protection for the industries within, based on scenarios for future flooding. While perhaps this will prove adequate to prevent future factory damage, the flooding of the surrounding area would prevent the factories from continuing to operate. Thus, the surrounding local and migrant communities still remain vulnerable, both to the physical impact of flooding itself, and to the loss of means to make a living during episodes of severe flooding. Indeed, arguably, they are now more vulnerable, as future floodwater would not be able to be redistributed across the industrial estate but will instead accumulate nearby.

Conclusion

Thailand's modern economy has largely been built on industrialization, commercialization of agriculture, and the growth of the service sector, with domestic and international migration of people a significant characteristic of this mode of development. Economic modernization has brought material benefits for many but has also produced new forms of inequality and vulnerabilities for rural and urban areas. In this context, this chapter has presented seven case studies in the Chao Phraya River basin and their experiences of severe flooding in 2011: three rural communities, three urban communities and one semiurban/industrial community. The chapter has considered the significance of migration and mobility in each case study.

Within Thailand's economic development pathway, water has been become a commodity necessary for economic production, ranging from producing hydroelectricity, to irrigation water in agriculture, to water for industrial processes. Thailand's water management regime, the operation of its associated infrastructure and the overall allocation of benefits, costs and risks has been much analyzed, including the modification of the landscape and waterscape (e.g. Molle and Srijantr, 1999; Molle, 2007; Lebel et al., 2011). Thailand's water policies generally have not paid sufficient attention to the ecological impact or vulnerability encountered by Thailand's smaller-scale farmers in rural areas and have contributed to growing socioeconomic inequalities in Thailand.

The countrywide severity of the 2011 flood has been linked to shortcomings in the water management regime, and more broadly to Thailand's economic modernization (Marks, 2015). Government policy at the time privileged the protection of urban areas over rural areas, and protecting industrial sites over agriculture farmlands, raising questions of social justice. They revealed deeper inequalities in Thailand as wealthy communities stayed dry. On occasion, tensions spilled over into protest and confrontation, as in the case of U-Chareon community and Tung Songhong housing estate. Media images of these communities trying to break down the large floodwall built of 2.5 ton sandbags after being inundated for over a month while the protected area behind it stayed dry became symbolic of what was perceived to be unjust about the country's flood management. Post-2011 flood policy has perpetuated urban-rural inequalities, emphasizing the protection of industrial estates and commercial areas from floods, while designating a 200 kilometer long swathe of the Chao Phraya's rural central plain as a 'floodway' and other areas as water retention areas (Fernquest, 2011).

Vulnerability to flooding, therefore, must be understood as relationally produced between rural and urban areas. Rural communities are accustomed to seasonal flooding, and thus have some experience to adapt, as well as resources such as stilted houses and boats. They draw upon the support of their tightly knit social structure. People in rural central plains generally plan ahead to live with flood. They put their belongings on higher places and prepare dried food in case of difficulties in transportation. However, in the 2011 flood, farming livelihoods were severely affected, ultimately reducing incomes, and other sources of livelihood, including factory work near the rural community areas that we studied were also undermined. This damage in rural areas was exacerbated by policies to protect the major urban and industrial areas, in particular Bangkok and Ayutthaya province.

In urban areas, severe flooding like that in 2011 is an exceptional event. Urban houses are not well protected against floods, and there is limited experience among urban populations to prepare for and manage living with flooding. While some stayed in their houses, to protect property or out of lack of other options, others were mobile and temporarily moved to higher locations or, for some, even back to their rural family households.

Our case studies showed how rural and urban areas organized themselves and lived through the flood. Overall, this sense of organizing was stronger in rural areas. Most rural communities have kin-based social structures and turned this into a strength to manage distribution of emergency relief relatively more equally than urban communities; this is because the people tend to know one another and recognize one another's needs. In addition, local leaders were more present and accessible, and they tended to listen to the voice of the people. In contrast in urban areas, many are former internal migrants with diverse occupations and do not share the sense of a closely knit community as kin-based rural farming communities. However, as revealed in our urban case studies, local leaders and politicians organized flooded communities, and drawing upon civil society and political networks was an important strategy for their ability to adapt to flooding and draw upon the resources of the state. Within communities that had longer-standing forms of self-organization within them, and who thus were already active members of wider networks, they had the ability to gain extra help or extend help to others; for example, Lan Takfa worked within the Tha Chin River Basin Network, and Poonsup community with the Urban Poor Network.

The linkages between flooding and migration in Thailand are subtle and tied to the interconnections between rural and urban areas. Migration has been a key trait of Thailand's modernization, with seasonal and permanent movements of people from rural to urban areas, as well as international economic migrations. For households in Thailand's rural areas, it has enabled a multilocal-livelihood strategy, where older household members remain in farming, while many younger members have sought education opportunities and waged employment in urban areas. While remittances may partially support rural households under everyday conditions, during the 2011 flood, similar to periods of major economic crisis, rural households and communities serve as social safety nets for family members who were affected, so instead of out-migration, there was a movement toward returning home during those difficult periods. In terms of the postflood period, the government policy for recovery and remedy barely recognized the issue of mobility and migration; for example, people whose names were not listed in the house registration for a particular flooded area could not claim compensation.

It is inevitable that Thailand will experience periodic severe floods in the future. Strategies for increasing resilience to flooding are therefore necessary, and under active discussion. These policies should range from supporting local community empowerment and building stronger local institutions for disaster management and recovery to structural changes at the national level that address the impacts of economic modernization on Thailand's vulnerability to extreme flooding and that consider not only hard infrastructure approaches to flood management but also institutional development, such as more inclusive and participatory river basin management. Integrated into these policies should be more specific consideration of the role that migration and mobility have played in producing vulnerability and capabilities in urban and rural areas in Thailand, and in particular how social interconnections between rural and urban areas (i.e. multilocal livelihoods) could be recognized and built upon as a resilience strategy in itself.

Acknowledgments

The authors would like to thank the following for their research support: Pichaya Surapolchai, Paladej Na Pombejra, Usa Kotsripetch, Surangrat Jumneanpol, Wichaya Komin, Bovorn Subsing, Nantiya Kakeya, Prapart Pintobtang, Kanokpan Ucha and Saikeaw Tippakorn.

Notes

1 There are 16 governmental units in four ministries that were involved in water resource management in one way or another (Boonyabancha and Archer, 2011).
2 *Rai* is a unit of land area in Thailand, equal to 1,600 square meters or 0.16 hectares.
3 Thailand Information Center website (in Thai) accessed on 23 March 2017: http://phranakhonsiayudhya.kapook.com/อุทัย/คานหาม
4 Estimate posted to Baanmaha web board at time of flooding accessed on 23 March 2017. www.baanmaha.com/community/archive/index.php/t-46869.html
5 During the 2011 flood in Ayutthaya province, 616 factories located in five industrial estates were inundated as follows: Saharatananakorn with 49 factories affecting 10,882 workers, Rojana with 236 factories affecting 99,751 workers, BannWa (high tech) with 143 factories affecting 51,168 workers, Bang Pa-in with 89 factories affecting 27,590 workers and Factory Land at Wang Noi with 99 factories affecting 6,015 workers. The total number of workers affected in Ayutthaya province was 195,406 people.

References

Boonyabancha, S., and Archer, D. (2011). "Thailand's floods: Complex political and geographical factors behind the crisis." Blog post. www.iied.org/thailands-floods-complex-political-geographical-factors-behind-crisis.

Fernquest, J. (2011). "Super express floodway." *The Bangkok Post*, 15 November 2011. www.bangkokpost.com/learning/learning-from-news/266424/super-express-floodway.

Hendow, M., Pailey, R.N., and Bravi, A. (2016). *Migrant in countries in crisis: Emerging findings: A comparative study of six crisis situations*. Vienna: International Centre for Migration Policy Development (ICMPD).

Lebel, L., Manuta, J., and Garden, P. (2011). "Institutional traps and vulnerability to changes in climate and flood regimes in Thailand." *Regional Environmental Change* 11: 45–58.

Marks, D. (2015). "The urban political ecology of the 2011 floods in Bangkok: The creation of uneven vulnerabilities." *Pacific Affairs* 88(3): 623–651.

Meesang, S. (2013). [In Thai] *A case study: Lessons from the movement of assembly for local reform – V-reform Thailand.* Bangkok: Reform Office and National Health Council.

Middleton, C., and Krawanchid, D. (2014). "Chapter 5: Urbanization and sustainable development in the Mekong region." (pp. 72–96) in Lebel, L., Hoanh, C.T., Krittasudthacheewa, C., and Daniel, R. (eds.) *Livelihoods, ecosystem services and the challenges of regional integration in the Mekong region.* Gerakbudaya: Strategic Information and Research Development (SIRD) Centre (SIRD).

Molle, F. (2007). "Scales and power in river basin management: The Chao Phraya River in Thailand." *The Geographical Journal* 173(4): 358–373.

Molle, F., and Srijantr, T. (1999). *Agrarian change and the land system in the Chao Phraya Delta.* DORAS Center Research Report No. 6. Bangkok: Kasetsart University.

Mustafa, D., Ahmed, S., Saroch, E., and Bell, H. (2011). "Pinning down vulnerability: From narratives to numbers." *Disasters* 35: 62–86.

Pintobtang, P. (2012). [In Thai] *Diversity of life and the communities drown in the flood: The case of Lantakfa, Nakhon Chai Si district, Nakhon Pathom province.* Bangkok: Thailand Health Promotion Fund and Social Agenda Working Group, Chulalongkorn University.

Pongsudhirak, T. (2011). "The politics behind Thailand's flood." *The Guardian*, 21 October 2011. www.theguardian.com/commentisfree/2011/oct/21/thailand-floods-bangkok.

Rojanaphruk, P. (2011). "Conflict over barriers: A sign of divide: Thailand flood." *The Nation*, 18 November 2011. www.nationmultimedia.com/news/national/aec/30170105.

Thairath Online. (2011). "Three rivers inundate Ayutthaya and Rojana industrial estate." *Thairath Online*, 9 October 2011. www.thairath.co.th/content/207859#cxrecs_s.

UNESCAP. (2015). *Asia-Pacific migration report 2015: Migrants contributions to development.* Bangkok: The Asia-Pacific RCM Thematic Working Group on International Migration including Human Trafficking.

World Bank. (2012). *Thai flood 2011: Overview, rapid assessment for resilient recovery and reconstruction planning.* Bangkok: World Bank.

6 Generating vulnerability to floods

Poor urban migrants and the state in Metro Manila, Philippines

Edsel E. Sajor, Bernadette P. Resurrección and Sharon Feliza Ann P. Macagba

Introduction

Migration is a major dynamic of urban population growth in Southeast Asia's mega-urban regions, such as Jakarta, Manila, Ho Chi Minh City and Hanoi. Since the 1980s rapid economic growth in the region's major cities has accelerated rural-urban migration and migration between the urban core and peri-urban areas (Kelly and McGee, 2003; Yap, 2012). Rapid urbanization and urban poverty combine to influence the mushrooming of informal settlements and slums in cities, often in hazardous and flood-prone areas. The urban poor and low-income migrants have little choice but to inhabit these risky spaces, having been subject to continuing eviction from safer areas in other parts of the city. Moreover, such groups have been priced out of the formal housing market in relatively safe locations where urban livelihood and economic opportunities are easily accessible, and where land values have increased by as much as 6,000 percent (Yap et al., 2002 cited in UN-HABITAT, 2012). The urban poor and migrants thus move to sites that remain cheap or 'free' because they are hazard prone and therefore unattractive for commercial and private business (Jha et al., 2013; Jha et al., 2011; Satterthwaite et al., 2007, Hardoy et al., 2013).

This chapter examines internal migration in Malabon City, part of the Metro Manila mega-urban region in the Philippines, where low-income migrants occupy risky flood-prone areas. We explore factors underlying settlement in obviously high-risk areas and the resource structure that constrains the urban poor from doing otherwise. The chapter assesses the core orientation of the city's current disaster preparedness program, which focuses on relocation of migrants, but with limited attention paid to patterns of mobility and livelihood strategies. Interventions thus fail to prevent relocated poor migrants from returning after flooding episodes or new waves of migrants from occupying recently vacated spaces. Thus, the generation of vulnerability to flooding disasters for poor and low-income migrants continues as an accretive process.

This case study shows that vulnerability to flood hazards should not be seen purely as a function of biophysical and geographic variations in exposure to the natural stressor of flooding caused by extreme precipitation. It is a generated vulnerability, undergirded by a socially constructed marginality in the allocation of land and housing resources in the city. As other studies show, such marginality influences poor and low-income city migrants to knowingly live in places that are exposed to flooding risk so as to have easier access to livelihood opportunities in given areas (Pelling, 2011). This marginality is socially and politically generated in society, especially in cities, through inequitable distribution of economic and political power between and within social groups (Leichenko and O'Brien, 2006; Moser and Boycoff, 2013). We also argue that differential vulnerability to flooding is a function of underlying social vulnerability, which is in turn created by past and ongoing development processes in the wider political economy of the Philippines. These have resulted in the unequal distribution of income, land access, capacity and power (Bankoff et al., 2004). Thus, vulnerability to flooding is produced through chains of influence and trends in the wider political economy.

To this we would add that a migration perspective means examining these chains of influence across the different spaces that migrants occupy over the course of their livelihood-driven mobility. For the people in this study, migration has been the strategy they have adopted to resolve livelihood stresses in their places of origin, taking advantage of informal-sector work opportunities in Malabon, but this has heightened and accumulated their exposure to flooding. Their vulnerability is then compounded by a lack of access to tenure security and adequate housing, which, in turn, is influenced by development trends that have regressive effects on the allocation of land and housing resources.

Rather than base solutions and remedies around the present-day locus of flood event impacts, a wider frame of reference is needed that takes account of a series of vulnerabilities that map on to the complexities of people's life course and everyday mobilities. Our Malabon case study shows there is a need to go beyond an exclusive focus on an adaptation policy response of simply forcibly relocating these communities to safer places, and instead to address livelihood concerns of the mobile poor, and more fundamentally address the broader structural influences and development processes that currently inhibit land tenure and housing security.

In the following we will first present the geographic and demographic profile of Malabon City and also its poverty and flood mapping. This will be followed by a discussion of the characteristics and patterns of migration and of the informal settlements in the city's floodways. Then, we focus on the reasons and conditions for the migrants' settling in the floodways and a discussion and assessment of government response to flooding in these settlements. We end with a conclusion that wraps up our findings and overall arguments.

Malabon City: urban growth and flood hazards

The city of Malabon is a coastal town located in northern Metro Manila, adjacent to a narrow coastal strip town of Navotas, which directly borders Manila Bay, as shown in Figure 6.1. Together with Navotas, Valenzuela, Pateros, Taguig, Pasig and Muntinlupa, Malabon forms the outer ring towns of Metro Manila,

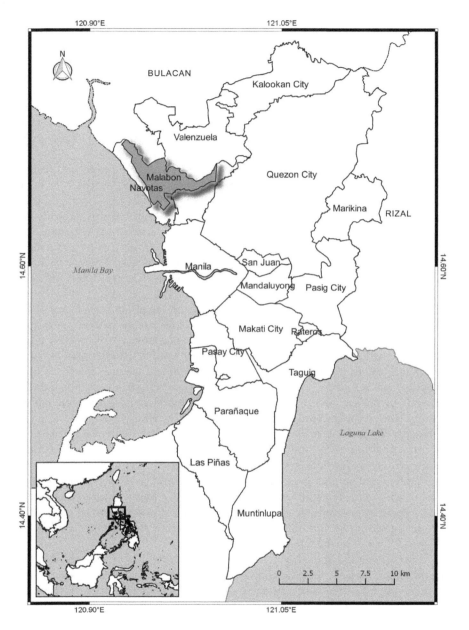

Figure 6.1 Location of Malabon City

with the City of Manila as its center. It has population of 353,337 (Census of Population and Housing, 2010). Though it is highly urbanized and part of the national capital region, Malabon is in the bottom-ten cities of the Philippines in terms of per capita income. It is ranked 128 out of a total of 136 cities in the entire country, with a per capita income of 2,111 Philippine pesos (PHP) in 2009, roughly equivalent to US$46 (NSCB, 2012), well below the national average of 3,844 PHP, or US$85 (NSCB, 2009). All of Metro Manila's municipalities and cities, unlike in most of the other regions, are within the Philippines statistical authority's 'least poor' category, and have a poverty rate that is below than 20 percent.[1] However, among the five poorest places in Metro Manila, Malabon ranks third poorest (3.8 percent), after Port Area in Manila City (10 percent), and Navotas (6 percent) (Business Mirror, 11 April 2015).

The city of Malabon has a total land area of 1,571 hectares, which is divided into 21 barangays, or village politico-administrative jurisdictions, the bottom of the administrative hierarchy in the Philippines. Technically, city and municipality social welfare programs cascade to the barangay level, but this depends on the delivery capacity and logistics available at higher levels of government for supporting this. Malabon's land area is currently divided into the following land uses: residential, 38 percent; commercial, 19 percent; industrial 33 percent; institutional, 6 percent; agricultural/fishpond, 1 percent; open space, 1 percent; and cemetery, 1 percent.

These proportions reflect an accretive process of actual land use rather than planned utilization of land based on an effective government land-use plan and official development strategy. Malabon City is no exception to a historically typical characteristic of land use in the country, where even as a master plan for land use formally exists, planning institutions and operational mechanisms for implementing it are not in place, and regulatory practices and enabling guidelines do not exist to prevent spot zoning and other pervasive forms of exceptionalism vis-à-vis the formal land-zoning provisions (Sajor, 2003).

Roughly 71 percent of the total land use of the city is for residential and industrial functions. Land for residential use is mostly in the form of low-density housing areas (characterized mainly by single detached dwellings with the usual community ancillary uses on a neighborhood scale and relatively exclusive subdivision with support facilities) and medium-density housing areas (characterized by two-family dwellings, townhouses, accessories or row houses) and other low-area medium-rise multifamily dwellings with more limited support facilities designed for needs at the village scale.

On the other hand, industrial zones are made up of light industries whose manufacturing products are for local consumption or distribution within the city, and medium-size industries whose products are for regional consumption. Floodways in the city, as elsewhere, are legally considered to be government-owned and controlled land and are therefore excluded from alienable and disposable land. However, as discussed later in this chapter, these have become sites for large concentrations of informal settlements of mostly poor and low-income migrants to the city.

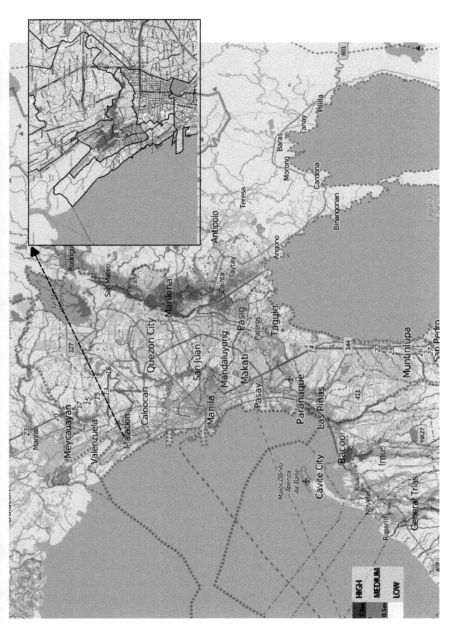

Figure 6.2 Flood hazards and informal settlements in Malabon City
Source: Lagmay, 2013

Malabon is one of Metro Manila's most flood-prone areas. It has 18 rivers and waterways, 16 of which have scores to a hundred of families living in informal settlements (see Figure 6.2). Out of the city's total 21 barangays or villages, 18 are in waterways. Rivers and tributaries that in the sixteenth century linked the old town and trading center of Malabon to other neighboring towns have over time been largely filled in and transformed into a network of feeder roads to serve delivery of locally produced or processed goods to various markets. Without a planned and systematically laid-out drainage system in this area, settlements in former waterways are easily flooded through the combined impact of continuous or heavy precipitation and high tide in Manila Bay.

Migration and informal settlements in floodways

The present-day population of Malabon City has grown dramatically in recent years. In 1903, the city registered a total population of just 20,136. In the succeeding 58 years (i.e. 1903–1960), growth was modest, at 2.3 percent per year. Two boom periods followed. From 1960 to 1975, the city's population increased by 98,000, from the 1960 base number of 29,983 to 175,000. A second period of population boom followed when it increased by 156,000, from 191,000 in 1980 to 347,000 in 1995 (NSO, 2010).

The 1960–1975 population boom was largely made up of rural-to-urban migration, with families coming from the poorest provinces of Bicol region, islands in central Philippines and in northern Luzon. However, the 1980–1995 population boom would be a mix of three in-migration streams: urban-to-urban migration for livelihood and employment; urban-to-urban migration resulting from enclosures of private and government city properties to make way for major real estate and infrastructure developments in the more central areas of Metro Manila; and, a continuing rural-to-urban migration for livelihood (although the latter is at a far lower rate than that observed between 1960 and 1975). It was during these two periods of in-migration that informal settlements in the city of Malabon grew dramatically.

The combination of extremely high migration rates in the period from 1960 to 1975, and then later from 1980 to 1990, caused a great increase in demand for housing. By the year 2000 it was reported that the city had a backlog in demand of 4,119 housing units (NSO, 2000). Around 81 percent of this constituted 'double-up households', where a household with a separate arrangement for food preparation and consumption shares the dwelling unit of another household, a form of hidden homelessness. Under the present Urban Development and Housing Act, government units are supposed to provide underprivileged and homeless citizens in their localities with decent housing, secure tenure at affordable cost and with basic services. The presence of thousands of people living in double-up housing in mostly informal settlements attest to the big scarcity of mass housing in Malabon City. Housing scarcity is also indicated by the reported 4.45 percent of families in the city who were living in unoccupied housing units without the consent of the owner (Ibid).

Table 6.1 Migration to the floodplains, 1961–2012

	Number of households	%
1961–1970	7	3.6
1971–1980	25	12.8
1981–1990	60	30.6
1991–2000	55	28.1
2001–2012	49	25
Total	196	100

Source: Authors' survey (September 2013)

Table 6.2 Points of origin of migrants living in Malabon floodways

	No. of households	%
(1) Within Metro Manila		
a. Other urban communities in Malabon City	70	34.3
b. Other urban communities in Metro Manila	83	40.7
(2) Outside Metro Manila	51	25.0
Total	204	100

Source: Authors' survey (September 2013)

By June 2009, there were about 27,202 families in the city reported to be living in informal dwellings. Out of these, 46 percent were built on privately owned lots and 26 percent were on government lots. However, 28 percent of these informal settlers live in the danger areas of the city's waterways. Based on the data collected by the Community and Urban Poor Affairs Office of Malabon City (MMDA, 2010), there were 5,485 families living in 18 informal settlements in Malabon City waterways.

Floodways in Malabon City have become an important destination for poor urban settlers in search of somewhere to live. Based on the random survey by the authors conducted in 15 communities in September 2013, densification of the poor migrant population in the floodways was most intense from 1981 to 2000. In this period, nearly 59 percent of present informal settlers set up home in risky areas (see Table 6.1). The rates of migration to the floodways in the survey also strongly suggests an overlap between the peak period of in-migration to Malabon from 1980 to 1995 mentioned earlier, and the peak period of urban poor migrants moving to the floodways from 1981 to 2000. More recently, migration to floodways has slowed slightly. This reflects the implementation of housing and relocation projects: as of 2011, there were three housing projects organized by the city government of Malabon. However, our survey found 69 percent of the informal settlers living in waterways disagreed with the plans to resettle them in new locations, citing the lack of livelihood opportunities and lack of basic services in the relocation sites as reasons.

In 2012, a poverty mapping study was undertaken in all but one of the 18 communities living along the waterways of Malabon, involving a large random sample of 3,859 respondents (FDA, 2012). The study concluded that rural-to-urban migration has not been the key process contributing to the densification of the urban poor population of the waterways of Malabon City. Nearly 84 percent of respondents came from other areas within Malabon City itself and other cities in Metro Manila. Only about 25 percent have come from the provinces, from both rural and urban areas (see Table 6.2). Our survey also shows that most of those coming to Malabon floodways to settle from other communities in Metro Manila come from the neighboring urban municipalities and cities of Navotas, Caloocan, Quezon City, Manila and Valenzuela. Navotas and Caloocan contribute 30 percent and 24 percent, respectively, of the total of migrants whose points of origin are cities outside Malabon but within Metro Manila.

Our data suggest that movement is livelihood driven and is mediated by social networks. The fact that double-up households constitute a major phenomenon in the informal settlements implies that kin who had previously migrated into Malabon often facilitate the mobility and shift of employment of other poor kin staying elsewhere in nearby cities in Metro Manila, by providing immediate housing through shelter sharing. Further, based on informal interviews, the fish market trading and processing activities, which have traditionally been concentrated in Malabon, provide easy access to informal employment for these migrants, despite providing only low wages. In-migration from far-flung rural provinces does not commonly have this advantage of house sharing by kin and quick access to specific employment opportunities in Malabon. Without these advantages, migration entails high risks for potential migrants from more distant points of origin. Moreover, a major proportion of migrants had been forcibly evicted from elsewhere in Manila, implying that Malabon City is a better alternative destination for these migrants, vis-à-vis the livelihood options of leaving Metro Manila or returning to rural provinces.

Reasons and conditions for settling in the floodways

The FDA's poverty mapping study in Malabon City also showed how the employment profile of settlements along the waterways of Malabon City is characterized by the pervasiveness of the informal sector and by a high rate of unemployment in informal occupations (FDA, 2012). In our survey, this was also confirmed (see Table 6.3).

The informal settlements in Malabon City's floodplains are usually located on top of a river or canal, or in low areas that are seasonally flooded during the rainy season. These settlements are at the front line of disaster when floodwaters rise during heavy precipitation. Most houses are standing on stilts and made of very light housing materials. Under the Water Code of the Philippines, these floodways of Malabon fall under the category of

> banks or rivers and streams. . . [that] throughout their entire length and within *three (3) meters in urban areas* . . . along their margins, are subject to

Table 6.3 Employment profile of household members in floodplain settlements

	Female	%	Male	%	Total	%
Formal (government sector)	11	1.7	4	0.6	15	2.3
Formal (private sector)	38	5.8	47	7.1	85	12.9
Informal (employed)	27	4.1	168	25.5	195	29.6
Informal (self-employed)	40	6.1	39	5.9	79	12.0
Unemployed (without any economically gainful or self-employment at all)	229	34.8	56	8.5	285	43.2
Total	345	52.4	314	47.7	659	100

Source: Authors' survey (September 2013)

the easement of public use in the interest of recreation, navigation, flotage, fishing and salvage. *No person shall be allowed to stay in this zone longer than what is necessary for recreation, navigation, flotage, fishing or salvage or to build structures of any kind.*

(Chapter IV, Article 51 of the Water Code of the Philippines, Presidential Decree No. 1067, December 31, 1976. Authors' emphasis)

Thus, the fact that these areas are only designated for flood control and management and not for human settlements underscores the physical vulnerability of these locations to flooding due to the rise in the water level of the rivers and canals. According to our survey, in some of these inhabited areas along Malabon City's 18 rivers and waterways, flooding is experienced up to eight times a month.

But despite physical vulnerability to flooding, demand for housing in this place is high, so much so that some informal settlers rent out their living spaces and small adjoining lots to others, even though they do not and would not own this land. Population remains high, even though basic services are marginal or substandard, due to deliberate marginalization by local government in public provisioning for these illegal settlements.

A large proportion of households (43 percent) that have moved to and continue to remain in these floodways have devised their own autonomous ways of coping and preparing for constant flooding risks. Based on the authors' survey these include putting their appliances, furniture, and important things on higher places, preferably at the second floor of their houses; staying indoors while waiting for the floodwaters to subside; and stocking enough food and water for days. Further, the respondents also said their respective barangay officialdom enforces evacuation and rescue operations, as well as early warning systems and relief operations. Also, cleaning of waterways, proper garbage disposal, and a campaign against leptospirosis form parts of the IEC campaigns in their barangays for disaster reduction and preparedness. Both autonomous and government-initiated measures for disaster preparation and response apparently give the residents a measure of security against severe casualties or damage from local floods.

Living conditions in informal settlements are substandard. In recent years, settlements have been provided with water from common standpipes, as well as electricity from the local public utility company. However, houses do not have any improved sanitation. Fecal wastes are discharged by the residents directly to the water body below or nearby. Solid wastes, on the other hand, in some communities are collected by municipal trucks, but in some they are not collected at all. For 2,737 households in these places, solid wastes are collected by garbage trucks only once a week (FDA, 2012). Moreover, due to crowding in houses, tuberculosis and respiratory diseases are very common.

Despite the generally high risk of flood disaster and substandard living conditions in the informal settlements in the floodplains, over the last 3 decades such settlements have grown. Data from the FDA's poverty mapping study, and from our own surveys on employment opportunities in these areas, suggest that while floodways may be characterized as spaces of risk, for migrants, they also represent spaces of opportunity. To understand the migrants' risk-taking behavior and apparently high tolerance of substandard living conditions, one should focus on the common reasons that attracted the migrants to these places. At the same time, recognition needs to be given to the factors that 'pushed' or drove them into these places from their former locations of residence.

Based on the authors' own survey in 2013, the principal reason why migrants have chosen to stay in these floodplains is work or livelihood related. This is very much interconnected with the two other factors that rank second and third in importance to the migrants' decisions to move and stay in flood-risk areas – that is, kinship ties and accessibility of land and affordability of rent. In addition, a substantial portion of the migrants (34.3 percent) currently occupying the floodplain's informal settlements have come from other places in Malabon City itself and from the adjacent urban municipalities of Navotas and Caloocan. It is likely that certain earlier individual migrants or families in the decades of 1980s, when migration to Malabon City was at its height, had occupied safer or non-flood-prone areas of the city. Subsequently, other kin members coming from other places or new couples of the second generation in the original households have had to build a new house or move into the city's floodplains, where land or room renting is the most affordable, cheap or free. This would explain why kinship ties, the accessibility of land and work-related factors run close in the multifactor order of importance.

The urban-poor settlers in the floodplains are attracted by the easy access to low-paying unskilled informal jobs in Malabon or in an adjacent municipality, such as, for instance, Navotas. From the surveys, a principal reason for moving residence to the Malabon City floodplains is 'due to its proximity to their present employment or main economic activity'. For poor migrants to make a viable living in Malabon City, informal job occupations that are obviously very insecure and characterized by poor working conditions and low pay have been complemented by free and accessible, albeit disaster prone and substandard, living conditions in the floodplains. The most common occupations of men in the place are as workers in small manufacturing firms, daily construction workers, motorcycle transport drivers and haulers in salt factories. Economically active women, on the other hand, are commonly street vendors, recyclable-garbage collectors, laundry women, domestic helpers and paper lantern makers. Both women and men are also employed as helpers in cottage-size fish-drying shops, which is a very pervasive industry in the city. Unemployment and underemployment are high, particularly among women.

The availability of jobs and livelihood combined with accessible and affordable housing is a strong source of motivation for poor migrants to move to Malabon City's floodplains, and this is further supported by our exploration of the factors that 'pushed' current urban-poor migrants to move from their place of origin and into Malabon's floodways. In the survey, the factors of unsatisfied need for employment and livelihood sources in the place of their origin, and the need for a new place to live registered 38.7 percent and 14.7 percent, respectively. Together these two factors already make up 53.4 percent of the sample (see Table 6.4). Furthermore, most, 74 percent, of the migrant respondents were married or had common-law partners at the time of the survey, indicating a likelihood of whole families migrating or establishing a new family in informal floodway settlements.

Further, it should also be noted that of the 25 percent of migrants in the floodplains of Malabon City who came from provinces outside Metro Manila, 44 percent came from provinces with high rates of poverty, notably Samar, Masbate, Negros Oriental and Lanao del Norte, which are the poorest provinces in the Philippines, and the main senders of internal migrants looking for livelihoods, especially in the urban areas (NSCB, 2012). Samar, Masbate and Negroes Oriental are island provinces with mountainous and highly rugged terrain, where arable lands are relatively scarce. Municipalities of these provinces are composed mostly of upland towns dependent on upland farming and agro-forestry, and narrow-strip coastal towns characterized by the pervasiveness of small fisherfolk livelihoods.

Developments in the land market, particularly in the real estate sector in Metro Manila, have also had a major influence in the densification of the migrant population in the floodplains of Malabon City. In Southeast Asian cities, urban poverty remains substantial but has been generally on the decline from 1993 to 2002. However, statistics show that urban inequality is increasing within most countries in the region, and population in urban slums, while slightly decreasing in proportion, has been increasing in absolute numbers (UN HABITAT, 2010). Moreover, urban employment within cities is growing but is largely composed of

Table 6.4 Reasons given for migrating to Malabon

Respondents reasons for migrating to Malabon	Number of responses
Peace, order and community solidarity	39
Benefits provided by the city government	9
Accessibility of land and affordability of rent	123
Kinship related	146
Work related	188

Source: Authors' survey (2013)

precarious, self-employed informal-sector work (Yap, 2012). At the same time, urban-planning institutions and land development management in the region are considered generally ineffective. Rather than being an outcome of planning processes, urban development and land-use practices result from negotiations over individual projects between private business developers on one hand, and the local government on the other hand. The former often work together with local politicians and administrators to promote profits for the few rather than benefits of all, in ways that are prejudicial to redistributive housing and land tenure policies in the city (Yap, 2012; Sajor, 2003; Goldblum and Wong, 2000). Part of the dynamics are powerful economic and political interests wanting 'their city' to continue attracting new investment (Huq et al., 2007), and a government-dominant focus on economic growth rather than reducing inequality through redistribution (UN-HABITAT, 2010).

Government policy and actions are biased toward and clearly encourage high-end real estate investments by big private domestic and foreign property developers. With demand rising because of aggressive and unregulated high- and middle-end residential and commercial real estate development projects in Philippine cities, the price of urban land has increased dramatically, pricing out the poor and low income from formal land and housing markets in safer locations and near workplaces. Thus, in this case, a regressive policy pursued in the domain of urban land development aimed at encouraging inward investment and a high economic growth rate has led to the unintended outcome of generating vulnerability in spaces to which dislocated urban poor and low-income informal settlers have moved. Metro Manila's property boom from the mid-1980s to late 1990s was characterized by market speculation and the overbuilding of high-end residential and commercial complexes (Magno-Ballesteros, 2000). This has led in many instances to massive forced eviction of informal settlements in prime locations, forcing their occupants to reestablish their homes elsewhere (Sajor, 2003).

After the property market bust of 1997–2001, real estate development has again been on a continuous upswing in the country, especially in Metro Manila, promoted and encouraged by a favorable policy environment of the Philippine government on investments and land development. Since 2003, property development of high-end and middle-end residential estates and buildings, office and commercial complexes and industrial zones have been constantly on the rise in the national capital region (Colliers International, 2012). Fast-track property developments have resulted in the massive eviction of occupants in squatted private lands. There are also cases reported in the media in recent years of forced burning of informal settlements in private lands to clear the huge urban lot and immediately begin construction of high-end residential-commercial complexes by big developers. Thus, the Malabon floodways have served to absorb this stream of forcibly ejected people from private lots in the national capital region. In our survey, eviction from private property has accounted for 14.1 percent of migrants' 'push' factors from their original place. Related to this land market development is the rise in house rent and land price in migrants' areas of origin. This factor accounts for another 10.4 percent of the reasons compelling these urban-poor migrants to move to the riskier floodways.

While there are structural factors that have been driving the mobility of urban poor to settle in the disaster-risk floodways of Malabon City over a period lasting at least 3 decades, it should not be imagined, however, that the decision to migrate into these risky places for livelihood and for cheap and free housing has been made autonomously and independently by individual migrants. Social ties of migrants have often played a big role in their consideration and final decision to take the risks and the opportunity posed by moving into floodways. Preexisting family ties, as well as marital needs and obligations, seem to be the most important considerations of migrants in deciding to relocate to the floodplains (See Table 6.5).

Often, a sibling or a close kin member already residing in the informal settlement would provide initial support for a newly entering migrant coming from outside to join in and occupy a space in the house. In due time, this new migrant would be constructing his/her own makeshift shelter. The need for new couples to establish their own affordable new shelter, after sharing space in the house of another household temporarily, is also a reason to resettle on a more permanent basis. This happens as an individual's employment in the city becomes more secure over time. These spontaneous resettlement actions that gradually accumulate over time are not regulated by the local authority at all, neither registration

Table 6.5 'Push' factors for migrants in place of origin

	No. of households	%
Livelihood-related need	63	43.8
Immediate need for a new place to live*	24	16.7
Kin-related need	23	16.0
Eviction from private property	17	11.8
Increase in house rent or land price in original place	6	4.2
Eviction from government land for infrastructure development	5	3.5
Education	5	3.5
Others	1	0.7
Total	144	100

*Under this category are the following: sale of former shelter, destruction due to fire and a new couple's need for a separate living space.
Source: Authors' survey (September 2013)

Table 6.6 Mediating social factors in the decision to move into the floodplain

Influencing agent	No. of households	%
Kin	77	47.8
Workmate	9	5.6
Partner or spouse	51	31.7
Own decision	24	14.9
Total	161	100

Source: Authors' survey (September 2013)

nor prior notification to officials being required. Once a settler has de facto occupied a place in the area, they are welcome to register as voters of the city.

Government response to flooding in informal settlements

Government response to flooding risks in the waterways can be divided into local government–initiated and national government–initiated programs, with the latter purportedly offering a more long-term and comprehensive adaptation.

Immediate local government flood-related responses

Evidence from this study suggests that local government response to address flooding vulnerability and risks in Malabon City has been grossly lacking in coverage of all communities at risk and confined or limited only to short-term predisaster and postdisaster rescue and relief operations. From our survey, only 44 percent of households reported being covered by or encountering local government–initiated activities related to flood disaster. The majority have had to rely on their own autonomous actions and resources in coping with flooding episodes. Moreover, to date, local government–initiated activities related to flooding problems have been confined to two immediate foci: (1) flood disaster preparedness, and (2) rescue and relief operations during local flood disaster events. The first consisted of early warning measures and seminars conducted with selected community members for disaster preparedness. The second focus is on rescue operations, evacuation and distribution of relief goods during the flooding episodes. There is no local government–initiated program that provides medium-term or long-term solutions to the social vulnerability of households and communities in the floodplains. This aspect is touched upon explicitly only in recent policy rhetoric of the national government concerning informal settlements in the floodways and the urban poor.

National government–initiated programs regarding informal settlers and flooding

National government–initiated programs that directly affect informal settlers in flood contexts include the Informal Sector Relocation Program (ISRP). The Informal Sector Relocation Program is one of the five housing development programs under the National Housing Authority (NHA). It involves the acquisition and development of large tracts of raw land to generate service lots or housing units for families displaced from sites earmarked for government infrastructure projects and those occupying danger areas such as waterways, city water canals and railroad tracks.

In the last decade, the NHA has focused on the resettlement program in line with the relocation need of the North and South Rail Infrastructure Project, which required the relocation of close to 100,000 families (Ballesteros and Egana, 2012).

However, a series of intense typhoons that hit the country also during this period caused major disasters, especially in the Bicol region and Metro Manila. Hazard-affected families were among the first beneficiaries of NHA resettlement projects. Between 2001 and 2011, the resettlement program received the largest budget and accounted for about 75 percent of NHA production outputs for the period.

In December 2010, under the umbrella of this program, a presidential directive was issued for the Department of Interior and Local Government (DILG) to take the lead in a package to ensure immediate, safe and flood-resilient permanent housing solutions for informal settler families (ISFs) living in danger areas of the national capital region (NCR). This directive has a proviso that states that flood-resilient housing should be developed without sacrificing the basic human rights of the affected ISFs. Relocation of the affected families shall be on-site, near the city, and in the city, and in accordance with the 'People's Plan' in which the affected ISFs had been adequately and genuinely consulted.[2] Relocation outside the city shall only be resorted to in accordance with the People's Plan or when directly requested by the affected ISFs themselves, which must satisfy that they have been offered adequate and genuine consultation prior to relocation. An ISF fund amounting to 50 billion PHP has been allocated for the purpose. In the operation guidelines of DILG, 400,000 PHP is the ceiling amount to be allocated for the construction of one house per family (Interview with Office of Undersecretary of DILG, 3 July 2013). The current estimate of families living near canals and floodways in Metro Manila is around 104,000. The program target is for 20,000 families to be relocated in 2013, 40,000 in 2014 and 40,000 in 2015.

While the task of creating viable livelihood projects in relocation sites has been widely acknowledged as an important component agenda of the project, to date no operational planning at has been made on how this can be addressed. It is understood by the various participating agencies of the government that the office of the NHA will shoulder the task of packaging the resettlement project in a manner that includes developing livelihood activities for the resettled families. However, to date, there is no published report yet regarding the latest performance of the relocation project. Based on news articles quoting the NHA, around 19,000 families are identified by the Department of Public Works and Highways (DPWH) and the Metro Manila Development Authority (MMDA) for relocation to NHA housing sites in Bocaue, San Jose del Monte and Balagtas in Bulacan province; in Rodriguez and Baras in Rizal province; and in Trece Martires in Cavite province. Others are in-city housing and in partnership with Civil Society Organization (CSO) proposals.[3]

However, the agency maintains that its role is only in the building of physical small-market structures and basic infrastructures such as local roads and bus stops. Beyond this, no single agency or group of agencies has seriously problematized how to assist in developing sustainable livelihoods in the planned resettlement areas. Without government-initiated and funded measures to immediately kick-start livelihood opportunities in relocation sites, targeted or actual beneficiary families of these flood-safe sites have faced a dilemma that those being resettled describe as transferring from 'flood zone to dead zone'.[4] The latter refers to insufficient basic services like water supply, electricity and education facilities, as well as the lack of livelihood opportunities. This research has shown there is a lot of resistance therefore to the relocation program by local people because even though its flood-safe shelters are available, sites are located at far away from the municipalities that they presently work in. For example, the relocation sites identified by the government for the Malabon City relocatees are in Bulacan, Rizal and Cavite municipalities, which, say interview respondents, are 2–3 hours away from Metro Manila. Thus, the program provides disaster-proof housing to flood-vulnerable groups but exacerbates their vulnerability to livelihood stress and shocks and reduces their long-term general resilience in the new area because of the lack of employment opportunities. This illustrates a grossly incomplete and delinked package on disaster preparedness that neglects social vulnerability of the target relocatees living in the floodways.

While the earlier-cited national water code prohibiting permanent settlements in floodways has been in place since 1976, today's unprecedented aggressiveness and haste by the national government to clear the floodways of informal settlements has been spurred by the Philippine government's official commitment to international agreements on the Climate Change Adaptation Agenda. It also reflects national response to several extreme precipitation episodes that buffeted the country in recent years (e.g. Typhoon Ketsana). In the face of a strong-arm and no-compromise stance of the national government as it implements a Metro-Manila-wide clearing of informal settlements in waterways, communities and households find it difficult to bargain for better deals in resettlement locations that balance safety with sustainable livelihood goals. In the face of powerful, national-level climate-change adaptation policy discourses and programs, informal settlement communities have lost any leverage they may once have had to stay put and bargain with local officials.

When the ISRP was initially planned for the informal settlements in the waterways of Malabon City, the residents strongly opposed the plan. In the authors' survey in September 2013, a total 69 percent of current residents have registered their categorical opposition to the program, citing the reason that it is easier to find work in Malabon. Only 25 percent of settlers in the floodplains are in favor of the program. Of the respondents who were in favor, reasons cited included safety from disasters and floods (20 percent), as well as tenurial and housing security (72 percent), and livelihood improvements (8 percent). A major proportion of those opposing the program cited a lack of livelihood resources and opportunities in the relocation sites under the program (43.2 percent), a lack of basic services in the relocation sites (29.7 percent), a disconnect of relocation sites with local municipality and indigenous communities (5.4 percent), the physical remoteness of relocation sites relative to Metro Manila cities (8.1 percent) and the target relocatees' lack of reliable information and knowledge of the conditions in the relocation sites (13.5 percent).

Legitimate and urgent livelihood needs of the relocatees could have been addressed by existing national poverty alleviation programs, if only they could be specifically focused and flexibly adjusted to directly serve the ISRP in localities. However, these programs, which come under the remit of another national government department, the DSWD (Department of Social Welfare Development), continue to be implemented and designed separately with no integration or adjustment to serve the target beneficiaries of ISRP. These two programs predate the former and could have been deliberately harnessed to address the lack of a concrete employment and livelihood component of the ISRP, an element absent that has been the main source of opposition of the target relocatees to the ISRP.

Conditional cash transfer (CCT)

CCT is a program directly implemented by the Department of Social Welfare and Development (DSWD). Under this program, poor households are identified by DSWD, primarily based on indicators such as income, employment status and number of children. Those qualifying receive monthly cash subsidies for 5 years in exchange for their commitment and monitored compliance to send their children to public schools and to have mothers and children regularly undergo checkups in the local or municipal health centers. The maximum monthly subsidy per family is 1,200 PHP (i.e. 300 PHP per child, for up to three children, and 300 PHP for the mother). An immediate objective of the program is to increase the school participation rate among children of poor households. The long-term objective is to increase employment opportunities for children in households taking part in the program, with the view that they in turn can eventually lift their families out of poverty.

In its Program Implementation Status Report of 1st Quarter of 2013, DSWD reported that CCT is being implemented in 143 cities and 1,484 municipalities in 79 provinces. A total of 3.9 million households have been enrolled, exceeding the target for 2013. The Philippine government plans to continue increasing the budget for the program until 2015 until 4.6 million families have become beneficiaries. However, particularly in the case of the poor migrants occupying the floodways of Malabon City, these people have not been beneficiaries of this program at all.[5]

Sustainable livelihood program (SLP)

The SLP is the current repackaging of an earlier Self-Assistance Program for Progress in the 1980s undertaken by the DSWD. The SLP is a poverty-alleviation project of the department that has targeted the poor in general. The program has two components: (1) community-driven enterprise development (CDEV) and (2) employment facilitation. Both components have a public-private partnership dimension. CDEV requires organizing poor communities to collectively identify appropriate livelihood and employment opportunities for local households under a community enterprise scheme, managed by representatives of the community.

Of late, the program has evolved into a public-private partnership, with a private bank providing 1 million PHP as capital seed funds for 1,000 beneficiaries. These beneficiaries undergo training on financial literacy, microenterprise development, basic business management and bookkeeping, before they are given a maximum of 10,000 PHP each. The amount is not a grant but should be repaid after 2 years. The priority beneficiaries under this program are walk-in poor persons requesting assistance from DSWD offices, or referrals from local government officials.

As mentioned earlier, this particular program has not been encountered at all by the residents of the floodplains being targeted for relocation under the ISRP. A big factor that accounts for lack of uptake among survey respondents is that this is a walk-in program, often availed by those individuals who have the appropriate information and bureaucratic connection to the main office of the DSWD in Quezon City, a place quite distant from Malabon. Also, the program's funding is limited and prioritizes the critically poor or very poor (e.g. street vagrants).

The employment facilitation component of the SLP is also a public-private partnership endeavor. DSWD keeps a record of potential poor beneficiaries – or employable people who have contacted the office and are looking for work. The record includes educational background and current occupation. DSWD then coordinates with participating small and medium business enterprises (SMEs) to understand their workforce needs. It also conducts a focused job-skills training program, for which employable people are selected to participate from its list. Afterward it endorses and sends people to the relevant SMEs to apply for the vacancies. In this component, DSWD also utilizes the database of the CCT program, which is also under its wing.

However, like the previously discussed program of CCT, the SLP program is not being effectively linked and deliberately harnessed to address the poverty and livelihood situation of urban-poor migrants in the floodways. Limited funding of these national programs and the selectivity of scoping has prevented these being transformed by design to provide specific livelihood safety nets for the relocatees in Malabon's floodways.

Conclusions

Studying the migration histories of poor urban migrants and their reasons for settling in risky city floodways highlights the need to go beyond assessing their vulnerability to the physical dynamics of floodwater and potential disaster impacts in their current location. As the case of poor migrants' settlements in the floodplains of Malabon City demonstrates, their current vulnerability to flooding has been generated and is continuously being shaped by wider economic, social and political processes. These processes have determined their marginality in access to urban employment and livelihood and to affordable and secure urban housing and land tenure both in their places of origin and the places in which they have settled. Certain factors causing marginality underpin these urban migrants' experiences of vulnerability, manifested during their urban-to-urban or rural-to-urban migration.

The characteristics of urban migrants' mobility thus underscore a need to view their vulnerability to flooding and limited adaptive capacity both as an existing state during their exposure to flood hazards and as outcome of processes occurring prior to their settling in these flood-prone areas. These causal processes are translocal and include vulnerabilities in other spaces, outside of the flood-prone places that they currently occupy. The mobility of urban migrants from place to place provides us with an understanding of the circumstances and conditions shaping their decision to move to flood-prone areas, despite a clear prior knowledge of these places' danger of disasters. Further, a focus on mobility and migration provides an open window to peer into wider processes and structures at work in the urban development of the city region and in rural places that generate the vulnerability and limited adaptive capacity to flooding of the urban poor.

In the case of Malabon City, needs and aspirations for livelihood security and urban employment and for accessible, cheap housing are the strongest drivers in migrants' decisions to settle in flood-prone areas, even though these insecurities remain in the floodways. The floodways, albeit also insecure, are perceived to be considerably better than what these migrants had access to in their places of origin.

Thus, current causes of vulnerability of urban migrants in the floodways of Malabon must be examined not only *in situ*, but equally – and perhaps more importantly – in the context of the urban region and rural provinces from where migrants originate. Thus, a wider and broader spatial analysis is needed to complement a better understanding of *in situ* vulnerability of migrants. Moreover, implicated in the case study are issue fields of poverty and urban employment and inequity in land development and housing for the poor that are determined by distinct economic development logics and priority goal setting, and problematized in different (and often separate) policy arenas. Thus, vulnerability and limitations of adaptive capacity of migrants to flooding not only are multilocal and multilevel but also emerge from actions and influences of government in other sectoral policy domains. Effective actions for adaptation that address migrants' vulnerability to flooding risks therefore require linkages and integration with these policy domains that lie beyond disaster management and climate change concerns. These involve government agencies, public actors and strategies addressing (or ignoring) poverty alleviation and creation (or failure to create) adequate urban employment, and housing and urban land development concerns and programs that are redistributive and equitable (or not).

In the Metro Manila urban regional context and in the Malabon case, government actions, such as the ISRP, which is designed as a major adaptation and grand risk-reduction scheme for protecting lives and properties of settlements against disasters in the flood-prone areas, do not touch upon nor harmonize or integrate at all with the aforementioned policy domains and their respective goals. This program has been focused only on immediate and direct measures related to flooding risks, such as disaster preparedness and relocation of these settlements to flood-safe areas. However, the relocation sites are considered by those to be relocated as 'dead zones' due to a lack of livelihood opportunities, themselves a source of vulnerability for migrants in the first place.

Since fundamental processes generating vulnerability have not been addressed by government, poor urban migrants in turn respond negatively and oppose current resettlement programs. They would rather risk experiencing flooding in the floodways than be deprived of more fundamental needs related to livelihood and housing security. Further, goals and priorities set in another policy domain (i.e. the development of the real estate sector and land market management) undermine the goal of decongesting the floodplains of informal settlers. The current government promotion of high-end private commercial and residential real estate development in Metro Manila commonly entails forced eviction of informal settlements from private lands to make way for this type of development. An associated rise in urban land values has further priced out the urban poor and low income from tenure security. In the absence of any special redistributive measures coming from government for land and housing allocation, the urban poor are forced to move into and densify population in the floodways. Further, priorities in certain poverty alleviation programs may have marginalized or totally ignored targeting urgent livelihood needs of migrants in the floodplains because of the illegal nature of these settlements, thus further contributing to social vulnerability to flooding risks.

Conventional adaptive actions of governments that are directed toward people living in 'risky spaces' are often confined to a single recipe – a relocation program to physically safer places – and this is the case in Malabon city. Our analysis highlights the limitations of such an approach, and instead points to the need for a multiple-level, multiscalar analytical framework that identifies interacting policy domains concerned with climatic and nonclimatic vulnerability stressors. This can facilitate the apportioning of accountability and the locus of effective adaptation actions.

This case study advances the need for a two-pronged change in emphasis to disaster adaptation response by government: (1) a set of immediate measures in the locality for disaster preparedness and risk reduction vis-à-vis flood disasters to ensure immediate minimization of potential losses of lives and properties and (2) a set of transformative policies and measures addressing certain fundamental changes in the wider political economy of the urban region and rural provinces where urban poor migrants come from, particularly around issues of poverty, housing and urban land inequity. This requires a change in the structures of power and current allocative mechanisms that reproduce poor urban migrants' marginality and vulnerability. This approach certainly needs integration and harmonization of goals between and among conventionally separate sectoral policy domains and their respective concerned state agencies, a challenge in the more complex and larger scale agenda of 'transformative adaptation' (Moser and Boycoff, 2013). As Pelling (2011) notes, where vulnerability is an outcome of wider social causes and processes, then responsibility for change becomes broader, more diffuse and oriented toward addressing questions of power and authority. Examining the experiences of the urban poor in Malabon City through a migration lens indicates the urgency of addressing these concerns in Metro Manila.

Notes

1 Data are from the 2012 Philippine Statistics Authority poverty classifications: least poor (i.e. 20 percent poverty rate or less), mildly poor (i.e., 21–40 percent poverty rate) and highly poor (i.e. 61–80 percent). The worst poverty incidence rate in Metro Manila is in the Port Area of Manila, with 10 percent poverty rate recorded (Business Mirror, 11 April 2015).
2 'People's Plans' are formed by people's organizations, with or without the support of NGOs or NGAs and refers to a community development plan that has undergone a process of consultation with and endorsement by the beneficiaries, which contains a site development plan and may include nonphysical development such as livelihood, self-help development and capability building trainings, among others.
3 Interview with the Office of Undersecretary of the Department of the Interior and Local Government, 3 July 2013.
4 Interview with the Office of the Undersecretary of the Department of the Interior and Local Government, 3 July 2013.
5 The CCT is a nationally funded poverty alleviation program that is not universal in mandatory coverage (i.e. all households in the country considered poor become effectively covered), but selective and limited, based on the given budget allocation at a given time. Thus, the program prioritizes the poorest of the poor based on income and employment indicators and ensures the spread of the program to cover more of these core poor who are in the poorest regions and provinces in the Philippines. Thus, the poor in the floodways of Malabon City are not an urgent priority by these standards and practice.

References

Ballesteros, M.M., and Egana, J.V. (2012). *Efficiency and effectiveness review of the National Housing Authority (NHA) resettlement program*. Manila: Philippine Institute of Development Studies and Department of Budget and Management.
Bankoff, G., Frerks, G., and Hilhorst, D. (2004). *Mapping vulnerability: Disasters, development, and people*. London and New York: Routledge.
Business Mirror. (2015). "Rich-poor gap widened in 2012-PSA." 11 April.
Colliers International. (2012). *Research and forecast report: Philippine real estate market*. www.colliers.com.
FDA. (2012). *Enumeration of urban poor households along riverways*. Unpublished Data Report. Foundation for Development Alternatives, Manila.
Goldblum, C., and Wong, T.C. (2000). "Growth, crisis and spatial change: A study of haphazard urbanization in Jakarta, Indonesia." *Land Use Policy* 17: 29–37.
Hardoy, J.E., Mitlin, D., and Satterthwaite, D. (2013). *Environmental problems in an urbanizing world: finding solutions in cities in Africa, Asia and Latin America*. London and New York: Routledge.
Huq, S., Kovats, S., Reid, H., and Satterthwaite, D. (2007). "Reducing risks to cities from disasters and climate change." *Environment and Urbanization* 1(1): 3–15.
Jha, A., Boch, R., and Lamond, J. (2011). *Cities and flooding: A guide to integrated urban flood risk management*. Washington, DC: World Bank and GFDRR.
Jha, A., Mner, T., and Stanton-Geddes, Z. (2013). *Building urban resilience: Principles, tools and practice*. Washington, DC: World Bank.
Kelly, P.F., and McGee, T.G. (2003). "Changing spaces: Southeast Asian urbanization in an era of volatile globalization." (pp. 257–286) in Sien, C.L. (ed.) *Southeast Asia transformed: A geography of change*. Singapore: ISEAS.

Lagmay, A.M.F. (2013) Disseminating near real-time hazards information and flood maps in the Philippines through Web-GIS. *DOST-Project NOAH Open-File Reports* 1. http://center.noah.up.edu.ph/disseminating-near-real-time-hazards-information-and-flood-maps-in-the-philippines-through-web-gis/ [Last accessed 01/09/17]

Leichenko, R., and O'Brien, K. (2006). "Is it appropriate to identify winners and losers?" (pp. 97–114) in Adger, W.N., Paavola, J., Huq, S., and Mace, M.J. (eds.) *Fairness in adaptation to climate change*. Cambridge, MA: MIT Press.

Magno-Ballesteros, M. (2000). *The urban land and real estate market I metro Manila: A socio-economic analysis*. PhD Dissertation: Faculty of Social Sciences, Catholic University of Nijmegen.

Metro Manila Development Authority. (2010). *Unpublished data of the community and urban poor affairs office*. Philippines: Malabon City.

Moser, S., and Boycoff, M. (2013). "Climate change and adaptation success: The scope of the challenge." (pp. 1–34) in Moser, S. and M. Boycoff (eds.) *Successful adaptation to climate change*. London and New York: Routledge.

NSCB. (2009). *Population data*. Unpublished data of the National Statistics Coordination Board, Philippines.

NSCB. (2012). *Population data*. Unpublished data of the National Statistics Coordination Board, Philippines.

NSO. (2000). *2000 census of population and housing*. Philippines: GRP. National Statistics Office.

NSO. (2010). *2010 census of population and housing*. Philippines: GRP. National Statistics Office.

Pelling, M. (2011). *Adaptation to climate change: From resilience to transformation*. London and New York: Routledge.

Sajor, E. (2003). "Globalization and the urban property boom in metropolitan Cebu, Philippines." *Development and Change* 34(4): 713–741.

Satterthwaite, D., Huq, S., Pelling, M., Reid, H., and Romero Lankao, P. (2007). *Adapting to climate change in urban areas: The possibilities and constraints in low-and middle-income nations* (Human Settlements Working Paper Series Climate Change and Cities No. 1. London: IIED.

UN HABITAT. (2010). *The state of Asian cities 2010/11*. Nairobi: UN-HABITAT.

UN-HABITAT. (2012). *Innovative urban tenure in the Philippines*. Nairobi: UN-HABITAT.

Yap, K.S. (2012). "Challenges of promoting productive, inclusive and sustainable urbanization." (pp. 10–80) in Yap, K.S. and Thuzar, M. (eds.) *Urbanization in Southeast Asia: Issues and impacts*. Singapore: ISEAS.

7 Responses to flooding

Migrants' perspectives in Hanoi, Vietnam

Nguyen Tuan Anh and Pham Quang Minh

Introduction

Urbanization, migration and flooding are intimately connected in Hanoi. The city has grown rapidly since the introduction of economic reforms in the 1980s. In recent years, the development of export-oriented labor-intensive industries has encouraged further migration, and this has been enabled by the relaxation of the household registration system (*hộ khẩu*), which was intended to control spontaneous rural-urban migration (Dang, 2003: 31–33).[1] By 2013, the city had a population of 6.9 million (General Statistics Office of Vietnam, 2014), of whom 6.6 percent were migrants (General Statistics Office of Vietnam, 2011: 41). Along with migration, there has been an urbanization boom, creating many new urban spaces across a large land area (Labbé, 2010).

Amid this rapid change, flooding has become a significant phenomenon in the city. From 30 October to 4 November 2008, the city was subject to the most intense and heavy rainfall in 100 years. Over a 10-day period, many sites were covered by up to 2.5 meters of water, resulting in loss of life (Trinh, 2010). Flood events have become an annual occurrence, bringing hardship through disruption to livelihoods, damage to property and infrastructure and impacts on human health (Trinh, 2010; Tuyết Mai, 2011; BáoMới, 2012; Tran et al., 2011). Impacts have been particularly felt by communities in Hanoi's riverside urban areas (Hoang et al., 2007), low-cost but risky spaces that are often settled by migrants from Hanoi's rural hinterland.

Residents, government officials and researchers have paid attention to many dimensions of flooding in Hanoi, which is seen as one of the most serious and frequent disaster events affecting the city (Oanh et al., 2011). Factors relating to urbanization such as old and poor underground sewage irrigation, the replacement of lakes and land areas by buildings and inefficient solid-waste disposal are identified as contributory factors to inundation of the city (Global Facility for Disaster Reduction and Recovery, 2009). Government effort has thus focused on tackling infrastructure failures, principally by redesigning the city's drainage system, for example through 'Hanoi's Master Plan/Project for Drainage System (*Dự án thoát nước Hà Nội*)', which has involved relocating and compensating residents in 60 communes of the city where land was needed for the project (TTXVN, 2008; Huy Nam – VOV, 2014).

This chapter examines the linkages between migration, rapid urbanization and floods in Hanoi in a context where government interventions have sought to 'manage migration' through policies designed to restrict entry to the city, and 'manage floods' by reengineering the city's infrastructure. The chapter argues that flooding is an integral part of Hanoi's migration dynamic in that it creates the conditions that have made certain areas of the city affordable, thus enabling settlement by low-income people. At the same time, experiences of flooding in such risky spaces means that people who have secured a better livelihood move on to more expensive but less environmentally challenging parts of the city. Amid this dynamic, those most vulnerable to flood disasters include migrants who have settled without registering in the city, and in so doing, place themselves outside circuits of government support when floods arrive. It is unclear how engineering infrastructure and population mobility will be able to address the specific vulnerabilities of this group.

The chapter is organized as follows. The next section introduces the study sites and presents the methodology used in the study. This section includes a brief discussion of the factors causing floods in Hanoi. The chapter then explores migrants' livelihoods and reasons for living in flood-stricken areas of Hanoi before outlining specific vulnerabilities in flood-affected communities. The main part of the chapter considers peoples' responses to flooding and how these are augmented (or otherwise) by interventions by local and higher-ranking leaders. The chapter concludes with a discussion of ways migrants' vulnerability to flooding is being addressed, and what a better understanding of the flood-migration dynamic could contribute to better policies and planning in this area.

Research methods and study sites: socially produced floods

Research was undertaken in two areas of Hanoi that experience heavy floods, and where migrants make up a large proportion of the population (see Figure 7.1). Tan Trieu is a representative commune located on the outskirts (peri-urban area) of Hanoi, and Tan Mai is a representative ward of inner urban Hanoi. Populations in each comprise local residents (who were born and lived in each site) and migrants, defined as those who have moved to live in the area. Migrants also comprise those who have arrived with the past 5 years (new migrants) and those who have lived in the areas for more than 5 years.

Tan Trieu has an area of around 297 hectares including agricultural land, residential land and other kinds of land. In December 2013, this commune had 26,475 people living in 6,339 households. The commune has 14 clusters of households living in two villages (*thôn*), namely Trieu Khuc and Yen Xa. The residents in Tan Trieu follow several occupations such as small industries and handicrafts, small trading and services and agricultural production (Ban chỉ đạo xây dựng nông thôn mới xã Tân Triều, 2014: 1–2). During fieldwork it emerged that few local residents cultivated their fields; rather, fields were left fallow or leased to migrants who grew vegetables.

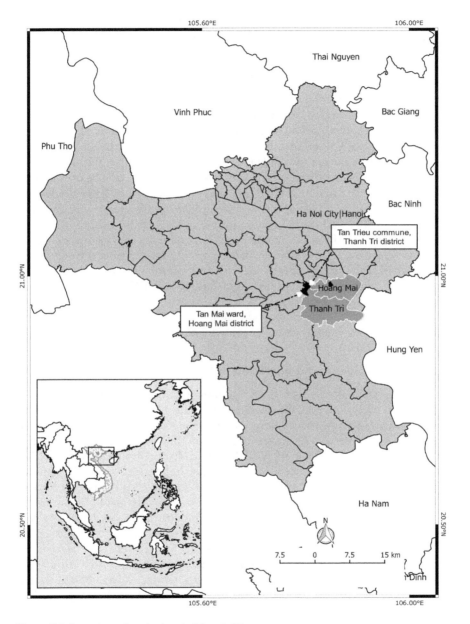

Figure 7.1 Location of study sites in Hanoi, Vietnam

Tan Mai has an area of 0.53 square kilometers. In 2012 this ward had 23,658 residents.[2] Tan Mai has 11 groups of residential households (*cụm dân cư*) that are divided into 53 clusters of households. Doing fieldwork in Tan Mai, we learned that this is an area of many low-income laborers. Occupations included work in government departments, work for companies, petty trade and services at markets and on streets and renting out their houses.

Both qualitative and quantitative methods were used to collect data in Tan Trieu and Tan Mai. Secondary data included written materials and reports relating to the commune and ward.[3] Besides collecting written materials, we also conducted in-depth interviews, focus group discussions and a structured household survey in July 2013. In each site, interviews were conducted with four informants (two men and two women, two migrants and two nonmigrants). We also carried out in-depth interviews with one male migrant in Tan Trieu, one head of household renting out apartments in Tan Trieu and one head of a group of residential households in Tan Mai. Along with these in-depth interviews, the researchers also had many long and short conversations with local leaders such as the vice-president of the Tan Trieu Commune People's Committee, the vice-president of Tan Mai Ward People's Committee and some staff and cadres of the commune and the ward. Focus group discussions with five informants were carried out in each site. A survey questionnaire was undertaken with 100 households in each site. The sample was stratified to include 23 percent of households that are new migrants' households; 47 percent of households that are old migrants' households; and 30 that of households that are local households.

Floods, urban change and migration in Hanoi

According to natural scientists, flood and inundation in Hanoi are caused by a combination of intense rainfall, elevation and slope of terrain. Hanoi has a low terrain with an above-sea-level elevation of 3–5 meters. Most flooding is caused by heavy rainfall inland, with high surface runoff that is in excess of local drainage capacity (Nguyễn Hiệu et al., 2013). Thus, risky environments in both Tan Mai and Tan Trieu are produced by both natural and human factors. Blame was placed by study participants on the infilling of the lakes and ponds in Hanoi, which in the past had helped mitigate the risks of floods. Rapid urbanization and population growth in Hanoi, coupled with industrialization, has led to the infilling of lakes and ponds to create residential zones and other buildings. From 1997 to February 2013, Hanoi had 152 projects to construct new residential zones, totaling an area of around 44,406 hectares (Thông tin KHCN, 2014). Ten years ago Hanoi had more than 40 lakes with a surface area of 850 hectares; this number was reduced to 19 lakes with a surface area of 600 hectares in 2013 (Nữ Quỳnh, 2013). In Tan Trieu, there were 14 projects that requested giving compensation to remove residents in order to construct housing and commercial projects, converting agricultural land to urban uses.[4]

Respondents also suggested that flooding could be caused by the upgrading or repairing of the drainage system. Quantitative data showed 49 percent of the respondents thought that poorly planned construction of the drainage system was among the major causes of flooding. For instance, Tan Mai had a project on transforming open-air channels into drains. However, the implementation of this project brought about heavy floods due to slow progress in building work, which affected drainage, and the new design was inadequate for the volume of water.[5] Floods were also attributed to waste treatment, including throwing household waste and building materials from house repairs into channels. Some links between migration, land-use change and flooding were made by respondents from the communities. A resident in Tan Mai said that 10 years ago, when she moved here, there were a few households and the ward was thinly populated. Since then there had been a big increase in the number of nonnative residents, students, independent workers and state officials.[6]

The link between rapid urbanization, migration and flooding is one that is made by lawmakers. High levels of recent migrations are apparent in both the study sites, as well as the city more generally. In response to increased numbers of migrants into inner Hanoi, in 2012 the Vietnam National Assembly issued the Law on the Capital City (effective from July 2013) in order to stem immigration flow into Hanoi. Article 19 of this law stipulates that in order to register as permanent residents in Hanoi, people have to meet two criteria: living continuously in Hanoi for at least 3 years and owning house or renting a house, provided that the location of the house meets the regulation of Hanoi City People's Council (Quốc Hội, 2012).[7]

This law effectively reversed the earlier law on residence, issued in 2007, which was blamed by the minister of justice for increased population and pressure on infrastructure and public services. With the 2013 Law on the Capital City, the Ministry of Justice calculated that there had been a reduction of 14,000 people registering as permanent residents in the inner city (Thảo, 2012). While migration to Hanoi has continued, migrants do not apply for residential registration with the local authority when they move. The significance of this point is explored in a later section. In summary, however, the social production of floods and inundation arises from poor drainage, urbanization and poor waste treatment, associated with the mass construction of housing. As a factor contributing to urbanization, extensive rural-urban migration forms part of the suite of causes of flooding in Hanoi.

Migrant livelihoods, residency and risk in flood-stricken areas

Migration to the city of Hanoi is a strategy of many people living in rural areas of other provinces. When living and working in Hanoi, migrants have many ways to develop their livelihoods in order to increase their income, and for many, this is life changing (Rigg et al., 2014; Nguyen et al., 2012). The case of one young migrant couple illustrates the ways in which livelihood risks and opportunities are negotiated in making the move from rural areas to Hanoi. Duc (not his real name) was born in 1989, and originates from a rural area of Nong Cong district, Thanh Hoa province. He and his other two siblings migrated to find jobs in cities as the wet rice land allocated to his parents was insufficient to meet the needs of the household. Duc's livelihood history reveals a number of moves, initially to Hanoi, then to Binh Duong to work in a rubber plantation, then back to Hanoi, where he now works as a laborer transporting construction materials. Duc's work every day is to drive a small tractor trailer to transport construction materials to construction sites – usually the places in Tan Trieu and surrounding Tran Trieu areas where private houses are being built. His wife Sam (not her real name) is also a migrant: she arrived in Tan Trieu in 2008, where she works as a scrap iron and waste material collector. The couple returned to their homeland to marry in 2010, and afterward came back to work in Tan Trieu. They have a child who stays with Sam's parents. Every month, Duc and Sam send home 1,000,000 VND (around US$50) along with canned milk, baby clothes and candy to support their child. Duc and Sam have lived in Tan Trieu for many years. However, up to now they have not registered with the Tan Trieu local authority. They also do not participate in collective activities at the commune. At the present time, through a verbal agreement or contract, Duc and Sam rent a small, low-quality apartment belonging to a local Tan Trieu resident. The apartment costs 600,000 VND (around US$30) per month. After deducting all their living expenses, Duc and Sam save around 2,000,000 VND (US$100) per month.

The apartment where Duc and Sam live is affected by flooding every year, usually in July and August, when the floor is inundated with floodwater and floating garbage to a depth of about 0.5 meters. During these days, Duc and Sam cannot work and therefore have no income. They stay at the apartment and put all baggage and furniture on their bed to avoid getting it wet. They also have to buy bottles of pure water at a nearby grocery to use because the tap water and faucet are unusable. After inundation, they have to clean the apartment and rearrange their belongings. Duc and Sam could rent a better apartment in Tan Trieu with the price of around 1,500,000 VND (around US$75) per month. The floors of those apartments are raised and are not often flooded. However, they choose to live in the current apartment in order to save their money. About the plan for their future, Duc and Sam said that they continue to live and work in Tan Trieu and do not have other plans at the present time.

The experience of Duc and Sam is echoed in the quantitative data. Among the 100 households surveyed, 23 percent arrived within the past 5 years, 47 percent are migrant households who have been in Hanoi for more than 5 years and 30 percent of households are local households. Migration histories reveal that although most have only migrated once (46 percent), 24 percent have moved more than twice. The survey explored reasons for living in such flood-prone locations as Tan Trieu and Tan Mai, as shown in Table 7.1.

Despite having to face floods each year, the reasons given by many migrants for settling in Tan Mai and Tan Trieu included following or joining other family members, the availability of work opportunities and opportunities to buy or rent houses. The kinds of work undertaken by migrants and local people in the two study sites (Table 7.2) showed that most had only one occupation, and this varied depending on whether people were more established migrants, recent migrants or local people.

Responses to flooding in Vietnam 133

Table 7.1 Reasons for moving to live in Tan Mai and Tan Trieu

Reason		First reason	Second reason	Third reason
Follow or join	Percent	33%	5%	0
family	Count	27	2	0
Work related	Percent	19%	24%	3%
	Count	16	9	1
Bought land or	Percent	27%	57%	69%
house here	Count	22	21	20
House allocated	Percent	16%	5%	21%
here	Count	13	2	6
Others	Percent	6%	8%	7%
	Count	5	3	2
Total	Percent	100%	100%	100%
	Count	83	37	29

Source: Authors' survey (July 2013)

Table 7.2 Main occupation of heads of households

Residence		Occupation					
		Retiree	Professionals in all fields	Skilled manual worker	Unskilled or low-skilled laborer	Other occupations	Total
New	Count	7	8	1	7	0	23
migrants	Percent	30%	35%	4%	30%	0	100.0%
Established	Count	24	14	5	4	0	47
migrants	Percent	51%	30%	11%	9%	0	100.0%
Local people	Count	7	3	2	13	5	30
	Percent	23%	10%	7%	43%	17%	100.0%
Total	Count	38	25	8	24	5	100
	Percent	38%	25%	8%	24%	5%	100.0%

Source: Authors' survey (July 2013)

Survey findings shows that unskilled and low-skilled laborers make up a third of new migrants and about half of those described as local people. Those in the professional category include a large proportion of both new and established migrants. Retirees account for significant numbers, especially among the group of old migrant household heads, which relates in part to how 'household head' is defined locally.[8] To a certain extent, this occupation classification provides a foundation to examine the types of vulnerability and responses to flooding among new migrants, established migrants and local people.

Survey data revealed that all households are affected by flooding, usually in July and August. Small differences in the extent of flooding relate to differences in the conditions of houses, roads and drainage systems within areas of the commune or ward. So, while a household may face flooding in one rainy reason, small improvements in these can mean the household is not flooded next time. Both qualitative and quantitative research in Tan Mai and Tan Trieu reveal two main types of vulnerability caused by the impact of floods on households. *First*, floods badly affected the household property, especially vehicles, with motorbikes the most likely to be damaged. This is a significant contribution to economic and social vulnerability of households, as motorbikes are of critical importance as a relatively affordable form of transport for maintaining everyday mobility and commuting in Hanoi and the surrounding area. On average, each adult has one motorbike as their major means of transportation. Of the respondents, 58 percent said that floods had adverse impacts on their vehicles, particularly motorbikes. Experiences were similar across all three groups. Their traveling from work to home by motorbike was also hampered by flooding. They were forced to keep their motorbikes in a dry place and go home on foot, which was not only inconvenient but also wasteful in terms of time that could be spent earning a living. According to a resident in Tan Mai, it cost him 60,000 VND (around US$3) per day for three motorbikes to be kept.[9] Besides motorbikes, other household items were also affected. A respondent in Tan Mai said that if floods occurred when there was no one home, electrical items such as fans and refrigerators and furniture such as tables and chairs were all damaged. Household plumbing was also severely affected. In the wake of a flood, it could take them a whole day to tidy up their house after flooding, and again, this represents a significant loss of livelihood or time spent earning for those affected in this way.[10]

Second, floods reduced the income of many households surveyed. Of the respondents, 54 percent said that floods made their income decrease in different ways.[11] Those with small, informal-sector businesses said that floods reduced the number of their clients, or that their business was interrupted. In Tan Trieu commune, many households are involved in recycling plastic, or work as small traders in two commune markets.[12] In Tan Mai, many households work as small traders along streets or in small restaurants.[13] These kinds of businesses are often affected by flooding. In-depth interviews in Tan Trieu showed that small-sized traders were forced to cease trading temporally during the floods.[14] Some businesses involved in recycling plastic also closed when heavy rains fell. A respondent in Tan Trieu running a recycled-plastic business described how severe floods meant that trucks carrying plastic goods could not park near his house so he had to hire pulled rickshaws to carry goods to his house. Overall, floods proved costly for this respondent. Moreover, the daily classification of plastic garbage had to be stopped as the open-air nature of this activity meant it could not take place during heavy rain. Similar impacts were felt by a resident in Tan Mai who described how her catering business was affected by floods, which hampered access to the market and delivery of food to customers, meaning hiring taxis at great expense.[15] Thus it can be seen that a variety of factors led to a decrease in income during and just after flood events.[16] At the same time, flooding provided small opportunities for many people, especially new migrants, to have temporary jobs as rickshaw drivers.

Despite the flood risks, the decision to live in the two study areas is because the price of housing is low. Many people considered these areas as temporary living places, as suggested in this extract from a focus group discussion in Tan Mai:

MR. DANG QUANG VIỆT: This area is inundated and polluted. Thus, the level of population mobility is high. Many people moved to live in this area and many people moved out. Many migrants lived here some years and then they moved out. Many houses had 3 or 4 owners in sequence over a short period.
INTERVIEWER: This area is inundated. Why do people continue to move to this area?
MR. DANG QUANG VIỆT: Because housing prices [buying and renting] in this area are cheap. This area looks like a place where many people like to live for a short period and then they move to other places.
MS. NGUYEN THI THUONG HANG: I intended to sell my house because of inundation. However, so far I have not sold yet because the buyers have been afraid of inundation. Many people bought houses here and then they sold after a period because of inundation. Many households could not sell their houses but they did not want to live here; they moved to live in other areas and rented out their houses to migrants. Many migrants lived here and then left after some heavy rainy seasons.
(Focus Group Discussion, Tan Mai, July 2013)

Many households in the flood-stricken areas of Tan Mai ward and Tan Trieu commune have moved sequentially through 'risky' spaces over several years. Most households had moved from other provinces, especially in poor rural areas where their livelihoods were not good. The city presented better income opportunities, but in order to be able to access low-cost housing, migrants had to contend with flood and inundation every year. Thus, it can be said that vulnerabilities related to flood and inundation were produced through mobility.

Responses to flooding

The way in which people respond to flooding depends on their capital, including human capital, financial capital, social capital and political capital, and these provide foundations for local people and migrants to respond to flooding. Our data show that there is a link between migration and both social and financial capital in the context of flood responses. According to survey, interview and focus group data and qualitative and quantitative data, several common ways to cope with floods were evident in both study sites. The first is to do house cleanup after floods (79 percent of survey respondents).[17] In-depth interviews showed that whenever floods occur, garbage also enters peoples' homes, and even sewage wells up. Therefore, the cleanup is time-consuming, impacting time that might otherwise be spent earning an income.[18]

The second is to raise the level of the ground floor. Of survey respondents, 26 percent chose this way to respond to floods. There was no variation between established migrants, new migrants and local people. Some families raised their floor by 55 centimeters.[19] In many cases, householders had to repeat these repairs several times in response to heavier floods. The third is to build small floodwalls to prevent water flowing through doorways, a strategy used by 17 percent of survey households in each of the three categories. Some had built cement walls right in front of their house. However, this would cause inconvenience in their daily activities so many of them built temporary walls to stop water flow. When rainfalls receded, they broke the walls to enable normal activities to resume.[20] The fourth is to locate household items in high places out of the way of floodwaters. Residents in both Tan Mai and Tan Trieu came up with this solution. They used available furniture such as tables and chairs as the base to place other items. Direct observation of the households that participated in in-depth interviews showed that households in Tan Mai prepared high shelves in their house. When it rained, they put smaller items on those shelves. With some household items, they added a base to elevate them away from the water. Other responses included preparing medicines, rebuying damaged personal items or using protective items.

Many of these measures to lessen the impacts of floods are relatively low cost, requiring limited material resources. However, such methods depended on knowledge and experiences they accumulated during the time living with flooding. Other solutions, such as raising the ground floor to avoid flooding, were costly, with some people spending up to 100,000,000 VND (around US$5,000) to raise the floors of their house.[21] Another established migrant said that for low-income households such as his, the cost of raising the floor level far exceeded his household's income of 4,000,000 VND per month (around US$200).[22] This means that low financial capital is an obstacle for people in coping with flooding and inundation.

Another solution is to relocate to another part of the city. Although only a small number of households mentioned this (6 percent), in-depth interview data reported that some families that had lived in Hanoi for 30 years had been pushed to move by recent serious floods, particularly those in very low-lying areas where inundation of rainwater and solid waste happens after just 15 minutes of rain. Selling affected houses was difficult, so these properties were either abandoned or rented out to new migrants. Families who could not sell their house or who were beset with financial troubles had to live with floods.[23] What has emerged, however, is a market for low-cost properties in flood-affected areas that new migrants use as a stepping stone to come to live in the city. When their families became better-off, they would move away. In this way, many houses in Tan Mai had changed their owners many times within several years.[24]

In Tan Mai ward and Tan Trieu commune, most of the population was born outside the area (78 percent in Tan Mai, 62 percent in Tan Trieu), and in both areas, people buy or rent apartments on a temporary basis, moving on to areas that are not affected by flooding once their household economy has improved. In Tan Trieu, the cost of a low-quality apartment is about 600,000 VND (around US$30) to 700,000 VND (US$35) per month, compared to high-quality apartments, which have been flood proofed (with raised floors), whose monthly rental value is 1,500,000 VND (US$75) per month. According to informants, low-income migrants choose to rent low-quality apartments, and as flooding has kept prices low, it has acted as an accelerant to immigration to this area by creating the conditions that make housing affordable for low-income people. At the same time, vulnerability to flooding causes migration as once people have improved their livelihoods sufficiently, they move on to less-risky spaces. In other words, flooding is inextricably entwined with the migration dynamics of Hanoi, not only as a factor that facilitates entry for low-income people, but also as a factor that causes them to move on, when the opportunity presents itself.

The qualitative and quantitative data presented here illustrate that there were many ways residents used to cope with flood and inundation. These ways not only reflect the way in which residential households deal with flood and inundation but also indicate the role of migration in coping with this socionatural phenomenon. Migration, in combination with the impact of flooding on property values, offers a pathway for building economic capital that then enables people to move away from risky spaces. Many households migrated to Tan Trieu and Tan Mai from rural areas when and where their economic situations were difficult. After a period of time living in Tan Trieu and Tan Mai, many of them improved their households' economies. However, along with the improvement of their households' economies, they have to live with flood and inundation. Thus, on the one hand, migration is an effective means for migrants to improve livelihoods; on the other hand, migration is necessary for coping with floods and inundation.

Nonregistered migrants and official flood responses

Following Article 110 of the Constitution of the Socialist Republic of Vietnam in 2013, administratively Vietnam is divided into provinces and centrally run cities. A province is divided into rural districts, towns and provincial cities; a centrally run city is divided into urban districts, rural districts, towns and equivalent administrative units. A rural district is divided into communes and townships, a town or provincial city is divided into wards and communes and an urban district is divided into wards (Quốc hội, 2013). Key local authorities or leaders in this case study are the leaders of Tan Mai ward and Tan Trieu commune, and it is at this level that most people experience 'government', in relation to dealing with flooding. However, more strategic decision making rests with the high-ranking authority and leaders, here understood as authorities or leaders of administrative levels, from district level to the central government.

The role of high-ranking authorities in response to floods and inundation in Hanoi is in policy making and funding large-scale engineering projects, a key arm of which is 'Hanoi's Master Plan/Project for Drainage System'. This project was approved by the prime minister of Vietnam, and the first stage started in 1998, with a second phase commencing in 2005. This involved engineering rivers, drainage channels and sewers to increase their capacity for coping with heavy rain, therefore reducing the risk of inundation (TTXVN, 2008; Minh Hạnh, 2014).

In contrast, the principal role of the local authority and functional agencies in responding to floods involves three elements: providing information related floods, such as early warning, to residents; considering residents' recommendations in responding to floods; and supporting the residents to overcome negative impacts of floods on their life. Survey results suggested that access to this kind of support was uneven within the populations of each case study community. *First*, in terms of providing residents with information related to floods, the survey showed that only 40 percent could access flood-related information from their local authority at ward or commune level. The most common means is community megaphone or loudspeakers in their ward or commune (22 percent). A very small proportion (4 percent) of respondents got the information via residential group meetings or residential group leaders (5 percent). Interviews showed that there is no direct channel between ward or commune leaders and the residents regarding flood-related information. To explain this, the interview respondents gave different answers. For instance, 15 percent said that they were too busy with their work; 17 percent blamed it on the irresponsibility of the local authority; 11 percent said that they did not care about this; and 7 percent got the information via the television. A large number (69 percent) said they had no flood-related information from commune or ward leaders.

In terms of access to flood-related information from the district level or beyond, survey responses showed that the majority (64 percent) had no opportunity to access any information from district-level authorities. Of those that did receive information, this was largely through official residential group meetings, television, community megaphones or through direct contact with the local authority. Around 12 percent of respondents were of the view that the authorities paid no attention to the issue, while another 8 percent said that they personally took no notice of flood-related information from district-level authorities. The limited effectiveness of existing methods is therefore further reduced by a lack of engagement by residents themselves. The survey also investigated the ways in which respondents engaged with local authorities, revealing a number of strategies adopted in each community. This included accessing the local authority through residential group leaders, by submitting petitions to the local authority or by telephoning the local authority.

The authority itself adopted different strategies when floods occurred. This included visits to affected areas to assess damage, or helping residents with drain dredging or road-bed lifting, but these were viewed as *ad hoc* solutions. According to a Tan Mai resident in an in-depth interview, in the past, whenever it rained heavily, the street was submerged up to 50 centimeters. Previously, the local government assisted them to increase the road-bed height by 20 centimeters and to dredge the drainage system. This helped them overcome floods temporarily, not permanently. Other residents appreciated the assistance of commune and ward leaders in dealing with floods. However, at ward or commune level, they could only offer temporary and small-scale solutions, and were unable to address problems originating beyond the commune or ward (e.g. drainage, waste treatment or restrictions on migration and urban land-use change).[25] A variety of forms of support are offered by the local government after floods, although respondents viewed this as rather limited. For instance, after floods, the commune or ward leaders and officials visited each household to console them. But this is where the support ended.[26] In terms of the authority's support during floods, the survey showed that families received instant noodles in the historic great flood of 2008, but in other floods households got almost nothing. In summary, it can be seen that the role of the local government in supporting the residents to overcome adverse impacts of flooding is still limited.

The unevenness of access to flood-related information and support from the local authority is due in part to exclusions and differing treatment of migrants who have been unable to register as residents in the commune or ward. The survey showed that a small number of recent migrants had no access to flood-related information from their local authority because they did not take part in communal meetings. A resident in Tan Trieu said that she had lived here for 2 years but she hardly attended any meetings or social events in her residential cluster. The reason given was that migrants were not informed about those meetings. However, when there was an announcement on road repairing, she and other migrants had been invited to the meeting to contribute financial support for road construction. At first, they were required to contribute twice as much as households with permanent residence status (hộ khẩu). However, this was opposed by migrants as they felt they should be treated equally. In the end, the residential group decided to assign the contribution equally to each family with 2,000,000 VND (US$100) per household. She added that although her house had been submerged before, she did not know whom to report to.[27] In addition, one more significant point here is that many migrants living in Tan Mai and Tan Trieu did not register with the commune or ward authority. Without residential registration, migrants do not participate in collective activities of the commune such as household meetings, and are not eligible for support from the local authority, including that related to coping with flooding and inundation. For them, when flooding and inundation happens, they stay in their apartment and wait until the floods have subsided.

As an example of power, patronage and unequal access to political, environmental, social and economic assets, flood-related information from the local authority in Tan Mai and Tran Trieu reveals the ways in which migrant status intersects with general vulnerability to floods to create exclusions and the potential for adverse inclusions (having to pay more than permanent residents). It can be said that after many years living with flooding and inundation, residents in Tan Mai are still waiting for a promising significant project to deal with flooding and inundation in this area, and residents in Tan Trieu can hope for the finish of the ongoing drainage system project.

Conclusion

This chapter has explored the ways in which those moving to the city of Hanoi are getting by in the context of severe flooding. In Hanoi, a very particular relationship between flooding, livelihoods and migration is playing out against a backdrop of high-ranking government attempts to reengineer the city and reduce flood impacts, and laws that aim to reduce rural-urban migration and therefore limit permanent settlement in the city. Migrants in Hanoi have come from many rural areas in Vietnam in search of a better livelihood, as urban incomes are generally better than those obtained in rural areas. Rural-urban migration is therefore a vulnerability-reducing strategy. However, living in Hanoi, many migrants have to face and live with flooding and inundation, particularly in the months of July and August, when heavy rains combine with nonporous surfaces and poor drainage in low-income areas of the city. The floods had negative consequences and impacts on local communities in several ways: damage to property, reduced incomes and adverse impacts on the environment and on peoples' health. Thus, what is gained in terms of strengthened livelihood is compromised by exposure to flood risks.

Many survey respondents were aware of the factors that had contributed to flooding in their immediate surroundings. Blame was placed on the urban drainage system and, in particular, the infilling of urban lakes and ponds and replacement of agricultural land by buildings, reducing water absorption capacity. Analysis of this data, in tandem with secondary reports, suggested that floods were caused by slow progress made in upgrading the drainage system, combined with poor solid-waste disposal, leading to the clogging of urban drains and waterways. Expanding rural-urban migration has also contributed to the circumstances in which flooding is becoming a more pernicious and regular event: more buildings, more waste and greater demands placed on sewage systems are a consequence of in-migration. For this reason, the government has attempted to stem the flow of rural-urban migrants by reversing the relaxation of the household registration system, which critics claim had led to expanding rural-urban flows of migrants.

An emerging connection between migration and flood-risk landscapes relates to the lower property prices found in those areas that are particularly vulnerable to flooding. These spaces have become areas in which relatively recent migrants settle, in low-quality but more affordable housing, with a view to saving on housing costs until in a position to move on again, this time to settle in an area of the city that is safe from floods (and as a consequence, where housing is costlier).

In terms of how local communities cope with floods, local people and migrants make use of a number of relatively low-cost methods, including doing a house cleanup after floods, raising the floor, building floodwalls to prevent water flows, placing possessions on higher ground and moving to another place to live. These measures depend on social capital, human capital and financial capital in terms of migrants' household economy and income, their social network and also their experiences of and knowledge about coping with flooding and inundation. What can be emphasized here is that migrants, especially unskilled or low-skilled laborers with humble income and few social connections *in situ*, have measures to cope with flooding but lack the capacity for taking long-term and significant measures. Moreover, a particularly vulnerable group are those who have not registered within a particular ward or commune, thus reducing their access to economic and social support in the event of flooding. Many migrants, especially migrants without residential registration, lack the support that is being offered to local residents from district-level government. The role of commune and ward leaders and high-ranking leaders in dealing with floods suggests three significant points. *First*, a large portion of the population surveyed did not access information on flooding and inundation through commune or ward leaders and high-ranking leaders. In addition, local and high-ranking leaders did not give information related to flooding to residents directly, but indirectly, mainly through commune or ward loudspeakers. *Second*, the actions of commune or ward leaders and high-ranking leaders in dealing with flooding and inundation, such as upgrading and repairing drainage systems, is locally limited and not effective. *Third*, solutions by the local government to support the residents after floods are to record the situations and to remind the residents to keep their house clean in order to prevent flood-borne diseases.

What this chapter suggests is that measures to mitigate flooding may have unintended consequences for the vulnerability of unregistered rural-urban migrants, as flood protection improves the environment of these low-income areas, creating in effect a form of flood-related gentrification that prices some of these migrants out of the housing market. Efforts to reduce rural-urban migration through household registration appears not to have prevented people from coming to the city. However, it has meant that those that do not register are unable to access the support that is offered at commune or ward level. Data discussed in this chapter suggest that this may be fostering new forms of vulnerability for people who have already moved, sometimes a number of times, using migration as a strategy to improve livelihoods.

Notes

1   Vietnam has an elaborate and complex KT system of classification for residents in urban and rural areas: KT1 indicates that a person is registered in the district where he/she resides; KT2 indicates that the person is not registered in the district where he/she resides, but registered in another district of the same province; KT3 indicates a person who has temporary registration for a period of six months or more; KT4 indicates a person who has temporary registration for less than six months. Only those with KT1 registration have full entitlements to government services, the rest must pay for them or are excluded.

   (Quoted in Deshingkar, 2006: 10)

2 Information from the portal of Hoang Mai district, Hanoi (2012) [Cổng thông tin điện tử Ủy ban Nhân dân quận Hoàng Mai, 2012].
3 For Tan Trieu commune, we analyzed the following reports: "Report on the results of implementation of socio-economic, security and defense affairs in 2014 and main objectives in 2015" (Ủy ban Nhân dân xã Tân Triều [Tan Trieu Commune People's Comittee], 2014) and "Report on assessment of implementation of the project on building new countryside in Tan Trieu commune in the period 2011–2013" (Ban chỉ đạo xây dựng nông thôn mới xã Tân Triều, 2014). For Tan Mai ward, we looked at

the following reports: "Report on the results of implementation of the economic and social development plan from 2005 to 2010", the "Plan for the economic and social development of Tan Mai ward from 2011 to 2016" (Ủy ban Nhân dân phường Tân Mai [Tan Mai Ward People's Comittee], 2012) and "Report on the results of implementation of socio-economic affairs in 2014. Directions to the implementation of socio-economic plans 2015" (Ủy ban Nhân dân phường Tân Mai [Tan Mai Ward People's Comittee], 2014).

4 "Report on the results of implementation of socio-economic, security and defense affairs in 2014 and main objectives in 2015" of Tan Trieu Commune People's Committee (Ủy ban Nhân dân xã Tân Triều [Tan Trieu Commune People's Committee], 2014: 4).

5 In-depth interview with Nguyen Van Than, 75 years old, retired worker, Tan Mai ward (10 July 2013).

6 In-depth interview with Nguyen Thi Thuong Hang, 53 years old, caterer, Tan Mai ward (10 July 2013).

7 According to section 3 of article 20 of the law on residence, citizens may register their permanent residence in centrally run cities if they are

> [b]eing transferred or recruited to work in agencies or organizations, who are salaried from the state budget or under labor contracts with an unspecified term and have lawful domiciles. Where their lawful domiciles are leased, lent or let for free-of-charge stay by individuals, written consent of the lessors, lenders or such individuals is required.
>
> (Quốc Hội, 2006)

8 This is partly due to how household heads are defined. The household registration system (hộ khẩu) tends to define the head as the oldest person in the household.

9 In-depth interview with Dang Quang Việt, 59 years old, carpenter, Tan Mai ward (10 July 2013).

10 In-depth interview with Nguyen Thi Thuong Hang, 53 years old, caterer, Tan Mai ward (10 July 2013).

11 According to the survey, the incomes of 57.1 percent of new migrants, 48.9 percent of old migrants and 74.1 percent of local people were decreased. However, a chi-square test for independence indicated no significant association between residence (new migrants, old migrants and local people) and changes in incomes of residents; χ^2 (2, n = 93) = 4.405, p = 0.111.

12 From the report of the Tan Trieu Commune People's Committee, in 2014 the commune had 1,820 households working as small private traders or providing services. Earnings of the commune from recycling plastic and providing small guest-house services accounted for 26.7 percent of the households (Ủy ban Nhân dân xã Tân Triều [Tan Trieu Commune People's Committee], 2014). "Báo cáo kết quả thực hiện nhiệm vụ phát triển kinh tế – xã hội, an ninh – quốc phòng năm 2014 và mục tiêu, nhiệm vụ trọng tâm năm 2015 [Report on the results of implementation of socio-economic, security and defense affairs in 2014 and main objectives in 2015]").

13 Ủy ban Nhân dân phường Tân Mai [Tan Mai Ward People's Committee]. 2014. "Báo cáo kết quả thực hiện nhiệm vụ phát triển kinh tế – xã hội năm 2014. Phương hướng thực hiện nhiệm vụ phát triển kinh tế – xã hội 2015 [Report on the results of implementation of socio-economic affairs in 2014. Directions to the implementation of socio-economic plans 2015]."

14 In-depth interview with Truong Thi Xinh, 67 years old, retired worker, Tan Trieu commune (11 July 2013).

15 In-depth interview with Nguyen Thi Thuong Hang, 53 years old, caterer, Tan Mai ward (10 July 2013).

16 In-depth interview with Cao Xuan Do, 49 years old, scrap collector, Tan Trieu commune (9 July 2013).
17 The survey results show that 88 percent of new migrant households, 93 percent of established migrant households and 100 percent of local households do house cleanup after floods. However, a chi-square test for independence indicated no significant association between time of living in the research sites and doing house cleanup after floods.
18 In-depth interview with Nguyen Thi Thuong Hang, 53 years old, caterer, Tan Mai ward (10 July 2013).
19 In-depth interview with Nguyen Thi Thuong Hang, 53 years old, caterer, Tan Mai ward (10 July 2013).
20 In-depth interview with Nguyen Thi Xinh, 73 years old, retired worker, Tan Mai ward (10 July 2013).
21 Information from Nguyen Thi Thuong Hang, 53 years old, caterer, at a focus group discussion in Tan Mai ward (11 July 2013).
22 Information from Dang Quang Việt, 59 years old, carpenter, at a focus group discussion in Tan Mai ward (11 July 2013).
23 In-depth interview with Nguyen Van Than, 75 years old, retired worker, Tan Mai ward (10 July 2013).
24 This and information in the next two paragraphs are from an in-depth interview with Nguyen Thi Thuong Hang, 53 years old, caterer, Tan Mai ward (10 July 2013).
25 In-depth interview with Nguyen Thi Xinh, 73 years old, retired worker, Tan Mai ward (10 July 2013).
26 In-depth interview with Nguyen Van Than, 75 years old, retired worker, Tan Mai ward (10 July 2013).
27 In-depth interview with Nguyen Thi Tuc, 67 years old, retired worker, Tan Trieu commune (8 September 2013).

References

Ban chỉ đạo xây dựng nông thôn mới xã Tân Triều. (2014). *Báo cáo đánh giá kết quả thực hiện các tiêu chí về xây dựng nông thôn mới xã Tân Triều giai đoạn 2011–2013* [Report on assessment of implementation of the project on building new countryside in Tan Trieu commune in the period 2011–2013]. Tan Trieu commune, Hanoi.

BáoMới. (2012). "Hanoi streets flooded while typhoon Kai Tak advancing." *BáoMới.com*. http://en.baomoi.com/Info/Hanoi-streets-flooded-while-typhoon-Kai-Tak-advancing/3/294655.epi [last accessed 12/05/17].

Cổng thông tin điện tử Ủy ban Nhân dân quận Hoàng Mai. (2012). "Phường Tân Mai [Tan Mai ward]." *Ủy ban Nhân dân quận Hoàng Mai*. http://hoangmai.hanoi.gov.vn/cgt/cgtdt/phuong_tan_mai.html. Truy cập tháng 12 năm 2014 [last accessed 12/05/17].

Dang, N.A. (2003). "Internal migration policies in the ESCAP region." *Asia-Pacific Population Journal* 18(3): 27–40.

Deshingkar, P. (2006). "Internal migration, poverty and development in Asia." *Promoting Growth, Ending Poverty ASIA 2015, Asia 2015 Conference*. www.asia2015conference.org [last accessed 12/05/17].

General Statistics Office of Vietnam. (2011). *Vietnam population and housing census 2009: Migration and urbanization in Vietnam: Patterns, trends and differentials*. Hanoi: Ministry of Planning and Investment.

General Statistics Office of Vietnam. (2014). *Statistical data: Population and employment*. www.gso.gov.vn/default_en.aspx?tabid=467&idmid=3 [last accessed 12/05/17].

Global Facility for Disaster Reduction and Recovery. (2009). *A primer on reducing vulnerabilities to disasters*. Washington, DC: World Bank.

Hiếu, N., Hiếu, Đ.T., Kinh Bắc, D., and Thu Phương, D. (2013). "Assessment of flood hazard in Hanoi city." *VNU Journal of Earth and Environmental Sciences* 19: 26–37.

Hoang Mai district, Hanoi (2012). [Cổng thông tin điện tử Ủy ban Nhân dân quận Hoàng Mai 2012]. "Phường Tân Mai [Tan Mai ward]." Ủy ban Nhân dân quận Hoàng Mai. http://hoangmai.hanoi.gov.vn/cgt/cgtdt/phuong_tan_mai.html.

Hoang, V.H., Shaw, R., and Kobayashi, M. (2007). "Flood risk management for the RUA of Hanoi – Importance of community perception of catastrophic flood risk in disaster risk planning." *Disaster Prevention and Management* 16: 245–258.

Huy Nam – VOV. (2014). "Hà Nội: "Gập ghềnh" GPMB dự án thoát nước giai đoạn II [Hanoi: The "Bumpy" Project for Drainage System – the Second Stage]." *VOV Giao Thông*. http://vovgiaothong.vn/tam-diem/ha-noigap-ghenh-gpmb-du-an-thoat-nuoc-giai-doan-ii/4204. Truy cập tháng 1 năm 2015 [last accessed 12/05/17].

Labbé, D. (2010). *Facing the urban transition in Hanoi: Recent urban planning issues and initiatives*. Institut national de la recherche scientifique, Centre – Urbanisation Culture Société, Paris.

Minh Hạnh. (2014). "Dự án thoát nước ì ạch về đích [The Project for Drainage System ploddingly to finish]." *Nhân Dân*. (http://www.nhandan.com.vn/hanoi/tin-moi-nhan/item/23740402-du-an-thoat-nuoc-i-ach-ve-dich.html). Truy cập tháng 1 năm 2015. [last accessed 12/05/17].

Nguyễn Hiếu, Đỗ Trung Hiếu, Đặng Kinh Bắc, and Đoàn Thu Phương. (2013). "Assessement of Flood Hazard in Hanoi City." *VNU Journal of Earth and Environmental Sciences* 19: 26–37.

Nguyen, T.A., Rigg, J., Luong, T.T.H., and Dinh, T.D. (2012). "Becoming and being urban in Hanoi: Rural-urban migration and relations in Viet Nam." *Journal of Peasant Studies* 39: 1103–1131.

Oanh, L.N., Nguyen, T.T.T., Wilderspinc, I., and Coulierd, M. (2011). *A preliminary analysis of flood and storm disaster data in Viet Nam*. Background paper for Global Assessment Report on Disaster Risk Reduction. UNDP and UN-ISDR, Geneva.

Quốc Hội. (2006). "Luật cư trú [Law on residence]." *Cổng thông tin điện tử Bộ Tư pháp* (http://www.moj.gov.vn/vbpq/Lists/Vn%20bn%20php%20lut/View_Detail.aspx?ItemID=14850). Truy cập tháng 12 năm 2014. [last accessed 12/05/17]

___. 2012. "Luật Thủ đô [Law on capital city]." *Cổng thông tin điện tử Chính phủ Nước Cộng hòa Xã hội Chủ nghĩa Việt Nam* (http://vanban.chinhphu.vn/portal/page/portal/chinhphu/hethongvanban?class_id=1&_page=1&mode=detail&document_id=164931), Truy cập tháng 12 năm 2014. [last accessed 12/05/17]

___. 2013. "Hiến pháp Nước Cộng hòa Xã hội Chủ nghĩa Việt Nam [The Constitution of the Socialist Republic of Vietnam]." *Văn phòng Quốc hội Nước Cộng hòa Xã hội Chủ nghĩa Việt Nam - Hệ thống văn bản quy phạm pháp luật* (http://vietlaw.gov.vn/LAWNET/). Truy cập tháng 1 năm 2015. [last accessed 12/05/17]

Rigg, J., Nguyen, T.A., and Luong, T.T.H. (2014). "The texture of livelihoods: Migration and making a living in Hanoi." *The Journal of Development Studies* 50.

Thảo, P. (2012). "'Phiếu thuận' cho đề xuất siết điều kiện nhập cư Hà Nội ["Vote for" fastening the conditions for immigration to Hanoi]." *Thư viện Văn phòng Quốc hội*. http://duthaoonline.quochoi.vn/DuThao/Lists/TT_TINLAPPHAP/View_Detail.aspx?ItemID=856. Truy cập tháng 12 năm 2014 [last accessed 12/05/17].

Thông tin KHCN. (2014). "'Khoảng trống' trong quản lý phát triển các khu đô thị mới tại Hà Nội ["Space" in management of new residential zone development in Hanoi]." *Cổng thông tin điện tử Bộ Xây dựng*. www.xaydung.gov.vn/vi/web/guest/thong-tin-tu-lieu/-/

tin-chi-tiet/ek4I/86/247376/%E2%80%9Ckhoang-trong%E2%80%9D-trong-quan-ly-phat-trien-cac-khu-do-thi-moi-tai-ha-noi.html. Truy cập tháng 12 năm 2014.

Tran, H.B., Ngoc, Q.L., Le, T.T.H., Tran, T.D.H., and Guha-Sapir, D. (2011). "Impacts of flood on health: Epidemiologic evidence from Hanoi, Vietnam." *Global Health Action* 4(s2–s1): 6356.

Trinh, T.P. (2010). "Urban flood and inundation in Hanoi capital: Problems, measures, and climate change adaptation." *Urban Flood Risk Management in a Changing Climate: Sustainable and Adaptation Challenges*, 6–10 September 2010, Macao, China.

TTXVN. (2008). "Dự án thoát nước Hà Nội (giai đoạn 1,2) chưa giải quyết úng ngập cho khu vực lưu vực sông Nhuệ [Master Plan/Project for Drainage System in Hanoi (first stage and second stage) have not solved the inundation of Nhue River valley]." *VOV Đài Tiếng nói Việt Nam*. http://vov.vn/xa-hoi/du-an-thoat-nuoc-ha-noi-giai-doan-12-chua-giai-quyet-ung-ngap-cho-khu-vuc-luu-vuc-song-nhue-99041.vov. Truy cập tháng 1 năm 2015 [last accessed 12/05/17].

Tuyết Mai. (2011). "Mưa lớn gây nhiều điểm úng ngập tại Hà Nội." *Ministry of Natural Resources and Environment* (http://www.monre.gov.vn/v35/default.aspx?tabid=428&CateID=25&ID=105586&Code=7PIL105586), accessed on 29 September 2013. [last accessed 12/05/17]

Ủy ban Nhân dân phường Tân Mai [Tan Mai Ward People's Committee]. (2012). *Báo cáo đánh giá tình hình thực hiện kế hoạch phát triển kinh tế xã hội 5 năm 2005–2010 và kế hoạch phát triển kinh tế xã hội giai đoạn 2011–2016 phường Tân Mai*. [Report on the results of implementation of the economic and social development plan from 2005 to 2010, and the plan for the economic and social development of Tan Mai ward from 2011 to 2016].

Ủy ban Nhân dân phường Tân Mai [Tan Mai Ward People's Committee]. (2014). *Báo cáo kết quả thực hiện nhiệm vụ phát triển kinh tế – xã hội năm 2014: Phương hướng thực hiện nhiệm vụ phát triển kinh tế – xã hội 2015*. [Report on the results of implementation of socio-economic affairs in 2014. Directions to the implementation of socio-economic plans 2015].

Ủy ban Nhân dân xã Tân Triều [Tan Trieu Commune People's Committee]. (2014). *Báo cáo kết quả thực hiện nhiệm vụ phát triển kinh tế – xã hội, an ninh – quốc phòng năm 2014 và mục tiêu, nhiệm vụ trTimes New Romanng tâm năm 2015*. [Report on the results of implementation of socio-economic, security and defense affairs in 2014 and main objectives in 2015].

8 Flooding in a city of migrants
Ethnicity and entitlement in Bandar Lampung, Indonesia

Rebecca Elmhirst and Ari Darmastuti

Introduction

Indonesia is marked by historical and contemporary migrations associated with changing regimes of environmental governance and access to land and livelihood resources. Nowhere is this more in evidence than in the city of Bandar Lampung on Sumatra's southernmost tip, where waves of migration from many different parts of the Indonesian archipelago have created a diverse socioecological urban landscape. In this chapter, we examine how historical migration and the social geographies these forms of mobility have produced have shaped vulnerability to flooding and responses to flood events. The chapter adopts a political ecology framework through which we explore the ways historical migrations prompted by precarity and conflict in other places have on the one hand shaped contemporary vulnerability to flooding but, on the other, have enabled the maintenance of extralocal ties that provide capabilities for dealing with flood hazards among at least some of the urban population.

The chapter shows that historical migrations and associated ethnic networks shape not only the contours of precarious everyday livelihoods and how these are addressed in the context of flooding but also the political capital people are able to actualize at very localized scales to attract assistance of various kinds. Migration and ethnicity carry particular significance in Lampung, and this has been amplified following the devolution of previously heavily centralized political and fiscal authority to regional and district levels following the reforms of the late 1990s. While the importance of ethnicity in shaping politics in Indonesia is the subject of intense debate (Schulte Nordholdt, 2008), there is general agreement that a form of 'soft ethnic politics', often figured around peoples' notions of 'place of origin', inflects political capital and the operation of patronage in multicultural provinces like Lampung (Aspinall, 2011; van Klinken, 2009). The chapter shows how this works at a very localized, everyday scale, and how this demands that the city is understood as 'relational' – a product of layer upon layer of different sets of linkages, both local and to the wider world, its social landscape woven out of a distinct mixture of wider and more local social relations (Massey, 1994).

The city's migration history and resulting social geography originate in early migrations associated with the precolonial and colonial pepper and spice trade;

the state-sponsored resettlement of landless Javanese, Sundanese and Balinese farmers from heavily populated islands of Java and Bali in the late colonial period and early twentieth century; and settlement in coastal areas of seafaring Bugis originally from Bone in southern Sulawesi. As an economic and political focal point for the province, the city of Bandar Lampung is emblematic of this historically sedimented ethnic diversity. In recent years, the city's cosmopolitanism has been extended through newer migrations, including the continued circulation of people between the city and West Java and Banten provinces, facilitated by better overland and sea transport links, and increasingly, migration from the city's rural hinterland by those displaced through enclosure and changing resource governance elsewhere in Lampung province itself. The city now has a population just short of a million (BPS, 2015). Its economy is based on a mix of manufacturing (agricultural processing) and services (transport, port services), combined with small-scale fishing, plantations and food crop agriculture, and this combination has produced a mix of peri-urban landscapes coupled with high-density residential development focused on the merger of three centers (formerly separate towns): the port of Teluk Betung, the international shipment port of Panjuang and the inland commercial hub of Tanjung Karang.

Amid a landscape of socioeconomic change, Bandar Lampung experiences regular flood events. These are linked in part to its physical geography, situated on the coast and surrounded by steep hills. The city is also subject to a tropical monsoon climate and experiences intense and heavy rainfall particularly from December to April, where levels can be up to 185 millimeters per day. Observers suggest that this rainfall is becoming more erratic, and that pronounced seasonality is being replaced by heavy rain at any time of year.[1] Floods are associated with the two large rivers (Way Kuala and Way Kuripan), which pass through the city, as well as with the city's 23 smaller rivers. Some of this flooding is attributable to seawater inundation in areas on the coastal fringe (e.g. in Teluk Betung). However, in other parts of the city, floods are associated with high rainfall, rapid urbanization and land-use change and inundation caused by the low capacity of drainage systems to remove excess surface water (e.g. in Tanjung Karang). These floods regularly cause damage to property, disrupt already fragile livelihoods and may be linked to health hazards. Many of the city's poorer neighborhoods are located on the banks of rivers and in the lower-lying poorer areas of the city close to the coast.

Bandar Lampung is regarded as 'at risk' from climate change (BAPPENAS and ICCR, 2010, 2014; Lassa and Nugraha, 2015). In recent years, the city has been a focus for international and national efforts to build resilience to climate change through an initial vulnerability analysis, and through better urban management, capacity building and environmental education efforts. Much of this work has been led and coordinated by the Asian Cities Climate Change Resilience Network (ACCCRN) and its partners (Brown et al., 2012; Friend et al., 2014; Lassa and Nugraha, 2015), and Bandar Lampung features as one of the pilot cities in the Indonesian government's National Action Plan on Climate Change Adaptation (BAPPENAS, 2014). This work is careful to acknowledge the prevalence of generations of migrants among the city's population impacted by climate change, but its focus has been on capacity building among stakeholders – policy makers, planners, decision makers, community leaders and educators – with regard to climate resilience, rather than in analyzing how migrants and migration figure within this.

While the research discussed in this chapter was conceived independently and had no direct link with the climate change resilience projects being undertaken by ACCCRN and partners in Bandar Lampung, our aim has been to complement this work, by focusing explicitly on the interconnections between migration, vulnerability and urban floods. Our starting point is that migration histories are intertwined with the wider social and political ecological processes contributing to both vulnerability and capability. Thus, a mobile political ecology of flooding requires the city to be viewed as a relational space rather than as a specific territory (or, in the context of floods, a hydrological basin), as well as a product of historical layerings that continue to be significant in shaping people's local and extralocal economic, cultural and political connections.

The chapter is structured as follows. In the next section, a brief summary of the research methodology and an overview of the study sites is provided. The section that follows outlines the city's migration history, and the implications this has for social geographies of vulnerability. Remaining sections explore the ways in which historical migration inflects trade-offs between exposure to flooding, access to employment and tenure recognition and the ways in which people are able to command networks of solidarity and support to address flood impacts and associated vulnerabilities.

Research methods and study sites

Primary research for this study was undertaken in August and September 2013 using a mixed-methods approach that combined both qualitative and quantitative data collection tools in three urban villages (referred to in Indonesian as *kelurahan*) located in different parts of Bandar Lampung city (see Figure 8.1).[2] While the study sites coincided with areas investigated in the ACCCRN studies (Lassa and Nugraha, 2015), our aim was to complement rather than replicate the analyses being undertaken by that group. Research focused on the urban villages of Kota Karang, Kangkung and Pasir Gintung. These were selected because of their contrasting migrant profiles and according to their characterization as areas subject to flood risks of different kinds (Lampung Disaster Preparedness Board (BPBD), 2013; ACCCRN, 2010). All three neighborhoods are relatively low income and the security of housing tenure is low.

Kota Karang is located in Teluk Betung (the port area) to the south of the city on the edge of the Way Belau River and frequently experiences river and tidal floods. It is home to long-term Bugis 'migrants' originally from Sulawesi, who maintain some ties with Bone, Sulawesi, regarded to some extent as a 'homeland'. Livelihoods focus on sea fishing and labor in the fish market, alongside casual labor of various kinds. Kangkung is also located in the southern part of the city,

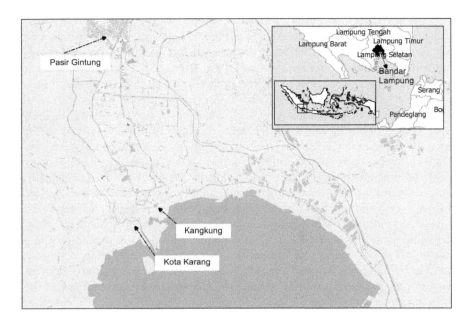

Figure 8.1 Location of study sites in Bandar Lampung, Indonesia

but directly flanks the coast. It also frequently experiences river and tidal floods. Much of the settled area is on recently reclaimed tidal land. It is home to low-income urban migrants, and is strongly associated with fishing and other natural resource–based livelihoods. Pasir Gintung is located inland in a hilly part of the city traversed by one of the city's smaller rivers, the Way Awi. It is subject to landslides and flash floods. It is home to low-income urban migrants, originally from Java, who are involved in informal-sector livelihoods, including trade associated with the city's 24-hour wholesale vegetable market, which is located close by.

First, data collection began with three key informant (KI) interviews with community leaders in each location to get a sense of the vulnerability profile of the area, including migration histories, recent experiences of flooding, engagement with city and central government for rebuilding and adaptation and a broad outline of the social characteristics of the community. In particular, topics around contemporary migration and the existence of multilocal livelihoods were explored.

Second, a focus group discussion (FGD) was held in each community with approximately 10 invited KIs representing different community organizations (including the youth group, women's group and subneighborhood leaders). Topics covered in the FGD included migration histories, recent experiences of flooding, coping and adaptation strategies, obstacles to overcoming flood hazards and the extent and efficacy of multilocal livelihoods. The latter topic proved particularly challenging for groups to discuss: reflecting the ways that migration in its various forms is played down in public and private discourse. Everyday practices of moving between spaces within and beyond the city are rarely articulated as 'migration' when this term tends to be associated with cross-border movement. Following this, greater attention was paid to the role of social capital: the kinds of patron-client networks evident within communities, and the ways in which such networks are shaped by area of origin and ethnicity at different levels.

Finally, a survey was undertaken, with a sample of 100 households in each urban village, defined in the study according to administrative boundaries. As far as possible, respondent selection was random, but in the absence of a population sampling frame, a particular effort was made to include those living in more marginal and difficult-to-access parts of each locality. A number of respondents in each community were selected to participate in an in-depth interview to explore the links between migration, floods and vulnerability in an unstructured way. All surveys and interviews were undertaken and analyzed in Bahasa Indonesia. Transcripts from the FGDs and KI interviews were analyzed using thematic coding that linked to the conceptual framework (see Chapter 1). Secondary data from the Bandar Lampung bureau of statistics were also analyzed, with an emphasis on data concerning urbanization, population change and migration. Each of the tools sought to uncover the historical relationship between migration and landscape change at the basin level and beyond, the experience of flooding in terms of vulnerability and capability to address this and how engagement in migrant-ethnic networks shape experiences of and responses to urban flood events.

Histories of vulnerability, migration and urban development

The importance of migration as a strategy to address vulnerability has been well established through numerous studies (de Haas, 2012). Types of migration may involve displacement (due to conflict or sudden-onset environmental hazards), managed resettlement by governments or other agencies to address landlessness (e.g. the Indonesian government's transmigration program) or through self-managed relocation to improve livelihoods. The history of Bandar Lampung city is tied up with all three of these types of migration, beginning with migration associated with the precolonial spice trade. During the mercantile period, the area that now forms the city was part of the sultanate of Bantam (centered on West Java and including the area that has now split off to form the province of Banten). During this period, movement into the port of Teluk Betung (now incorporated into Bandar Lampung city) revolved around the circulation of commodities, and included Bugis maritime traders from Sulawesi. Migration to Lampung from Banten began as early as the seventeenth century, establishing a migration stream that continues to this day, evidence for which is most notable in the urban villages of Kangkung and Kota Karang (in which people identifying as Bugis are clustered).

Under the influence of the Dutch East Indies company (Vereenigde Oostindische Compagnie, or VOC), and later the Dutch colonial authorities, the port of

Teluk Betung was established as the administrative center of the colonial district of Lampung in the mid-nineteenth century (1851). Migration to new areas does not necessarily result in reduced vulnerability: in August 1883, the eruption of nearby Krakatoa killed 36,000 people in total: the Bay of Lampung was devastated, and a wave reaching 20 meters in height wiped out much of Teluk Betung and its inhabitants, many of them recent migrants. The restoration of the port as a population center continued into the late colonial period, and Teluk Betung's character as a 'city of migrants' became most apparent by the 1930s, when, according to the colonial census, the population expanded through in-migration. This included interisland migrations of Bugis (from Sulawesi), Madurese (from Madura) and Javanese, Sundanese and Banten (from Java).

These migrations reflect a need to address economic and political vulnerabilities in places of origin, but in different ways. First, migration from Java was largely associated with the Dutch *'Kolonisatie'* resettlement program. While this was largely a rural phenomenon involving the provision of land to landless farmers from Java, Madura and Bali, *Kolonisatie* (and the postindependence transmigration program that followed) had a marked impact on urban growth and the ethnic profile of the city. In the 1930s, large population densities were found in the Teluk Betung area, corresponding with the arrival of landless Javanese migrants. According to the census of 1930, within the district of Teluk Betung, 62 percent of its 25,000-strong population was Javanese (from Central and East Java) and Sundanese (from West Java), including a proportion from Banten (Sevin, 1989). Second, migration of Bugis people from South Sulawesi in the 1960s was associated with the civil war that devastated large parts of South Sulawesi from 1950 to 1965, where people had been subject to violence from both the Indonesian national army and Islamic separatist forces (Acciaioli, 2007). Many of the respondents in the urban village of Kota Karang had originally come to the city from Bone and Wajo as internally displaced people in the late 1950s and early 1960s, after having spent some time in a refugee camp in North Java. Third, second-generation transmigrants, unable to find land because of the closure of Lampung province's agricultural frontier and the establishment of protected forest areas from the early 1980s onward (Elmhirst, 2012), prompted further migration into the city. This, combined with unprecedented migration from Java (often based on kinship ties with former transmigrants) by people seeking to address precarious livelihoods, contributed to a trebling of the city's population in the decade between 1980 and 1990. For some older participants in Pasir Gintung, migration to the city from rural areas of Lampung province was itself part of a strategy to mitigate vulnerabilities produced by changes in resource governance in rural areas. Thus, a complex history links enclosure, economic precarity and conflict in other regions of Indonesia with migration for improved livelihoods, and the geographies of these migrations have given shape to the social and ethnic profiles of the three study areas, as summarized in Table 8.1.[3]

These past migrations have contributed to the changes Bandar Lampung has seen over recent decades. While in-migration has historically contributed to the social geography of Bandar Lampung and its urban villages, unlike the Hanoi or

Table 8.1 Contrasting migration histories in Bandar Lampung

Urban village (kelurahan)	Migration history and social characteristics
Kota Karang	Approximately 40% of the population is Bugis (originating from Sulawesi), while 40% are Banten (from what is now Banten province, western Java). The remaining 20% comprise Pesisir (original Lampung population), Minangkabau from West Sumatra, Chinese and Javanese. The Bugis population is well established, having arrived as internally displaced people from Wajo and Bone in South Sulawesi in the 1960s when the area was still forested, and not yet fully incorporated into the city. Formerly farmers. Few new migrants; change is due to natural growth.
Kangkung	Population is either Sundanese (from Cirebon, North Java) or Banten (from Banten province). Banten migrants came originally from Cilagong, Kota Kosong, because of clove projects that were initiated in rural Lampung in the late 1960s by the family of Indonesia's former president Soeharto. When this monopoly failed, many returned to Banten but those who stayed settled in Kangkung, seeking laboring jobs in the port and fish market. Those originating from the coastal city of Cirebon were fishermen seeking better opportunities off Lampung's coast. Few new migrants; change is due to natural growth.
Pasir Gintung	Majority of the population are from Java, especially West Java (ethnically Sundanese). Many came to Lampung through the Indonesian government's transmigration resettlement program, are descendants of transmigrants or came to Lampung in the wake of the program. They therefore have links with rural areas in the province. In-migration continues from rural areas, and there is also substantial natural growth.

Source: Authors' survey

Manila cases (Chapters 6 and 7 in this volume), contemporary urban-landscape change is not attributable to any sort of current large-scale in-migration of the sort planners and urban managers tend to see as a problem (Tacoli, 2009). Rather, the city's recent growth and expansion are the result of a combination of natural population growth and the extension of built-up areas into surrounding peri-urban and rural communities. Bandar Lampung's changing economy, its role as a regional center and wider changes in urban lifestyles and consumption practices, particularly among a growing urban middle class, have in turn brought significant land-use change, and it is this, rather than rapid in-migration, that is associated with the increased frequency and impacts of urban floods.

Land-use change has largely involved the conversion of forested slopes and low-lying marshland for housing, retail and industrial development (Utoyo, 2015; BPS, 2015).[4] The built-up area of the city continues to expand, having grown from 620,979 hectares in 2008 to 664,058 in 2012 (BPS, 2015), creating a blurring between villages and the city as the former are incorporated. As is the case with other small and medium cities in Indonesia, this brings a juxtaposition between urban and rural activities in seemingly heavily urbanized spaces (Firman, 2003). The expansion of the city's built-up area westward and northward is in part associated with the city's population growth, but it is also attributable to construction of middle-class housing on larger plots of private land, in areas of the city such as the area of Way Halim to the north.

Aside from housing development, there has also been a proliferation of shopping malls and shophouses (known locally as *rumah-toko*), and hotel construction, on occasion in areas close to rivers where building is prohibited under local regulations. Overall, as is the case in many fast-growing small and medium-sized cities in Southeast Asia, all urban residents must contend with severe urban housing, infrastructure and service deficiencies, as well as various forms of urban congestion (Tacoli et al., 2015). Communities taking part in this study saw themselves as having to contend with the downsides of rapid urban development. High levels of intra-urban mobility are required because of the geographical separation between residential areas and areas where most economic activity is located (Malik, 2013), and this has continued to encourage road building as a politically popular effort to ease pressures. The impact on city dwellers of Bandar Lampung's traffic problems means road development is one of the most politicized issues in Bandar Lampung, for which many politicians fight for policies, programs and funds, and expenditure is higher in this sector than on flood prevention measures.[5] In the absence of a mass transportation system in a city with almost a million inhabitants, private ownership of cars and motorcycles has mushroomed, enabled by relatively low-cost loans that allow people on low incomes to buy motorcycles.

Rapid and unplanned urban development in Bandar Lampung has contributed to flooding in recent years, which results from a combination of intense seasonal rainfall patterns, landscape topography and recent land-use changes within the city and at basin level. Specifically, flooding is compounded by the expansion of impervious surfaces (surfaced roads, areas given over to housing development), coupled with poor drainage systems. Moreover, urban activities (particularly poor waste management) compound the problem as waterways become blocked with rubbish and therefore flood on a frequent basis (Lassa and Nugraha, 2015). Two of the study areas, Kota Karang and Kangkung, experience a combination of runoff and tidal floods, which, according to study participants, was due to poor waste management and a need to keep dredging the river so water can easily flow (Table 8.2). Other kinds of flooding were the focus of study participants in Pasir Gintung, where housing development and deforestation of slopes in the past has also meant that runoff from rainfall in the hills that flank the city is not slowed down by vegetation. This has exposed the community to frequent and powerful flash floods. In addition, the area's steep hill slopes coupled with intense rain means that landslides are common.

A widespread public discourse around the causes of flooding in Bandar Lampung's local media has meant that people in the study communities were clear in their explanation of how urban development had brought specific types of

Table 8.2 Characteristics of flooding in the study areas

	Type of flooding	Underlying causes
Kota Karang	Seasonal rain early in year raises level of Way Belau River. Flooding occurs when this coincides with high tides. Study participants report a worsening situation over the past 5 years. Floods subside within a day but impact lasts longer.	Waste blocks river channels and drains, preventing river flow. Increased housing development in upstream areas means water descends through the basin very quickly. Problems with sedimentation.
Kangkung	Floods in December and January, when high tides and heavy rain coincide. High tides also result in silting, which amplifies the flood problem. The flood reached 1 meter all through the market and slum area. Floods normally subside after 2 days, but impact lasts longer.	Waste from market and upstream areas blocks river channels and drains, preventing river flow. Increased housing development in upstream areas means water descends through the basin very quickly. Problems with sedimentation.
Pasir Gintung	Frequent intensive flash floods of Way Awi River, usually during seasonal rains in December and January. Steep slopes in area are prone to landslides. Floods often 3 meters in height lasting a few hours.	Urban development in upstream Sukadanakan area (a former transmigration settlement), removal of vegetation and replacement with nonporous surfaces. Waste dumped in rivers causes blockages.

Source: FGDs and key person interviews, Kota Karang, Kangkung and Pasir Gintung (August 2013)

flooding to their respective neighborhoods. However, it is the combination of urban development patterns and the specific nature of floods that produce a range of experiences and responses in the three study areas. The next section of this chapter explores how social geographies produced by past migrations underlie experiences of flood risk in the urban villages of Kota Karang, Kangkung and Pasir Gintung.

Contemporary social geographies and vulnerability to urban floods

There are some common features to vulnerability in each of the study communities, taken here to mean 'the social precarity found on the ground' when the floods arrive (Ribot, 2014: 667). In terms of material and economic vulnerabilities, all three areas are relatively low income. While figures are not available at village level, there are data on poverty for the administrative subdistricts (*kecamatan*) in which each urban village is located, namely in Teluk Betung Barat (Kota Karang), Bumi Waras (Kangkung) and Tanjung Karang Pusat (Pasir Gintung). The Indonesian government's SUSENAS 2015 poverty and well-being survey shows that 32 percent of households in the subdistricts in which Kota Karang and Kangkung are located, as well as 23 percent of households for the relevant subdistrict for Pasir Gintung, fall into the lowest category, defined as 'poor'. This means they are unable to meet one of five basic needs (food, shelter, clothing, health, religious practice) (BPS, 2015). Households in these categories are likely, therefore, to be vulnerable to shocks such as food price increases, ill health and factors that reduce income-generation capacity, making them vulnerable to the impacts of flood events.

A closer examination of how precarity is constructed in each community, however, reveals a more nuanced social geography, which reflects the interplay between work and livelihoods, risky living spaces and ways of living with floods that may paradoxically build security in otherwise precarious circumstances. In both questionnaire responses and FGDs, lack of regular paid work was by far the most important immediate source of vulnerability noted by study participants.[6] Participants suggested that employment opportunities are restricted, and this accords with secondary data sources that show Bandar Lampung has relatively few large-scale industries that might provide formal-sector wage work. Middle-class employment opportunities tend to hinge around work within local government, education and nongovernment organizations, while the expansion of retailing has also brought employment opportunities.

Most people in the study areas are engaged in what might be defined as rural employment (as laborers on offshore fishing boats, in fish processing and trading), alongside urban informal-sector employment (market trading, small shops and street-food vending) and laboring jobs.[7] There is a strong association between area of origin (which maps broadly onto ethnicity) and employment. While in FGDs people associate this with the 'characteristics and orientations' of particular ethnic groups (e.g. 'Banten people like physical work; Javanese tend to be more cerebral and business oriented'), the survey data suggested this pattern was more a reflection of the social networks through which people find work and support each other, a feature common to many low-income urban areas (Carpenter et al., 2004). For example, in Kangkung and in Kota Karang, the main types of work associated with people with family origins in Banten (western Java) relate to the fishing industry (as laborers on fishing boats, as building workers, fish-market laborers and in garbage removal). Women also work in the fish market and in processing fish. Work tends to be casual and precarious, and when there is no work locally, people will go to work in other parts of the port area of the city, in warehouse jobs or in the fish auction house. In Kangkung, key person interviews suggested that education attainment in the area was relatively low because so many children were also drafted in to work to supplement precarious household incomes.[8]

By contrast, in Kota Karang, Bugis people, originally from Sulawesi, work in slightly better-paid jobs also in the fishing industry, and most of the owners of the large fishing boats in Kota Karang are Bugis. Other employment is in retail or small businesses. In Pasir Gintung, populated largely by Javanese and Sundanese descendants of transmigrants, livelihoods revolve around informal-sector work and trade, and are focused on the wholesale vegetable market that serves the whole of Tanjung Karang. The market is open all hours, so men and women tend to work together, men at night and women during the day, taking turns. Women may also work selling cooked foods or by having a small shop at the front of the house (*warung*). Because of its location close to the commercial center of Bandar Lampung, Pasir Gintung is a sought-after area for informal-sector workers, and family and neighborhood social ties continue to be the main way through which people gain access to work in the area. In FGDs, the area was described as 'a little Jakarta', reflecting the possibility of economic opportunity afforded here. There has been a direct impact of dangerous flash floods on livelihood security in Pasir Gintung for some members of the community. According to survey responses, several households had sustained damage to their *warung* (small shops) because of the flash floods, meaning they had lost stock and had to rebuild portions of their property. However, for this community, dealing with floods is a risk worth taking because of the advantages of living close to the commercial hub of the city and reducing travel costs, which as the preceding section has suggested, is an important consideration in a city with limited public transport infrastructure.

In the other study areas, the precariousness of casual employment is worsened during floods, which at certain times of the year can have an acutely damaging impact on household livelihoods. First, this is due to having to take time off to clean up, as suggested by survey participants in Kangkung, for example, who regularly experience floods associated with heavy rain and high tides, limiting their availability as laborers at the fish market or on fishing boats. Second, floods restrict peoples' ability to maintain the connections needed to acquire work. In Kota Karang, focus group participants said most work was acquired on a daily basis, requiring the maintenance of social networks linking neighborhood and workplace. Finding work in other parts of the city was more difficult because of limited social ties. It was also noted as being expensive and time-consuming as travel costs and income lost to travel time needed to be factored in to overall costs. Finally, where people did need to commute to workplaces further afield, regular surface flooding added to the difficulties of crossing an already-congested city with limited public transportation. The impact of floods on everyday mobility is a critical issue for all residents of the city, but particularly for those on relatively low incomes who are unable to afford vehicles capable of safely traversing the flooded city.[9] Responding to this, one dealership in Bandar Lampung is marketing the 'Honda-Beat-Flood' motorcycle, which is designed for driving through floods (Saibumi.com, 2015). This is thus one of the reasons why people continue to live in otherwise 'risky' flood-prone areas in the downtown area of Pasir Gintung and the port and warehouse areas of Kangkung and Kota Karang, in an effort to avoid livelihood vulnerability, but being exposed in turn to geographical vulnerability.

Turning to vulnerabilities relating to security of tenure, while these are long-established communities created through historical migration flows, ongoing work is required by those on low incomes to maintain a 'space' in parts of the city that afford the benefits of localized kinship networks and access to employment opportunities. Studies from elsewhere have highlighted the contribution that insecure land tenure makes to vulnerability in the context of urban environmental hazards, such as floods (UN-HABITAT, 2010; Baker, 2012). Voorst and Hellman's (2015) study of flood responses in riverside settlements in Jakarta highlights the very specific issues evident in 'illegal' settlements where severe flooding is a regular occurrence. However, in the three communities studied here, the question of legality was somewhat ambiguous. Few households in any of the three study sites are in possession of official certification for their housing, and instead, hold a letter of recognition (*surat keterangan*), which has been issued by the community leadership. This is a form of tenure that is recognized by the community, but not formally recognized by the state. Thus, rather than there being a clear-cut distinction between legal and extralegal forms of tenure in the communities, there exists instead a continuum of formal and informal tenure rights (Reerink and Van Gelder, 2010).

The right to space in this form is akin to what von Benda-Beckmann et al. (2006) refer to as a bundle of rights, which includes the right to reside over time, to construct and to be present in a particular space. Forms of mutual recognition in claiming space range from physical edifices, land-tax receipts and the maintenance of particular sets of relationships (with different government agencies, with community leaders). For example, in Kangkung, even the government building that houses the urban village administrative leader's office (*kantor kelurahan*) does not have official tenure. As Nurman and Lund have written with regard to urban tenure in Bandung, West Java, 'security and certainty of tenure are less a question of right and wrong, and more one of actively building a contextually persuasive argument and of establishing as many relations of effective recognition by significant institutions as possible' (Nurman and Lund, 2016: 48). In the study sites, these relations of recognition are more readily realized through kinship and neighborhood linkages that relate in turn to a sense of common migration history expressed in the built environment, as well as in participation in neighborhood associations (examined in a later section).

In Kota Karang, most people regard themselves as rightful owners of their properties, and the neighborhood is not regarded as a 'squatter area' by residents themselves.[10] Over time, people have built wooden elevated houses in areas flanking the river and coast. These traditional houses, known as *rumah panggung*, are familiar in coastal areas across Indonesia, particularly in Bugis communities, and are designed especially for living on the edge of the sea, with the ground level used as a storage space for fishing gear. Relations of recognition are clear in the levels of state social provision that exist in the area. This includes the provision of physical infrastructure, for example, in the construction of flood defenses and dredging of the river to prevent the banks from being breached.[11] It is also evident in 'soft' forms such as, for example, the provision of a regular family clinic, but also, importantly, in peoples' inclusion in the electoral roll. When there was a proposal to relocate households from flood-prone areas of Kota Karang as part of a plan to create a 'waterfront city' in Bandar Lampung, a successful protest and lobbying effort enabled people to stay put.[12] However, as was expressed in FGDs and through the survey, people living in traditional houses on the edge of the river did not want to be moved because there was nowhere in the new houses for them to store their fishing equipment and the units were too small to accommodate the very large families most fishermen have. Subsequently, a new mayor took office, whose approach to city management was considered to be more inclusive. The program was halted on the grounds of being too expensive and because it was unpopular with the electorate in areas from which people were to be evicted.

In Pasir Gintung there has been a similar if slightly more ruptured process of incremental recognition as the area has become established. Much of Pasir Gintung is located on land 'belonging' to the railway company. The status of this kind of land is very unclear in Indonesia. Following independence, railway property established by colonial authorities became '*tanah negara*', or state land. However, privatization of Indonesia's railways meant the land was ceded to the railway company. However, according to KIs and also from the FGD in Pasir Gintung, the community is on *tanah adat* (customary land of the original Lampung clans). Describing a similar case in Bandung, Indonesia, Nurman and Lund write, 'who held the rights to the land was far from a settled fact; it became a fact to settle' (Nurman and Lund, 2016: 49). There are ongoing disputes with regard to tenure, and in recent years, a public hospital won its case against the railway company enabling it to remain on the site. Acceptance of this legal ambiguity in the area appears to be widespread, with some investment in flood management by local government to protect houses that seemingly have no tenure. The community itself has established its 'recognition' through community-level flood adaptations including construction of walls to protect housing areas, the creation of a community garbage collection and clearing service and the establishment of a warning system: a loudspeaker from the mosque warns of the immediate prospect of a flash flood so people have time to prepare and get to safety.

One of the biggest challenges in both Kangkung and Pasir Gintung is how to 'create space' for second- and third-generation households, as both areas have acute land shortages and are highly sought after because of their proximity to work opportunities. 'Creating space' has thus led people to inhabit ostensibly risky spaces, and it is therefore among this group that the combination of urban environmental hazards and informal tenure security leads to particular forms of precarity. In Pasir Gintung, overcrowding, as well as a desire to avoid the flash floods in the lower elevations of the neighborhood, has meant people have begun to build on steeply sloping land to the west of the Way Awi River. This land is regarded as customary land (*tanah adat*) by local Lampung people, and the right to inhabit is the outcome of negotiation between the people of Pasir Gintung and *adat* (customary) leaders. While this area affords the advantages of being close to livelihood opportunities, landslides are commonplace, damaging property and risking lives. In the coastal community of Kangkung, a land shortage has led people to attempt to reclaim land from the sea, by building low walls that are then infilled with waste to create 'land' on which simple wooden houses can be built. Although there is no formal recognition of tenure on this reclaimed land, those living here have been able to mobilize the kinds of relations needed for tacit recognition, which includes access to government resources (including social safety-net payments), and thus a perception that the current city mayor is unlikely to relocate them.

In contending with floods, those residing in the three study communities are being squeezed, on the one hand, by urban development, limited work opportunities, traffic congestion and poor infrastructure and, on the other, by the impacts of flood events. In each case, a trade-off is made between exposure to flooding and the livelihood advantages afforded by each of these localities in a context where commuting is expensive, time-consuming and frequently disrupted by surface water flooding. While limited security of tenure contributes to overall vulnerability, the complexities of tenure arrangements in these areas of Bandar Lampung, which is similar to other cities in Indonesia, provide an opportunity to secure 'space' through relations of recognition. To some degree, material adaptations to floods are one way in which recognition of entitlement is being signaled. with informal-sector jobs. The next section of this chapter considers the role social networks play in this regard, including those relating to migration-related solidarity and lines of patronage through which people access support and assistance after flood events.

Ethnic and migrant networks in dealing with flood hazards

Within communities created through historical migrations, social networks are significant in two related ways: first, through extralocal ties that connect urban communities with the places from which people (or their forebears) originated, and second, through more localized networks through which people can mobilize material support in the face of floods or other livelihood shocks and stresses. In a multicultural city such as Bandar Lampung, historical migrations have a hand in shaping both kinds of networks, and in lending them an ethnic dimension. For example, in Kota Karang, more than half the community has family origins in South Sulawesi, and these connections are still evident in terms of how people identify (as Bugis), and how they relate to others, including decision makers, within the community.

Other studies have demonstrated how extralocal ties may play a role in helping households mitigate vulnerabilities, by spreading labor across a number of sites, or in mobilizing resources (financial capital, social capital) from different geographical locations (Rigg, 2012). During Indonesia's economic crisis, these kinds of extralocal networks were important in low-income communities when dealing with financial insecurities and job losses (Silvey and Elmhirst, 2003). In the study areas, however, the extent to which extralocal ties could be mobilized for dealing with floods was very context specific. In Kangkung, for example, Banten respondents described the connections they maintained with relatives back in Banten province in Java as important – during Idul Fitri at the end of Ramadan, many people return to their areas of origin to visit family, and they sometimes return to the city with relatives looking for work as fishermen. At the same time, many families sent their children back to Banten to be educated in *pesantren* in Java, making use of kinship networks to do this (and thus altering the dependency ratio of children to adults in their households).[13] In addition, some households included family members working overseas as migrant workers in the Middle East (in construction, as domestic workers), but there was limited evidence of this having a financial impact on flood responses. Family ties were important for maintaining morale during and following floods, but there was limited prospect of relatives providing material help 'because they are even poorer than we are'.[14] During floods, people were more inclined to look to close relatives and neighbors for help.

A similar pattern is found in Kota Karang, where the community maintains links to places of origin; in this instance, for Bugis people the connection is with Bone and other areas in South Sulawesi. Although the distances and cost of travel are much greater for Bugis people than for those originating in Banten, there is still a tendency for even very low-income people to make the journey back to Bone for Idul Fitri. Solidarity networks are more visible in this community through the Kesatuan Keluarga Sulawesi Selatan, a family-ties organization akin to a hometown association, which facilitates annual visits back to Sulawesi, and which offers social solidarity if there is a death in the family. KIs noted that this organization also provides social support and solidarity in response to flood impacts, and during the last serious flood, it organized a group visit (from Sulawesi to Kota Karang) to inspect the damage and provide social attention and support: an informal means of empowerment and 'visibilization' of the community.

A different formation of extralocal ties is found in Pasir Gintung, which relates to the migration history of the families residing in this area. Almost all the residents surveyed originated from Java, including areas such as Banten, West Java and East Java, but many had also come from rural areas in Lampung province to which their families and forebears had moved as part of the Indonesian government's transmigration resettlement program. According to responses in FGDs, there is limited migration between the city and areas of origin, but, as was the case with the other areas, people retained a connection with their home area, to which they returned during Idul Fitri. However, in survey responses, it emerged that a number of households did maintain strong rural connections with other parts of rural Lampung, generally in the form of land ownership. In one case, for example, the family had planted a small plot of rubber in the area from which they originated. It was guarded and cared for by a family member, and treated as a 'pension investment'. Thus, as a multilocal livelihood strategy, this represented an effort to mitigate vulnerability across the life course, rather than a strategy specifically for coping with floods.

More localized networks of support are evident within the communities. These include both horizontal forms of social capital (access to support and assistance from neighbors and others in a similar socioeconomic bracket) and vertical forms of social capital (more hierarchical access to formal kinds of support, assistance and compensatory payments, usually from government bodies, and some from politicians for electoral reasons). In each of the communities, these two forms of social capital converge around the role of the leader of the neighborhood association, the *Kepala Rukun Tetangga* (*Kepala RT* hereafter). This is the lowest tier of the state governance hierarchy – each urban village (*kelurahan*) comprises a number of *Rukun Tetangga* (RT), or neighborhoods. During the Soeharto era, the RT was part of a hierarchical system to surveil and control populations, and to transmit messages from government at regular meetings. As democratization has progressed in Indonesia, this has altered somewhat in that the head of the *Kepala RT* is locally elected, but many top-down functions remain (Kurasawa, 2009).

In the study communities, the *Kepala RT* was seen as being closer to people than the urban village head (*Lurah*) and for that reason played an important gate-keeping role in communications and actions relating to flood relief, including assessing access to state resources of various kinds. In addition, the *Kepala RT* acts as a kind of 'broker' for communicating community needs back to local government (and, it should be stressed, to nongovernmental organizations). The kinds of state 'resources' that are relevant in this context include social safety net payments such as the RASKIN program (Beras Untuk Orang Miskin, or Rice for the Poor), a program through which people qualify for a monthly allocation of 15 kilograms of subsidized rice. Observation and interview data in each of the study sites suggest that success in lobbying the *Lurah* (head of the urban village neighborhood) and the *Kepala RT* (head of the neighborhood association) depends on 'closeness' and being able to enact clientelist connections, many of which were more secure when there was a coincidence of family place of origin between the claimant and the village hierarchy. The *Lurah* and *Kepala RT* thus wield considerable influence at the community level in defining who has access to official safety nets and to disaster funds.

Qualification is based on poverty definitions as used in the SUSENAS survey (as referred to on page 154), and this is assessed in part by the *Kepala RT*. Payment is based on having an identity card, for which people qualify after 6 months in residence, and again this decision rests with the *Lurah* in consultation with the *Kepala RT*. In Kota Karang, for example, officially, about 75 percent qualify for RASKIN, but what was decided in the *kelurahan* was to provide RASKIN to all but 5 percent of the population, and to just divide the rice into 7 kilograms per family, rather than the usual 15 kilograms, the idea being to make it go further. In addition, the Bandar Lampung city government has a program that people can access to help them to repair their houses if damaged by the flooding. This ranges from 500,000 Rp to 1,500,000 Rp, and 20 million Rp if there is serious damage.[15] Accessing flood assistance is brokered through the *Kepala RT*. In all three communities, the neighborhood association head (*Kepala RT*) compiled a list of who had been affected, and this was then reported to the higher-tiered head of the urban village (i.e. the *Lurah*). In Kangkung, following the floods last year, each person that was victim of floods received 500,000 Rp (approximately US$38) to help him or her restore belongings. Reports from the *Kepala RT* (neighborhood association head) established which houses were affected and how they would receive money.

In other words, the most important vertical social capital is via the head of the RT (i.e. the *Kepala RT*) – through this conduit people can access resources. In terms of how relationships between the head of the RT and the community relate to migration and ethnicity, across both horizontal and vertical forms of social capital, there is a strong sense of social embeddedness of patronage networks, as these are based around a sense of common origin and, by extension, ethnicity. In Pasir Gintung, the *Lurah* (head of the neighborhood village) was very active in mobilizing the community, but even here, the head of the RT was called upon to list those affected by floods and also to distribute any aid. There was therefore the potential for exclusion of people who didn't feel 'close' to the *Kepala RT* or *Lurah*. In effect, ethnicity-inflected patron-client connections operate at these very close scales (e.g. the neighborhood/RT) where the role of the RT *de facto* governed access to resources of various kinds, including flood assistance. It is at this scale that the politics of the flood-migration nexus is revealed, yet this is a scale that is generally below the radar in city government or NGO initiatives. RT leaders, through their everyday practices, take on a role as 'brokers', and this can lead to some inadvertent exclusions where certain members of a minority community may feel distant from the RT leader themselves. In sum, historical migrations and related social networks have sedimented a political geography at neighborhood level 'which combines themes of "traditional," family-like ethnic or religious community with modern techniques of mobilization as well as an interest in capturing the institutions of the state' (Van Klinken, 2009: 881) – in this instance, actualizing the political capital needed to access state assistance including flood relief and social safety-net payments.

Conclusion: historical migrations and contemporary vulnerabilities

As one of Indonesia's most multicultural medium-sized cities, Bandar Lampung is made through the layering of historical migrations. This chapter has suggested that the significance of these migrations continues to resonate through the city's social geography in ways that need to be taken into account when considering how to address the city's flood problems. As highlighted in Chapter 1, a political ecology lens enables attention to be centered on the processes and structures that give rise to and shape aspects of vulnerability and capability, and in this chapter, migration itself forms part of that generative social landscape in a number of important and perhaps surprising ways.

First, the migrants who first settled in and around Bandar Lampung (and indeed those that continue to arrive) have themselves been displaced by political, economic and environmental shocks and stresses in other parts of the archipelago, often related to wider processes of accumulation, dispossession and political conflict that make *in situ* livelihoods untenable. However, the contribution of in-migration to urban landscape change is relatively small compared to the broader impacts of marketization, investment and new consumption practices that underpin the growth of shopping malls, urban middle-class housing and traffic jams. Precarious employment opportunities, infrastructure failures and limited space for housing close to commercial centers make the city potentially 'risky' for those on low incomes. Thus, simple causal connections that could blame migration for creating the circumstances in which flooding has become more commonplace are misplaced in this context.

Second, historical migrations have led to ethnic diversity at very close scales, with particular groups clustering in specific neighborhoods, and this continues to be the case as social networks play a key role in enabling the urban poor to access jobs and for second- and third-generation migrants to access living space in the city that is close to where those jobs are located. What is evident is a complex interplay between different kinds of migration (migration to settle in particular parts of the city, a need for localized forms of mobility in order to access employment) and different kinds of floods (e.g. seasonal, large-scale inundations and flash floods that damage property, and the more regular surface flooding that disrupts daily commutes). In this context, 'making space' becomes an important strategy for people who need to live as close to employment opportunities as they can, even where this means living in places that expose them to floods.

Third, historical migrations and the social networks that these have given rise to are significant in the work people must do to 'make space', through the establishment and maintenance of informal tenure security. Networks are drawn on as people establish as many relations of recognition by significant institutions as they can, including representatives of government at localized scales (the *Lurah*, the *Kepala RT*). Everyday flood prevention measures are a concrete expression of this, seen in the investments people make in modifying their houses, and, at community level, in introducing warning systems and other flood management interventions (such as the embankment and desiltation project of the Way Awi in Pasir Gintung). Confirmation of 'recognition' is also found in the flood defenses provided by the city government.

Finally, the intersection of historical migration, kin networks and clientelism at very localized scales – in terms of recognition and qualification for social support, including postflood assistance – is illustrative of a need to consider how migration and ethnicity shape not only the contours of everyday precarious livelihoods in Bandar Lampung but also the political capital that people are able to actualize within their neighborhoods in order to attract formal assistance of various kinds.

For policy makers, there is a need for a more nuanced appreciation of the somewhat subtle ways in which past migrations remain significant in shaping vulnerability and in defining contemporary access to resources, often at very localized scales. This would be an important step in ensuring a just approach to addressing the causes and consequences of the frequent flooding that blights this rapidly changing city.

Acknowledgments

Surveys and FGDs were undertaken by Meli Anwar, Sari Indah Oktanti Sembiring, Alwansyah, M Adie Syaputra, Martaria Putri, Novianti and Nur Umi Peliawati, staff and students from the Faculty of Social and Political Science, University of Lampung (UNILA), Indonesia. We offer our thanks to all the communities for their participation in the study. We are grateful to Arizka Warganegara for his valuable inputs into this study, and to Carl Middleton for extensive comments on an earlier draft. All remaining errors rest with the authors.

Notes

1 Based on comments made in FGDs in all three communities, September 2013.
2 The city of Bandar Lampung is split into administrative subdistricts (*kecamatan*), which in turn are composed of a number of urban villages (*kelurahan*). While the city is led by a mayor (*Walikota*) who is directly elected by popular vote, each level in the hierarchy below are led by civil servants (*Camat* and *Lurah*, respectively).
3 'Precarity' is used here rather than vulnerability in that the term 'explicitly incorporates the political and institutional context in which the production of precarity occurs rather than focusing solely on individualized experiences of precarity' (Waite, 2009: 221).
4 The area under housing expanded by 44 percent in the decade from 1999 to 2010 (BPS, 2015). Most land conversion is on agricultural land, including former plantations (which was reduced by 1,500 hectares in this period). Very rapid change, albeit on much smaller areas, was seen for forests, which decreased by 32 percent between 1999 and 2010, and for marshy areas, which decreased by 43 percent. Conversion of forests and marshes has implications for managing the city's hydrology, and specifically flooding.
5 Interview with Handri Kurniawan, Member of Parliament of Bandar Lampung City, Member of Budgetary Board of Bandar Lampung House of Representatives, Member of Committee Responsible for Infrastructure, Bandar Lampung House of Representatives, October 2013.
6 Survey responses for Kota Karang, Pasir Gintung and Kangkung, September 2013; FGDs, August 2013.
7 Survey responses for Kota Karang, Pasir Gintung and Kangkung, September 2013.
8 KI interviews in all three areas, August 2013; FGDs, August 2013.
9 All data in this section are from FGDs, August 2013.
10 FGDs in Kota Karang, August 2013.
11 In Kota Karang this includes work by the public works division, which is aimed at protecting the city more widely, rather than just Kota Karang. Flood defenses include improved river embankments and strengthened sea defenses. At the household level, the city mayor's office has installed floodwater gates to prevent floodwater from getting into houses and causing excessive damage.
12 KI interview, Kota Karang, August 2013.
13 *Pesantren* or *pondok pesantren* are Islamic boarding schools that provide dormitory living at a very low cost for students. It is relatively common for those on low incomes to send children to be educated in these kinds of institutions.
14 FGD, Kangkung August 2013.
15 Five hundred thousand Rp is the equivalent to around US$38 at the time of the research.

References

ACCCRN. (2010). *Climate change vulnerability assessment of Bandar Lampung city*. Jakarta: Asian Cities Climate Change Resilience Network and Climate Change Working Group of Bandar Lampung City. www.acccrn.net/resources/climate-change-vulnerability-assessment-bandar-lampung-city [last accessed 2/04/17].

Acciaioli, G. (2007). "Legacy of conflict." *Inside Indonesia* 82 (April–June). www.inside indonesia.org/legacy-of-conflict [last accessed 21/04/17].

Aspinall, E. (2011). "Democratization and ethnic politics in Indonesia: Nine theses." *Journal of East Asian Studies* 11: 289–319.

Baker, J. (2012). *Climate change, disaster risk and the urban poor: Cities building resilience for a changing world.* Washington, DC: World Bank.

BAPPEDA Kota Bandar Lampung. (2011). *Rencana Tata Ruang Wilayah Tahun 2011– 2030. (Spatial Plan City of Bandar Lampung 2011–2030).* Bandar Lampung: Badan Perencana Pembangunan Daerah (Regional Body for Planning and Development). http://bappeda-bandarlampung.org [last accessed 2/04/17].

BAPPENAS. (2014). *National action plan on climate change adaptation.* Jakarta: BAPPENAS (Badan Perencanaan Pembangunan Nasional), Republic of Indonesia.

BAPPENAS and ICCSR. (2010). *Analysis and projection of sea level rise and extreme weather events.* Jakarta: ICCSR (The Indonesia Climate Change Sectoral Roadmap) *and* BAPPENAS (Badan Perencanaan Pembangunan Nasional), Republic of Indonesia. www.bappenas.go.id/files/2013/5229/9917/analysis-and-projection-of-sea-level-rise-and-extreme-weathe__20110217130224__1.pdf [last accessed 2/04/17].

BPBD. (2013). *Profil BPBD (Badan Penganggulangan Bencana Daerah).* http://bpbd.lampungprov.go.id/ [last accessed 2/10/13].

BPS. (2015). *Lampung Dalam Angka (Lampung in Figures).* Bandar Lampung: Badan Pusat Statistik Lampung. https://lampung.bps.go.id/website/pdf_publikasi/Provinsi-Lampung-Dalam-Angka-2016.pdf [last accessed 2/04/17].

Brown, A., Dayal, A., and Rumbaitis Del Rio, C. (2012). "From practice to theory: Emerging lessons from Asia for building urban climate change resilience." *Environment and Urbanization* 24(2): 531–556.

Carpenter, J.P., Daniere, A.G., and Takahashi, L.M. (2004). "Cooperation, trust, and social capital in Southeast Asian urban slums." *Journal of Economic Behavior &; Organization* 55(4): 533–551.

De Haas, H. (2012). "The migration and development pendulum: A critical view on research and policy." *International Migration* 50(3): 8–25.

Elmhirst, R. (2012). "Displacement, resettlement, and multi-local livelihoods: Positioning migrant legitimacy in Lampung, Indonesia." *Critical Asian Studies* 44(1): 131–152.

Firman, T. (2004). "Demographic and spatial patterns of Indonesia's recent urbanisation." *Population, Space and Place* 10(6): 421–434.

Friend, R., Jarvie, J., Reed, S.O., Sutarto, R., Thinphanga, P., and Toan, V.C. (2014). "Mainstreaming urban climate resilience into policy and planning: Reflections from Asia." *Urban Climate* 7: 6–19.

Kurasawa, A. (2009). "Swaying between state and community: The role and function of RT/RW in Post-Suharto Indonesia." (pp. 58–83) in Read, B.L. and Pekkanen, R. (eds.) *Local organizations and urban governance in East and Southeast Asia: Straddling state and society.* London: Routledge.

Lassa, J.A., and Nugraha, E. (2015). "From shared learning to shared action in building resilience in the city of Bandar Lampung, Indonesia." *Environment and Urbanization* 27(1): 161–180.

Malik, I.B. (2013). "Public transportation crisis in Bandar Lampung." *International Journal of Engineering and Technology Development* 1(3): 78–83.

Massey, D. (1994). *A global sense of place: Space, place and gender.* Minneapolis: University of Minnesota Press.

Nurman, A., and Lund, C. (2016). "On track: Spontaneous privatization of public urban land in Bandung, Indonesia." *South East Asia Research* 24(1): 41–60.

Reerink, G., and van Gelder, J.L. (2010). "Land titling, perceived tenure security, and housing consolidation in the kampongs of Bandung, Indonesia." *Habitat International* 34(1): 78–85.

Ribot, J.C. (2014). "Cause and response: Vulnerability and climate in the Anthropocene." *The Journal of Peasant Studies* 41(5): 667–705.

Rigg, J. (2012). *Unplanned development: Tracking change in South-East Asia*. London: Zed Books.

Saibumi.com. (2015). "Honda beat flood demo Serentak di Seluruh Lampung [Honda Beat flood demo simultaneously across Lampung]." *Saibumi.com*, 19 December 2015. www.saibumi.com/artikel-71104-honda-beat-flood-demo-serentak-di-seluruh-lampung.html [last accessed 20/04/2017].

Schulte Nordholdt, H. (2008). "Identity politics, citizenship and the soft state in Indonesia: An essay." *Journal of Indonesian Social Sciences and Humanities* 1: 1–21.

Sevin, O. (1989). "Lampung: history and population." (pp. 13–124) in Pain, M., Benoit, D., Levang, P., and Sevin, O. (eds.) *Transmigration and spontaneous migrations in Lampung*. Bondy, France: ORSTOM.

Silvey, R., and Elmhirst, R. (2003). "Engendering social capital: Women workers and rural – urban networks in Indonesia's crisis." *World development* 31(5): 865–879.

Tacoli, C. (2009). "Crisis or adaptation? Migration and climate change in a context of high mobility." *Environment and Urbanization* 21(2): 513–525.

Tacoli, C., McGranahan, G., and Satterthwaite, D. (2015). *Urbanization, rural – Urban migration and urban poverty*. IIED Working Paper. London: IIED. http://pubs.iied.org/10725IIED.

UN-HABITAT. (2010). *State of the world's cities 2010/11: Bridging the urban divide*. Nairobi: United Nations Human Settlements Program (UN-HABITAT).

Utoyo, B. (2015). "Manajemen pemamfaatan ruang kota: studi tentang dinamika penggunaan lahan dan pertumbuhan ekonomi di kota Bandar Lampung [The city utilization management: Case study of land use dynamics and economic growth in Bandar Lampung city]." *Spirit Publik* 10(2): 153–170.

Van Klinken, G. (2009). "Decolonization and the making of middle Indonesia." *Urban Geography* 30(9): 879–897.

von Benda-Beckmann, K., von Benda-Beckmann, F., and Wiber, M.G. (2006). "The properties of property." (pp. 1–39) in von Benda-Beckmann, F., von Benda-Beckmann, K., and Wiber, M.G. (eds.) *Changing properties of property*. New York: Berghahn Books.

Voorst, R.S. van., and Hellman, J. (2015). "One risk replaces another: Floods, evictions and policies on Jakarta's riverbanks." *Asian Journal of Social Science* 43(6): 786–810.

Waite, L. (2009). "A place and space for a critical geography of precarity?" *Geography Compass* 3(1): 412–433.

9 Vulnerabilities of local people and migrants due to flooding in Malaysia

Identifying gaps for better management

Mohammad Imam Hasan Reza, Er Ah Choy and Joy Jacqueline Pereira

Introduction

Malaysia has experienced several major floods and the intensity and frequency have increased over the past 2 decades. It has been observed that the occurrence of floods has become a yearly event since 1963 (DID, 2009). These floods are common hydrological phenomena in Malaysia affecting, on average, an area of 29,000 square kilometers, more than 4.82 million people (22 percent of the population) and inflicting annual damage of 915 million RM (DID, 2009). Flooding in Malaysia includes both riverine flooding and coastal flooding (Billa et al., 2006). Coastal areas and river basins are particularly susceptible to flood disaster due to their location and also the fact that vulnerable populations reside in these frequently affected regions. Many of these people do not have the financial capital to change their habitat to safer areas. Both urban and rural flooding has posed a serious threat to human livelihood (Mohammed et al., 2011). For example, in 1996, severe floods forced rural Malaysians and unskilled laborers from across the region into the country's booming city center in search of work. On arrival, it was impossible for displaced people to find affordable housing and better livelihoods on their limited, hard-earned pay. Therefore, one type of vulnerability was exchanged for another.

The floods that occurred in December 2006 and January 2007 in the state of Johor, a southern state of peninsular Malaysia, were particularly devastating, with an estimated total loss in terms of monetary value of 1.5 billion RM (around US$456 million) (Badrul et al., 2010). This was considered as the most devastating flood in terms of monetary loss in Malaysian history. In the state of Johor, one of the worst affected areas was Segamat district, where there was substantial loss of lives and property (NSC, 2011). More recently, in January 2011, severe flooding occurred in Segamat and other parts of upstate Johor and the neighboring state of Melaka, where 31,000 people were rescued from their flooded homes and where several people died. This flood displaced around 110,000 people who had to be sheltered in relief centers. A number of people also migrated to the urban areas to avoid suffering in the future (Reza and Alatas, 2013).

A hidden aspect of the flooding has been its impact on migrant populations that are resident in Johor. Malaysia's urban and industrial areas have become a destination of extremely mobile populations originating from other parts of the country, as well as from abroad. Migrant populations include many citizens of neighboring countries who are attracted by opportunities associated with Malaysia's economic prosperity and rapid economic growth over recent decades (UNDP, 2009). The UNDP (2009) report shows that, contrary to the popular public perception, migration can and has been a positive force for human development, improving opportunities for income, education and health care for the world's one billion migrants. Mobility is termed a basic element of freedom, bringing with it improved opportunities for work, education, political rights, safety and health care to migrants. Besides, migration brings large gains for source communities and countries, as well as destination countries, such as Malaysia, in terms of regional economic and sociopolitical development. However, it remains the case that in many destination countries, including Malaysia, migrants face particular forms of vulnerability when compared to the local population, by virtue of their status as 'migrants' or 'outsiders', and the lack of citizen rights that this often entails.

In relation to the impact of extreme events such as flooding, the study of the experiences and vulnerabilities of migrant populations is important in order to ensure that they are not disadvantaged, and in order to identify and classify different types of vulnerabilities that policy initiatives may need to address. Considering the aforementioned aspects, this chapter focuses on different village communities of the Segamat district to examine the experience of floods and to identify different types of vulnerabilities faced by migrants and local people. It will also discuss the nature and cause of these floods. National policy initiatives for reducing vulnerabilities of flood-affected communities will also be discussed so as to identify gaps in policy and to facilitate future attempts for better management, with migrants in mind.

Although some studies have assessed the vulnerabilities of people who have been affected due to these floods, particularly in the state of Johor (Chan, 2006; Shafie, 2009), most of these studies were confined to examining socioeconomic impact assessment, livelihood change, public health preparedness or the performance assessment of disaster management viewpoints (Billa et al., 2006; Sulaiman, 2007; O'Arabayah et al., 2008). However, no such study exists that considers the factors underlying the experiences, sufferings and vulnerabilities of either the flood-affected local people or migrants, or that draws a comparison of the experiences of these two population groups. Malaysia hosts a significant number of migrants, with foreign labor making up 21 percent of the Malaysian labor force (MOF, 2010). The Malaysian Department of Immigration estimates the number of undocumented migrants may account for nearly 1.8 million of the labor force. Overall, there is a dependence on foreign migrants for meeting labor demand and maintaining economic growth. As migrants are identified as one of the stakeholder groups in the United Nations' Sendai Framework for Disaster Risk Reduction 2015–2030, there is an onus on the Malaysian government to incorporate international migrants in its disaster planning, given the role this group may play in building the overall resilience of communities that experience flooding.[1] Therefore, the purpose of this chapter is to identify the types of vulnerabilities of people living in communities that experience flooding and to identify whether these vulnerabilities having a relationship with migration. The relationship and contribution of policy to these aspects will also be discussed.

The policy context

The National Security Council of the Prime Minister's Department is the coordinating agency for disaster management in the country. The primary policy instrument is Directive 20 on Policy and Mechanism for National Disaster Management approved by the Cabinet of Malaysia on 18 May 1994 (NSC, 2001). The directive provides guidance on the mechanisms, roles and responsibilities of government agencies in supporting the National Security Council to address disaster management. The directive is strengthened by standard operating procedures specific to the type of disasters that are common in the country such as floods, open burning, forest fires, haze and industrial disasters.

Disaster management is coordinated via disaster management and support committees at three levels (i.e. federal, state and district levels). At the federal level, the committee is chaired by a minister appointed by the prime minister with membership comprising 37 heads of federal agencies. At the state level, the committee is chaired by the state secretary, drawing on the support of some 24 state agencies. At the district levels, the committee is chaired by district officers or mayors, where relevant. The committee is supported by 20 relevant state and local agencies, as well as village heads of the respective districts. There are three degrees of disasters depending on severity and resource requirements. The lowest degree of disaster is handled by the district officers or mayors and the most severe by the minister at the federal level.

The Segamat district consists of 11 subdistricts and some 184 villages. There are 132 flood relief centers to cater to flood victims in the district. The standard operating procedure for floods is documented in the "Guidelines for Management and Disaster Relief (Floods) 2012/2013" (NSC, 2001). The Guidelines delineate the responsibilities of government agencies and village heads involved in managing flood disasters under the leadership of the district officer. The guidelines also list the names and contact details of all individual officers (regardless their race, ethnicity and religion), including the village heads, to facilitate communication during a disaster. The number of potential victims in each subdistrict, as well as facilities for relief operations such as the supply shops, equipment, vehicles, boats and other logistical aspects, is also listed in the document.

The migration context

Southeast Asia is a major hub for migration in the world, where almost 36 million people participate in intra-Asian migration. Among the different countries in

Southeast Asia, Malaysia has been experiencing rapid economic growth over the past few decades, becoming one of the fastest growing economies in the world. The increasing trends of urbanization are characterized by the rapid growth of cities, townships and conurbations that attract people from many different parts or states of Malaysia, as well as from many countries of developing Asia, particularly from the Southeast Asian nations.

Malaysia participates in two regional processes – the Bali Process and the Colombo Process – for which IOM serves as the secretariat. The Bali Process is a regional cooperation mechanism to combat people smuggling and trafficking in persons and related transnational crime. Malaysia has been a member since its launch in 2002. Malaysia also participates in the Colombo Process on the Management of Overseas Employment and Contractual Labour for Countries of Origin in Asia, as a labor-receiving country. In 2008, with 19 other countries, it signed the Abu Dhabi Declaration on Overseas Employment and Contractual Labour for Countries of Origin and Destination in Asia. Malaysian officials also regularly participate in a variety of migration-management training workshops that IOM organizes in the region and beyond.

The minister in the Prime Minister's Department of Malaysia who is responsible for migration, Tan Sri Nor Mohamed bin Yakcop, said,

> Migration has the potential to enhance economic development- both for source and destination countries and regions. Thus, policies need to be developed and adapted over time, to ensure that it continues to be mutually beneficial and in line with the evolving development needs of the economy.
> (UNDP, 2009)

In Malaysia, there are two types of migrant populations, internal migrants and international migrants (Migration Survey Malaysia, 2011). Historically, internal migration in Malaysia has been characterized as migration from rural areas to urban centers. Migration also occurs from the less developed areas or states to more developed areas or states (Jali, 2009). People migrate predominately to follow their family; to seek out better employment or career prospects; to move to a better environment; and for education opportunities, marriage and divorce (Department of Statistics, 2011). Wars, human rights violations, civil wars, environmental disasters, extreme drought or flood, nuclear disaster, earthquakes and tsunamis are recognized as factors contributing to migration (Idris, 2012). In the case of Malaysia, international migrants basically migrated to Malaysia for better livelihood, education and economic solvency. Hence, most of the migrant population comprises workers (Kaur, 2008). Table 9.1 shows the types and distribution of the migrant population in Malaysia between the periods 2009–2010 and 2010–2011.

Rapid urbanization and industrialization have generated large-scale internal migration and international in-migration in Malaysia. Migration patterns for the period 2010–2011 showed that the population tends to migrate within the

Table 9.1 Key migration statistics in Malaysia, 2009–2010 and 2010–2011

Description	Year	
	2009–2010	2010–2011
Percentage distribution of population by migration status	(%)	(%)
Total	100.0	100.0
Migrants*	1.9	2.5
Intrastate migrants	58.4	59.0
Interstate migrants	26.3	27.8
International migrants	15.3	13.2
Nonmigrants	98.1	97.5
Number of internal migrants by migration status	('000)	('000)
Internal migrants	449.1	617.9
Intrastate migrants	309.5	419.8
Interstate migrants	139.6	198.1

*Excludes migrants from Malaysia to other countries
Source: Department of Statistics Malaysia, 2013

same state. The recent national migration survey found that about 90 percent of the total migrants were internal and the rest international migrants into Malaysia. The survey found that the predominant internal migration was within the state (61.3 percent), followed by interstate (28.5 percent), while the remaining (10.2 percent) are international migrants. The intrastate migration rate (i.e. rural to urban) increased by 2.3 percent, whereas the interstate (from less developed states to more developed states) migration rate increased by only 0.5 percent in the last 3 years (Department of Statistics Malaysia, 2013).

Segamat has a negative net migration rate (−3.8 per 1,000 population) due to a high out-migration rate. Segamat district has a typical population mix and representation of peninsular Malaysia. A study reports that the proportion of males of working age is lower at the district level (Migration Survey, Malaysia, 2011). This gap is then filled by the international migrant workers who are mostly male.

For the period 2010–2011, the migrated population in the 15–35 age group represented more than half of the total internal migrants at 59.9 percent. This is because these young, educated people move to the cities to find better jobs or better education; they are not interested in agricultural jobs of the sort found in rural Malaysia (Jali, 2009; Hew, 2003). The percentage of female internal migrants in this age group was slightly higher (i.e. 60.0 percent) compared to male internal migrants (39.7 percent). This age group is most likely to migrate either for higher education or for work. The participation of internal migrants in the labor market was found to be higher than that of the local people (Migration Survey, Malaysia, 2011). The survey identified that almost half of the internal migrants in Malaysia migrated because they were following their family members (41.8 percent), followed by developing careers (21.9 percent) and for joining a new job or seeking new opportunities (20.3 percent). Environmental factors also influenced the internal migrants for the period 2010–2011 by 21.3 percent.

Study area

Segamat is a town, one of the eight districts located in the north of the state of Johor in Malaysia, bordering two other states of Malaysia (Negeri Sembilan on the west and Pahang on the northeastern side). After the formation of Segamat district, the government began to develop Segamat, mainly with agricultural activities to boost the district economy. This included the construction of the national railroad system passing the town of Segamat and also the construction of the main road known today as Federal Route 1. In the 1970s, Tun Razak Highway was constructed to boost the economy of Segamat as an agricultural hub, to shorten the traveling time to Kuantan and to speed up the development progress of the poorly developed areas in southern Pahang. The Johor branch campus of Universiti Teknologi MARA (UiTM) was constructed at Jementah (a town in Segamat district) at the end of 1980s and started its operation in 1991. The construction of the UiTM campus in Segamat district turned the area into another important educational hub in Johor besides Universiti Teknologi Malaysia at Skudai near Singapore.

The population of Segamat district is about 189,820 (2010 census), which is 8.6 percent of the total population of the state of Johor. The total area is 282.534.5 hectares (2.825.4 square kilometers) (Segamat District Council, 2016).

Agriculture was the main contributor to the Segamat economy, and accounted for 61.8 percent of the total employment in 1991. The second economic contributor is the manufacturing sector, with 13.1 percent of the total workforce in 1995. This is followed by the government service sector, with 12.2 percent of the total workforce in the same year. The trading sector includes wholesale and retail trade; hotels and restaurants were the fourth major sector in terms of labor absorption, representing 8.2 percent of the total labor absorption in Segamat. This district has great potential to become one of the vital industrial zones in Johor based on its existing agricultural and manufacturing, as well as educational, infrastructures. However, at the present time, the service and manufacturing sectors have overtaken agriculture. In 2014, this district receives the highest allocation among the districts of the state of Johor for infrastructural development, as well as for flood disaster mitigation development activities. These opportunities attract many internal and international migrants seeking work in this area.

Geographically Segamat is a flat area and situated in the Segamat River basin, which is characterized by slightly undulating terrain and hills (see Figure 9.1). The Segamat area is also surrounded by rivers such as Sungai Muar, Sungai Genuang, Segamat, Bekok and Jelawih. Segamat experienced floods during the 1950s; 1984; and recently in 2006, 2007 and 2011. The flood of 2006–2007, which was caused by Typhoon Utor in the Philippines, was generally considered to be the worst on record in Segamat and in the state of Johor. There is a strong public perception that the 2006 flood was caused by improper release of water from the Bekok Dam located at the upstream of the rivers that flow through Segamat. It was established in 1990 as a component of the Western Johor Integrated Development Project and its primary function is to mitigate flood downstream. The perception is based

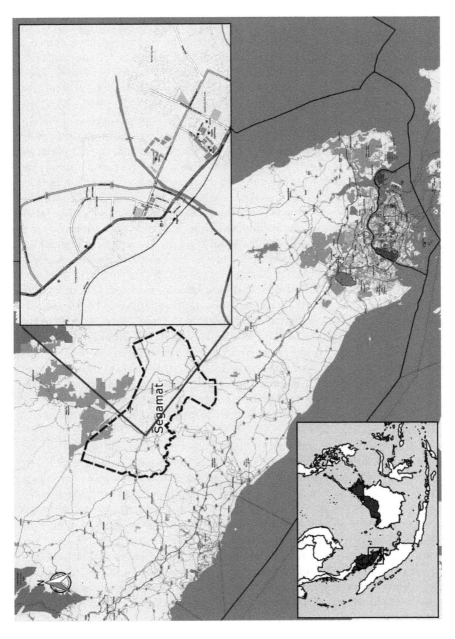

Figure 9.1 Location of Segamat in the state of Johor, Malaysia

on the fact that the water level of the Segamat River overflowed at a rate that was believed impossible to have been caused by rainwater only.

Methodology

Prior to data collection from the selected areas, the research team arranged a series of meetings with district administration, village leaders and also with different NGOs who have been engaged with community advancement and flood management programs. These meetings helped us to map and classify the area according to our research goal. At the same time, different stakeholders found the work was helpful for them in order to better manage flood disasters and vulnerabilities of people affected in that area. The information on the migrated population was based on discussion with the village leader, and prior to the sampling, we selected the area where internal migrants were living. We also found information regarding migrants from local respondents while we were collecting data from them, and those migrant households were also selected for data collection. In some villages, we found migrants reside in a cluster, and in other villages they are living randomly within the local population. To obtain data from the local people, we chose one person from a household and they were selected randomly.

Among the migrated people we searched to get both internal and international migrants. Some of the international migrants affected by the flood that occurred in 2006–2007 and 2011 were shifted to other places for work: none of them were found available in the vicinity at the time of our survey. This may be because foreign workers have little residential stability, given that they are not permitted to enter into marriage or to bring their families into Malaysia (Migration Working Group, 2013). Generally, a very insignificant number of international migrants reside at the study area, and those that do are mainly workers. Most of them work in construction sites, supermarkets and hospitals as daily laborers. They are predominantly from Indonesia, Bangladesh, Myanmar and Nepal. Normally, they work under recruitment agents and move frequently from one area to another, as well as from one agent to another.

Qualitative data were collected through field observation and semistructured interviews. Interviews were undertaken with 10 community leaders at different levels of the government hierarchy, from state parliament members to the village leaders, and five people from each category of local and migrant flood-affected people were interviewed. Village leaders are appointed by the government and are responsible for village administration. Interviewees of local and migrant flood-affected people were chosen according to their level of awareness and the degree of suffering. They were asked about their experiences and vulnerabilities, the causes of flood, the disaster management system and their opinion on how disasters can best be managed. A formal roundtable dialogue was conducted by the Segamat district officials where about 25 officers and staff of the district office participated. This meeting discussed the objectives of this study from the researchers' side and covered the various initiatives that the administration

Figure 9.2 Qualitative and quantitative data collection, clockwise from top left: (a) meeting with district administration, (b) interviewing the local disaster brigade where local people are involved and (c and d) data collection through questionnaires

usually performs as part of its disaster management cycle, including pre, during and postflood occurrences.

A questionnaire was used to collect data from 130 flood-affected local and migrated people in six parishes in Segamat that had suffered major floods in 2006 and 2011, these being Gemerih parish, parish Pogoh, Mukim Sungai Segamat, Chaah parish, Labis district and parish Bamboo Kasap. Questions covered demography, socioeconomic condition, income, household features, flood awareness, vulnerabilities and experiences of latest floods, experiences in shelter centers, flood governance, their expectations from the authority and their suggestions for better initiatives for disaster risk reduction. Information was also obtained from interviews and discussions with the state parliamentarian of the constituency, the Segamat district officer, the Social Welfare Department and the National Security Council Segamat Branch.

Findings

The survey, interviews and field observations reveal that the study area is prone to flooding and that the people of this area are suffering from both natural and anthropogenic vulnerabilities associated with flooding. The study area is situated within the basin of the Segamat and Muar rivers; therefore, it can be classified as an ecologically vulnerable zone for flooding. Development projects in Segamat replaced wetlands and marshlands, which previously had served as a holder of excess water. The people's perception is that development projects hamper the drainage system and cause floods in Segamat. Moreover, drainage and irrigation systems are not well constructed and managed in Segamat.

There is a general consensus that the Bekok Dam, which is used to release excess water in the rivers, caused flooding downstream in 2006 and 2011. In addition, the topography of the study site is low and naturally concave, which makes the area prone to flooding, and thus classified as a region of ecologically vulnerable. Inhabitants of Segamat also believe that most of the rivers are not properly maintained by the Department of Irrigation and Drainage, as silting causes the river basin to become shallower. As a result, rivers are not capable of holding large amounts of water, meaning floods are commonplace. Moreover, the survey reveals public perceptions that they are also suffering from socioeconomic and political forms of vulnerability. In particular, improper land-use policy, lack of drainage systems and inappropriate engineering of settlements were identified as causes of vulnerability that have produced the kinds of flood hazards that inhabitants suffer from frequently.

In Segamat, casualties and experiences were worst in the 2006–2007 and 2011 floods, although some respondents also said that they were affected in 2012 also. The majority of the respondents have multiple experiences of flooding and are frequently affected. About 45 percent of the respondents' families had to relocate to the flood shelter centers. In this case an equal proportion of locals and migrants were evacuated.

Sociodemography

In constructing a sociodemographic profile of the study area, 130 questionnaire surveys were undertaken in three *mukims* (subdivisions of the district); Gemerih, Pogoh and Segamat. Among them, 47 survey respondents (36.1 percent) are from Gemerih, 40 respondents (30.8 percent) are from Pogoh and 43 respondents (33.1 percent) are from Segamat *mukim*. Six parishes (union parishes) from these three *mukims* were selected for this study in order to consider the impact of the 2006–2007 and 2011 floods. These parishes are Gemerih parish, parish Pogoh, Mukim Sungai Segamat, Chaah parish, Labis district and parish Bamboo Kasap. Table 9.2 shows the sociodemography of respondents ($N = 130$) who experienced flooding in the study area. Of the sample, 46 percent were men, and the rest were women. The majority of the respondents were housewives (31.5 percent) and self-employed (30.8 percent), while a good proportion (28.5 percent) were doing other jobs (i.e. automobile worker, mobile shop owner, salesman). A few respondents were students and private workers (both about 9 percent). For the majority of the respondents, household income was reported as below 1,000 RM (60.8 percent), followed by 1,000–3,000 RM (31.5 percent) and 3,000–5,000 RM (6.2 percent); above 5,000 RM (1.5 percent) was the smallest group.

Table 9.2 Sociodemography of the respondents

	Classes	N = 130	Percentage (%)
Gender	Male	60	46
	Female	70	54
Local/migrants	Local	74	57
	Migrants	56	43
Mukim (administrative subdivision)	Gemerih	47	36
	Pogoh	40	31
	Segamat	43	33
Main occupation	Student	6	5
	Housewife	41	32
	Self-employed	40	31
	Private	6	5
	Others	37	29
Household income	<1000 RM	79	61
	1,000–3,000 RM	41	32
	3,000–5,000 RM	8	6
	5000 RM	2	2
Ethnicity	Malay	120	92
	Chinese	10	8
Education levels	Primary school	49	38
	Secondary school	72	55
	Diploma	3	2
	Bachelor's degree	6	5
Marital status	Single	10	8
	Married	104	80
	Divorced	1	1
	Widow	15	12

There was no significant difference recorded for the migrants, where 56 percent of respondents' household income was below 1,000 RM, followed by 29 percent who were within the income level 1,000–3,000 RM and about 12 percent who had income within 3,000–5,000 RM, while the remaining 3 percent had a monthly income of more than 5,000 RM. This compares with the majority of people in rural areas of Malaysia (51 percent), whose household income was between 1,000 and 3,000 RM and about 10 percent whose income was below 1,000 RM, while about 1 percent of the population was suffering from hardcore poverty (Department of Statistics, Malaysia, 2013). Ethnically, about 92 percent were Malay and the rest were Chinese. Most respondents had passed secondary school (55.4 percent), while 37.7 percent had passed primary school, 2.3 percent had a diploma and 4.6 percent were bachelor's degree holders. Similarly, 59 percent of migrants had completed secondary school and another 35 percent passed primary school. Of the respondents, 4.5 percent had a diploma degree and 1.5 percent had a bachelor's degree. Results show that 80 percent of the respondents were married; only 11.5 percent were widowed, 7.9 percent were single and 0.8 percent were divorced.

Although most of the local and migrant population had access to modern facilities, the majority of the inhabitants of the study area were within low-income groups. Access to facilities was made possible through government subsidies in many basic rights sectors (e.g. electricity, food, health and education). About 16 percent of respondents had air conditioning. Mobile phones were available to all and many households reported having more than one handset. Some of them have Internet facilities as well. Safe and pure drinking water was available and all respondents owned a motorized vehicle (e.g. motorcycle or car). Sanitary toilets and good sewage systems were also available.

Moreover, a good number of the local and migrant population had an acceptable level of education. The majority of the respondents had passed secondary school, reflecting the fact that this level of education represents a minimum requirement for getting a suitable job. Higher levels of education for women also contributed positively in enabling women to respond to societal needs (i.e. representation, leading a local community or founding an enterprise). Results show that the respondents were living in a good family conditions with a negligible proportion of divorced or broken families.

In summary, findings from the survey suggest that both migrants and local people had a reasonable standard of welfare, even if household incomes were relatively low. There was little difference in the characteristics of migrants and local people: this reflects the nature of employment in the area and the levels of education required of workers. In other words, the migrants in this study do not constitute the 'poorest of the poor'; rather, they are relatively well-qualified work-seeking migrants. The impact of flooding has been critical, however, with respondents experiencing multiple flood events that are significant enough to warrant relocation to evacuation centers. The survey suggested that both migrants and local people had access to such facilities.

Peoples' adaptation and vulnerabilities

Economic vulnerability

A considerable proportion of the respondents are aware of the possible dangers of flooding. Many of the affected people with sufficient wealth have themselves built alternative infrastructures (i.e. elevated houses) to save them from probable future sufferings that flooding may cause. However, as survey findings showed, most of the inhabitants have low incomes and are struggling to fulfil their basic needs: adaptive modifications to houses are expensive and difficult for people to accomplish on their own. Figures 9.3a and 9.3b show people built elevated houses themselves to avoid the risk of flood. The researchers recorded many such structural adaptations in the study region.

However, on the other hand, government planning contrasts with such adaptations. Figure 9.4a shows a very narrow and shallow channel beside a village that is not capable of holding excess rainwater as it flows through, which is therefore likely to result in flooding. As this is one of Malaysia's states where the regional economy is dominated by oil palm, intense and prolonged rainfall leads to rapid

(a)

(b)

Figure 9.3 Different types of structural adaptation in the study area; elevated housing to avoid flood risk (a) very close to the river Segamat and (b) closer to a river that causes floods

(a)

(b)

Figure 9.4 Different types of artificial structural vulnerabilities in the study area: (a) narrow and shallow channel that is not well structured and spacious enough to hold and maintain water flow; (b) construction of roads along the riverside may produce a barrier to the usual flow of the runoff

Vulnerabilities due to flooding in Malaysia 181

runoff and can easily cause overflow and flood, which cannot be contained within a shallow and narrow channel such as this. Figure 9.4b is an example of ongoing road construction work undertaken by the federal government beside a major river that was overloaded and flooded several times. Many people around the area were relocated for their own safety because of this area's flooding. Observations and survey data suggest that people on low incomes have limited access to physical flood-avoidance measures, and that structural adaptations undertaken by the government may have inadvertently exacerbated their level of risk.

Social vulnerabilities

As shown in Figure 9.5, the majority of respondents (86.8 percent) owned a home located less than 100 meters from the river, and 11.6 percent of respondents owned a between 101 and 500 meters from the river. Of the respondents, 1.6 percent owned a home located more than 500 meters from the river. This shows that the majority of the respondents resided within the flood-risk zone.

NTC: Figures 9.5 and 9.6 are in the "Revised figures" folder in the production file.

The impact of flooding on people in the area was severe. In some cases, respondents had lost family members during the floods of 2011 (12 lives were lost from households within the study sample alone). The majority of the respondents opined that floods affected their financial assets. About 77.5 percent of the respondents claimed that the loss of their assets was enormous and they had to pay a significant amount of money to start their livelihood after the damage had

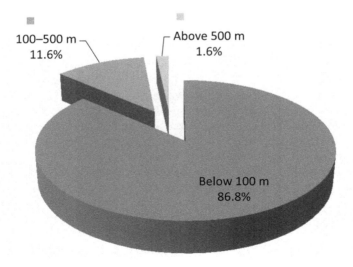

Figure 9.5 Proportion of people living in the danger zone, which is vulnerable to flooding

occurred. To manage this money, they had to take bank loans, sell property and also borrow money from their relatives.

Social capital

It was observed that some respondents rebuilt their elevated houses to be spacious so that they may help their neighbors during flood events. This suggested very good social interactions within the community. Social capital of this kind is a significant and strong element required to build up resilience within the community in order to face flood hazards collectively. Recognition by policy makers of existing collective efforts is important in future efforts to help build up peoples' capacity so that they will also be able to adapt in the face of flooding. As poverty and low incomes are the main source of vulnerability in this area, this is an important example of social capital particularly where there are differences in relative wealth and economic capacity within the community.

Engineering vulnerabilities

Many of the respondents have been trained to be aware of the dangers of rising flood levels and they are well aware of what to do in emergency situations. The government is credited with arranging such awareness and training programs. Having said that, respondents are not happy with the mitigation measures taken by the government to reduce flood risks. Moreover, they opined that most of the government initiatives were confined to the awareness program and to relief and sheltering programs over the duration of flood events. Although the government has built up more than 100 shelter centers in the Segamat district, flood mitigation initiatives are regarded as inadequate. Therefore, it is crucial to take robust and holistic, long-term planning measures for flood mitigation, integrating various departments, agencies and institutions.

Despite the state government having taken some measures to build riverbanks and barrages (through the Irrigation and Drainage Department), peoples' perception was that they were not well evaluated and would not reduce the flood hazards. For example, according to respondents, the river management project on a portion of the Segamat River lacked a scientific impact assessment prior to the infrastructure being built. Many respondents regarded it as a populist political gesture rather than as a robust plan to mitigate flood impacts.

Respondents also felt that it was important to dredge rivers to take out silt so that the channel can hold and flow large volumes of water. Many pointed out that major rivers were not managed by silt dredging, with the result that they become shallow and prone to flooding. It was observed that a big river become narrower due to siltation and people do agriculture on that silted mini island (see also Lebel and Sinh, 2009). Respondents pointed to that area as a major cause of flooding. It is important to dredge such areas to reduce flood vulnerability. In this context, the efficiency and the management of Bekok Dam needs to be evaluated scientifically to avoid a probable future cause for flooding downstream in Segamat.

Moreover, it is well documented that the drainage system in various localities of Segamat district are not well structured. For example, Figure 9.4 shows a channel beside a village, and similar features also evident in many other localities suggest the construction of improper drainage systems, which will increase suffering in the future too. Such engineering and infrastructural vulnerabilities must be identified, and related departments or agencies need to take immediate action to reduce such vulnerabilities.

Political vulnerabilities

Political vulnerabilities like improper land-use planning, transportation networks and development activities intensify many vulnerabilities. In the study area, an example of such vulnerability is the construction of the highway along the Segamat riverside. Many people were displaced from the site in the name of shifting them into safer places to reduce their vulnerability. However, constructing the highway at that place raised a question among the local people as to whether their displacement was less about their own safety and more to do with infrastructure development. Their perception was that the road network would cause further flooding due to sand deposition in the river, which used to come downstream due to development activities and agriculture in the upland areas. On the other hand, people also believe that this road network will cause a barrier to the runoff and will then create flash flooding in the event of sudden and heavy downpours.

It is evident from the survey results that about 90 percent of the respondents are residing in a danger zone that is so close to the river, and thus they are vulnerable to flooding. There was a mixed response found from the respondents over whether they would be willing to shift from that zone to comparatively higher, safe zones. In some areas, the government has taken initiatives to shift people from danger zones. Many people are not happy with these initiatives; this may be due to a lack of awareness regarding the potential threat, or that people are scared of not having enough financial capital to shift to a new place. They may also consider that the new place may not be suitable for their livelihoods. Observations and survey responses revealed that the majority of the population do not need to reside closer to the river in terms of their occupation or a better living environment. This indicates that effective awareness-building approaches and initiatives are lacking. There may be scope for the government to address this awareness gap.

Peoples' perception, sense of governance and responsibilities

Knowing about local governance, a sense of leadership and responsibility is important to build up a resilient society, and thus the survey sought to find out peoples' awareness of leadership and government at local, state and federal levels. About 37 percent of the respondents were involved in the different hierarchies of the village organizations such as, for example, the heads of the village, as community leaders or as members of a management committee. Among the respondents, about 85 percent felt that they had enough proximity to the community leadership, while among migrants, the amount was slightly lower, at 75 percent. However, most respondents did not consider themselves to have enough proximity or understanding about the district, state and federal leadership structure (62 percent in the case of migrants). It is important to mention that flood disaster governance in Malaysia is a top-down process and thus it is important for local people to know who and which agencies are responsible for flood disaster management. Through such understanding, people may directly deal with their vulnerabilities and be enabled to take proper decisions in crisis moments.

About 69 percent of the respondents, including migrants (73 percent of the total migrants), claimed that they had enough knowledge about potential flood hazards. The majority of them have joined the training program conducted by the Malaysian Civil Defence Department (JPAM) on how to face a flood situation. People are aware and know who will announce the development of a flood situation and when people will have to come out for an evacuation.

Peoples' perceptions of which government department or agency is responsible for flood disaster management and providing assistance during the flood varied significantly. This is a simple example of the lack of awareness of the leadership structure. However, most of the respondents believed that the state government is most responsible for the tasks (31percent) followed by civil defense and police (10.8 percent) and the least is the Welfare Department (3.1 percent) (Figure 9.6). This may also indicate that people wanted to see the state government be more active in disaster situations. It has two meanings: either respondents want to rely

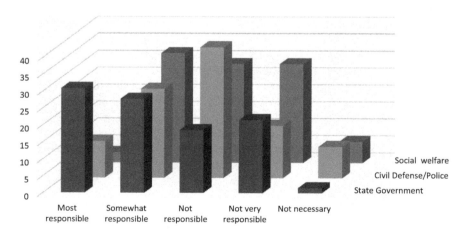

Figure 9.6 Perception of the flood-affected community about the responsibilities of different departments and agencies of the government

on the state government, or they want the state government to be closer to the local people than it currently is.

The majority of the respondents were of the view that the state government is most responsible for flood disaster management and for reducing different types of vulnerabilities. The responses of people on the scale of responsibilities shown in Figure 9.6 show a significant difference of opinion over which department is most responsible for disaster management. However, most of the people believe that it is the state government that should take the main responsibility during disaster time (Figure 9.6). This needs further study and validation to take necessary steps for improving the situation of flood-affected communities, including international and internal migrants. In-depth research on this perception may provide necessary guidelines to construct a better governance structure of the state and federal government.

Conclusion

Survey findings suggest that the respondents have a good relationship and interactive communication with the local authority or government (village leadership). However, many are not aware of the district, state or federal leadership or governance structure. People reported that state and federal leadership seldom visited their place and the leadership is not aware about respondents' opinions and needs. Like other parts of the developing world, it is difficult to for local people to establish easy access to state and federal leadership. Popular campaigns from the political leadership have been directed toward ensuring people are aware of their right to get the leaders among them to listen to their perceptions, opinions and needs. Both the local and federal leadership are responsible for ensuring peoples' voices are transmitted to the upper levels of government. Therefore, it is important to devise a suitable way to listen to them and satisfy them in terms of their opinions and rights. A hierarchical governance structure that values local people would benefit government, as it would provide greater legitimacy and an incentive for people to be on board and implement government initiatives.

This study identified vulnerabilities of flood-affected communities from a highly flood-prone area in the Malayan peninsula. It emphasizes peoples' perceptions about their vulnerabilities to flooding and also their experiences of governance and management. Findings show that there are three major types of vulnerabilities lying with the affected people. It also describes the underlying causes of those vulnerabilities. People voiced how they wanted to see the government eradicate their suffering from future disaster risks. Governance could be restructured according to the demand of the people, because a well-structured government must value peoples' perception, views and voices. If the government is able to devise a suitable initiative enabling them to relocate to a safer place, then this might address flood vulnerabilities. However, reliability and trust in the government is important and the government has to ensure this.

It is also worth noting that migrants in Malaysia are generally not discriminated against at the time of disasters and that they are provided with necessary supports where there is dire need. Moreover, it is also evident from the opinions of the lawmakers that international migrants are regarded as an important element in the development of the country. At the same time, Malaysia is a signatory of the Sendai Framework for Disaster Risk Reduction (2015–2030), which suggests the inclusion of migrants into the framework policy and implementation process since they are contributing to the resilience of communities and societies, and their knowledge, skills and capacities can be useful for disaster risk reduction. Such initiatives will certainly restore their basic rights, as well as enable them to contribute to Malaysia's economic and social development.

Empirical studies of this kind are a great resource to establish a welfare society that values its people and listens to their sufferings. However, it is more important that these findings will be used in policy making. Government should take the initiative where multiple stakeholders and experts should be involved and a comprehensive work plan will be taken into account. Local universities have multidisciplinary experts who can be a valuable part of this holistic effort.

Note

1 The Sendai Framework 2015–2030 is supported by the United Nations Office for Disaster Risk Reduction at the request of the UN General Assembly and is the successor instrument to the Hyogo Framework for Action (HFA) 2005–2015: Building the Resilience of Nations and Communities to Disasters (UNISDR, 2015).

References

Badrul, H.A.S., Marzukhi, M.I., and Daud, A.R. (2010). "The worst flood in 100 years: Johore experience." *Community Health* 15: 1–14.

Billa, L., Shattari, M., Mahmud, A.R., and Ghazalai, A.H. (2006). "Comprehensive planning and the role of SDSS in flood disaster management in Malaysia." *Disaster Prevention and Management* 15(2): 233–240.

Chan, N.W. (2006). "Increasing flood risk in Malaysia: Causes and solutions." *Disaster Prevention and Management* 6(2): 72–86.

Department of Statistics, Malaysia. (2011). *Population distribution and basic demographic characteristics 2010*. http://statistics.gov.my/portal/download_Population/files/census2010/Taburan_Penduduk_dan_Ciriciri_Asas_Demografi.pdf.

Department of Statistics, Malaysia. (2013). *Distribution of households by income class in Malaysia from 1970–2012*. Kuala Lumpur, Malaysia: The Household Income Survey (HIS), Department of Statistics.

DID. (2009). *Government of Malaysia department of irrigation and drainage Malaysia: Flood management manual volume 1*. http://smanre.mygeoportal.gov.my/smanre/aduan/Volume1_Flood%20Management.pdf.

Hew, C.S. (2003). "The impact of urbanization on family structure: The experience of Sarawak, Malaysia." *Sojourn* 18(1): 89–109.

Idris, A. (2012). "Malaysia and forced migration." *Intellectual Discourse* 20(1): 31–54.

Jali, M.R.M. (2009). *Internal migration in Malaysia: Spatial and temporal analysis*. Doctoral Dissertation, School of Geography, the University of Leeds.

Kaur, A. (2008). *International migration and governance in Malaysia: Policy and performance*. University of New England Asia Center, Asia Papers no. 22. Special issue on Migration and Security. http://pandora.nla.gov.au/pan/10530/20081020-0006/www.une.edu.au/asiacenter/UNEAC_Asia_Papers_21-28.html.

Lebel, L., and Sinh, B.T. (2009). "Risk reduction or redistribution? Flood management in the Mekong region." *Asian Journal of Environment and Disaster Management* 1(1): 25–41.

Migration Survey Malaysia. (2011). *Migration survey report*. Kuala Lumpur, Malaysia: Department of Statistics. www.statistics.gov.my/portal/index.php?option=com_content&view=article&id=1863%3Amigration-survey-report-malaysia-2011-updated-2912013&catid=166%3Amigration-survey-report&;Itemid=154&lang=en.

Migration Working Group. (2013). *A joint submission by members of the Migration Working Group (MWG) for the 17th Session of the Universal Periodic Review*, 24 October 2013. http://wao.org.my/file/file/Migration%20Working%20Group%20Joint%20UPR%202013%20Submission.pdf [Accessed 06/09/2017]

MOF (Ministry of Finance, Malaysia). (2010). *Economic report 2009/2010*. Kuala Lumpur, Malaysia: Government Printers, Ministry of Finance.

Mohammed, T.A., Al-Hassoun, S., and Ghazali, A.H. (2011). "Prediction of flood levels along a stretch of the Langat River with Insufficient Hydrological Data." *Pertanika Journal of Science and Technology* 19(2): 237–248.

NSC (National Security Council). (2001). *Standard operating procedures for flood disaster management*, Vol. 1. Kuala Lumpur, Malaysia: National Security Council, Prime Ministers' Department.

NSC (National Security Council). (2011). *Flood disaster report 2011*. Kuala Lumpur, Malaysia: National Security Council, Prime Ministers' Department.

O'Arabayah, D.A.R., Surinah, A., Noorhaida, U., Shaharom, N., and Rahim, A. (2008). "Public health preparedness and response to flood disaster in Johor, Malaysia: Challenges and lessons learned." *Malaysian Journal of Community Health* 15(5): 126–131.

Reza, M.I.H., and Alatas, S.M. (2013). "A decision support system to deal with contemporary issues of climate change induced vulnerability and human security in Malaysia." *Asian Journal of Environment and Disaster Management* 5(3): 275–285.

Segamat District Council. (2016). *Segamat background*. www.mdsegamat.gov.my/en/visitors/segamat-background [Last accessed 06/08/17].

Shafie, A. (2009). *Extreme flood event: A case study on floods of 2006 and 2007 in Johor, Malaysia*. Unpublished master's thesis, Colorado State University, Fort Collins, Colorado, USA.

Sulaiman, A.H. (2007). *Flood and drought management in Malaysia*. Paper presented at National Seminar on Socio-economic Impact of Extreme Weather and Climate Change organized by the Ministry of Science, Technology and Innovation. Putrajaya, Malaysia, 21–22 June.

UNDP. (2009). *Human development report*, United Nations Development Programme. United Nations, Geneva.

UNISDR. (2015). *Sendai framework for disaster risk reduction*. United Nations Office for Disaster Risk Reduction. www.unisdr.org/files/43291_sendaiframeworkfordrren.pdf.

10 Floods and migrants

Synthesis and implications for policy

Louis Lebel, Supang Chantavanich and Werasit Sittitrai

In the cases examined in this book, extreme floods are never the sole cause of long-term migration, but they are frequently a source of annoyance and hardship to migrants. The cases in this book have considered a *range* of different types of floods, as well as a range of relationships that people have with floods. Floods are not always a disaster. In rural areas, regular seasonal flooding increases productivity of fisheries and replenishes soils, and thus it benefits fishers and farmers. Slowly rising floodwaters that last for weeks, or even months, represent a different set of risks and opportunities to prepare than flash floods in an upland landscape that may come with very little warning. In urban areas, wealthier and well-connected households are much less vulnerable to floods and other disturbances to livelihoods and well-being than the poorest. Apart from vulnerabilities to flood, people also differ in their histories of mobility and capabilities for further migration.

This final chapter synthesizes the main findings of the previous chapters with respect to three lines of inquiry. First, is how floods impact ongoing processes of migration. The evidence from the case studies suggest that, apart from short-term evacuations, decisions to migrate are not usually a response to floods but a combination of many other factors, in particular economic ones. Second, is how floods impact the lives of migrants. Here the evidence is strong that migrants to peri-urban and urban locations are at increased risk, whereas in rural settings this was not the case. Third, is an analysis of why migrants end up in flood-prone places. Near cities that provide employment opportunities, high costs of housing are often the most important consideration, and affordable or informal housing tends to be in flood-prone locations. Based on these analyses of cases in the book, alongside some key recent literature, the chapter ends with a discussion of the implications for policy and planning. The findings argue strongly against overgeneralization about how people are affected by floods and whether or not mobility in response is a good tactic or not. Public policy needs to be nuanced to the differences between types of floods, geographical location, livelihood portfolios, and the capabilities and needs of migrants, as well as those trapped behind with few options to move or adapt.

Impacts of floods on migration

The impact of floods on the migration process overall is subtle, as many other influential factors act to motivate or discourage internal or international migration

(Black et al., 2013). Most cases discussed in this book find little evidence of outward long-term migration as a response to floods. The one exception is the Malaysian case study, which cites other work that claims a move from rural to urban areas occurred postflood (Reza et al., this volume). The cases examined are diverse with respect to type of flood, key livelihood activities, and history of migration, and these factors nuance most of the generalizations that can be made. In the case of Tonle Sap in Cambodia, for instance, normal seasonal flooding is a slow rising of waters that last months and benefits both farmers and fishers. Higher-than-usual floods create more wetland habitat that increases fish productivity and benefit fishers; this comes at a cost however to farmers whose growing season is curtailed (Middleton and Un, this volume).

The effects of stresses on mobility depend on whether or not these exceed an acceptable level (Sakdapolrak et al., 2014), as well as whether a household has other *in situ* options to turn to or not (Murali and Afifi, 2014). In several communities around Bangkok, temporary migration back to rural households was an important option for those who could no longer earn an income in the city because of prolonged flooding or loss of employment (Thabchumpon and Arunotai, this volume). In this case, the original source community for migrants provided a safety net for the urban migrants. Livelihood diversification through seasonal migration was not a common response to flooding in the case studies in this book, the one exception being the case in Cambodia. This contrasts with the Ganges-Brahmaputra Delta, Bangladesh, where yearly migration in the rainy season when agricultural lands get flooded is an important livelihood option (Ayeb-Karlsson et al., 2016). Migration of this type is a useful capability to have.

Floods can also reduce mobility. Floods disrupt transport systems, prevent people from going to work, and reduce incomes. They also prevent relief and customers from coming into a location for services. In the Poonsup community in Bangkok, deep floodwater covered key transport routes for months (Thabchumpon and Arunotai, this volume). In this situation floods increase vulnerability by reducing mobility.

Voluntary relocation in response to high or rising risks of floods may be a strategy for some households with sufficient funds, but even in these cases, decisions are tempered by social and emotional attachments to a place (King et al., 2014). In several studies in this book, migrants living in places impacted by floods indicated they would be reluctant to move from their homes, even for short periods (Salamanca et al., this volume). The reasons for this varied. In Cambodia, it related to rural households not knowing where to go or how to migrate resulting in a 'trapped population' (Black et al., 2013). In Thailand, urban residents worried about theft or damage to their property. In the study of upland and lowland villages in Laos, significant impacts of floods triggered evacuation as a short-term movement only (Salamanca et al., this volume). In this setting, men would often stay near their houses. Migration was not considered a response to flood impacts.

The case studies in this volume were not designed to evaluate the contribution of impacts or threats of floods on decisions to migrate, though this would have been a worthwhile extension. Nevertheless, the studies suggest that long-term, permanent forms of migration – as opposed to short-term evacuation – were not a common response to a range of flood types and livelihood relations with floods.

Consequences of migration on vulnerabilities to floods

The impacts of floods on migrants that move to flood-prone areas of major cities are significant. Migrants face the challenges of accessing their homes or leaving them to go to work. Floods also reduce customers for those who work in the informal sector (Thabchumpon and Arunotai, this volume). Damage to motorbikes, critical for work mobility in Hanoi, was another important impact (Nguyen and Pham, this volume).

Relatively low and unstable incomes make migrant households economically vulnerable to shocks, including losses and disruption to incomes caused by floods. In the Indonesian case study, in particular, 'precarious employment' meant the disruption of income during floods could have large impacts on a household (Elmhirst and Darmastuti, this volume). In contrast, in some situations floods may provide short-term employment opportunities for migrants. In Vietnam, for example, demand for rickshaw and motorbike transport services increased (Nguyen and Pham, this volume). In cases of prolonged flooding or where places of employment are damaged, migrants to urban areas may lose their jobs. This was a significant impact of floods on migrants in several of the communities studied around Bangkok (Thabchumpon and Arunotai, this volume).

The vulnerability of migrants to floods is also implied by health risks and outcomes. Polluted waters enter houses creating high risks of disease and other health problems. Poor sanitation increases risks of diarrhea, while cramped living conditions make tuberculosis and respiratory diseases significant risks (Sajor et al., this volume; Boutry, this volume). Poor waste management in migrant communities contributes to these health risks, and by blocking drains, increasing risks of flooding (Elmhirst and Darmastuti, this volume). Low-quality drainage infrastructure compounds the problems created by waste and low-lying positions. Almost all studies identified health impacts from flooding, and many noted that migrants often lived in low-quality housing as this was all that they could afford.

Floods impact some migrants much more than others. Differences in impact and social vulnerability arise for several reasons. First, is the degree to which the move was voluntary. This can be seen by contrasting the Yangon, Bangkok, and Manila, Philippines, cases. The history of forced resettlement in Yangon increased vulnerabilities, as there was little in the way of support networks to help migrants in their new location (Boutry, this volume). In the Poonsup community in Bangkok, which had relocated from an even riskier flood-prone location in the past, community members were able to use their connection to the Urban Poor Network to leverage support from the BMA (Thabchumpon and Arunotai, this volume). In the Manila case, migration was based on livelihood opportunities and supportive kin networks (Sajor et al., this volume), so moving did not increase vulnerabilities like it did in Yangon.

Second, the ability to draw on social capital and networks in source and destination locations influences the vulnerability of migrants. Migration often means a loss of personal connections that normally would be drawn upon when in difficult situations, such as extreme flooding. In the Bangkok case study, connections to rural households within Thailand had been maintained and were used (Thabchumpon and Arunotai, this volume); for migrant workers from Myanmar living in Bangkok, maintaining and making use of such links across international borders was much more challenging (IOM, 2016). The impacts of migration on vulnerabilities to floods may persist for long periods as a result of the ethnic and kin social networks they establish or disrupt. In Kota Karang, Indonesia, there were few employment opportunities, and maintaining social networks was crucial to securing precarious day-by-day work (Elmhirst and Darmastuti, this volume), whereas in Yangon the forced migration often cut economic networks, leaving migrants in a new location where agriculture was not possible, local employment hard to find, and flooding still a major risk (Boutry, this volume).

Third, information about floods does not reach many migrant households. In Hanoi, this was in part because such households were not registered, and thus members did not attend local commune meetings (Nguyen and Pham, this volume). Ethnic and language barriers are also important to information access and trust. In Bangkok, a special relief center was established with help from donations to assist the large numbers of migrant factory workers from Myanmar affected by floods, but migrants did not use it much (IOM, 2016). It should be underlined that recent migrants do not have the experiences or shared memories of past events that residents and their families can draw upon.

Although important differences among migrants, and between migrants and longer-term residents, were revealed in several case studies, this was not a universal finding. In the Malaysian study, residents and migrants were affected similarly by floods and recovery processes (Reza et al., this volume). In the Ayutthaya study site, residents moved to temporary shelters set up by the government or moved to high ground around the main highway where they also could safely leave their cars, whereas migrants from other parts of Thailand working in the Rojana industrial estate either returned to hometowns or sought work in factories elsewhere, as both the factories and their dormitories were completely inundated (Thabchumpon and Arunotai, this volume). Undocumented international migrants often did not return back home out of concerns of arrest and were worried that they may not get salaries due to them; as factories were closed for several months, this created substantial hardships (Hendow et al., 2016).

In popular public discourse migration is the cause of all kinds of ills. One version is that rural-urban migration increases vulnerabilities to floods. Few studies collect evidence about vulnerabilities in origin locations and compare them to those in destinations, and this is an important future research priority. Such a design is necessary as migrants may be more vulnerable than nonmigrants in general, but migration may still reduce vulnerability of those who move because they were highly marginalized to begin with or because migrants are healthier and more skilled than those that stay behind (Nauman et al., 2015). Some of the findings in this book indirectly suggest that having individuals that move decreases vulnerabilities of a household in general, if not always with respect to floods, for those in it who make the move. They also imply that migrants persist in their high-risk environments, in part, because they believe the benefits still outweigh the risks.

From a critical perspective this line of reasoning, especially if articulated by officials, needs to be scrutinized as it may be a ploy to reduce state responsibilities for providing services to vulnerable migrants. The problem with the argument that local communities need to prepare for floods *on their own* is that the reason they live in risky places and are vulnerable is often the product of other discriminatory government policies. In this situation it is not so much that individuals, households, and communities need to become more resilient, but rather that there is a need to transform the political structures and processes that made them vulnerable in the first place (Felli and Castree, 2012). In Thailand, for instance, vulnerabilities of migrants vary significantly with legal status, with the undocumented at greatest risk (IOM, 2016). In summary, the critical capabilities to move, and to be successful after moving, are from the start unevenly distributed, and continue to be socially and politically contingent.

Why migrants end up in flood-prone places

Migrants end up in flood-prone places for a couple of dominant reasons. First, informal settlements near the city are close to work and still affordable to rent or buy; the high cost of rent for legal dwellings in safer locations is beyond their reach. Second, people move to where they have family and friends; social networks pay an important role in migration, including migration into flood-prone places (Sajor et al., this volume). Third, people choose to live in flood-prone places because of the specific livelihood opportunities such locations provide – for instance, for fishers in rural areas (Middleton and Un, this volume) or as employees in factories in urban areas (Thabchumpon and Arunotai, this volume).

Ease of access to employment and livelihood opportunities in the informal sector were important drivers in all the urban case studies. As part of multilocal livelihoods, migrants evaluate income-generating opportunities in the city much higher than rural locations from which they move (Sakdapolrak et al., 2014). In the case of Bangkok, this is also true for international migrants seeking work in factories (Thabchumpon and Arunotai, this volume). Proximity of homes to employment is key.

Once settled in a flood-prone location, people may not want to move. In one of the Indonesian sites, traditional houses built on stilts and good boat access meant the option of living with floods or high waters was plausible (Elmhirst and Darmastuti, this volume). Flood-prone areas provide benefits to some households and livelihoods. Malaysian households living in a zone considered at high risk of floods were reluctant to relocate, in part, because of a lack of trust in the government (Reza et al., this volume). In Thailand, some people in flood communities around Bangkok were also reluctant to leave their homes unattended and organized themselves to lobby for assistance in draining away floodwaters and to accelerate recovery programs (Thabchumpon and Arunotai, this volume).

Two theoretical propositions raised in the introduction deserve reflection here. First, is the notion that migration *'involves exchanging one source of risk for another'* (Elmhirst et al., this volume). All the chapters in this book point to evidence that migrants were now living in risky places. In several studies, migrant narratives imply that the financial risks associated with low incomes in rural households were willingly being replaced with a higher risk of exposure to flooding and associated health risks (and lower income risks) in peri-urban or urban locations. In Yangon and certain communities studied in Bangkok, households had moved between locations that both had significant flood risks. The Cambodian case study includes examples of people moving toward places with greater exposure to floods because the benefits outweighed the risks. Taken together, these observations point to substantial complexity in the replacing or remaking of vulnerabilities, which is associated with how people relate to flooding, types of flooding, and capabilities to migrate.

Second, is the concern that *'framing migrants as adaptive agents can also feed into an apolitical and neoliberal discourse of self-help'* (Elmhirst et al., this volume). The cases in this book did find heterogeneity among migrants, as well as examples of how migrants self-organize to cope or adapt to floods. At one extreme, informants in Yangon reported families coping with flood impacts, in the worse cases, by taking children out of school so they can work or beg, or by young women entering commercial sex work (Boutry, this volume). At the other extreme were the responses of fisher households in Cambodia and Indonesia that turned highwater conditions into an opportunity (Middleton and Un, Elmhirst et al., this volume). Perhaps most antithetical to neoliberal-style reasoning were the rural communities in Laos, whereby many households simply waited for the floodwaters to recede (Salamanca et al., this volume). When officials refer to migrants as 'adaptive' or praise them for 'helping themselves' they off-load taking responsibility and deflect criticisms of government actions as a source of vulnerability. Care is therefore needed in taking such claims at face value. Even in the cases where migrants self-organize to respond to floods, it should be underlined that this may be because they have no choice – their plight is ignored by government.

Government plans and policies as sources of vulnerability

Government plans and policies, or the lack thereof, make migrants more or less vulnerable, and thus their lives in flood-prone locations easier or harder. There is a lot of evidence in the case studies in this book that government neglect or policies have made things worse for migrants.

It is common for authorities to call people living in risky places 'squatters' to underline they do not belong, even if they have lived there for a long time or were moved there by previous government projects, as was the case in Yangon (Boutry, this volume). In Hanoi, policies that discriminate against migrants included making them contribute more voluntary work on infrastructure projects than residents (Nguyen and Pham, this volume). Being classified as an 'informal' migrant, living in an 'informal' settlement, and working in the 'informal' sector completes the discursive marginalization of migrants.

Longer-term measures to improve drainage or build flood-protection barriers do not always work to the benefit of migrants in need of access to low-cost housing. Investments in flood-protection measures tend to amplify spatial differences in house prices and vulnerabilities (Husby et al., 2015). In Yangon, poor households now better protected found their rents increasing so much that eventually they had to move again to cheaper, more flood-prone places (Boutry, this volume). Infrastructure frequently redistributes floodwaters and risks into locations where vulnerable and marginalized households live, including migrants (Lebel and Sinh, 2009).

Some policies, in particular related to provision of low-cost housing, seem effective at reducing exposure to floods. A problem, however, is that by moving people into safe but 'sterile' locations, livelihoods may be undermined (Sajor et al., this volume). A recurrent theme in this book is that governments do not pay sufficient attention to livelihood security of migrants, often the main reason for migration in the first place.

While local officials are close to the community and respond quickly and sympathetically, many of the actions needed to make locations safer from floods need decisions by higher-level authorities who are less responsive and slower (Nguyen and Pham, this volume). In the Bangkok case, polarized national politics was a significant factor in a lack of cooperation between local communities, the Bangkok Metropolitan Administration, and national government (Marks and Lebel, 2016).

Floods are a political opportunity. Politicians in the Indonesian case used them to make a show of concern for constituencies, while making sure their actions were captured by the media (Elmhirst and Darmastuti, this volume). In Thailand, residents who stayed behind continually lobbied local politicians concerned with upcoming elections to help secure relief and other support for their communities' programs (Thabchumpon and Arunotai, this volume). The problem with this type of attention is that it is short-lived and focused on making promises to the electorate. Thus, it often does not translate into policies that reduce social vulnerabilities of migrants.

Implication for policy and planning

In this section, we focus specifically on policies at the intersection of migration and flooding, while acknowledging the importance of a broader policy environment related to natural disasters, human rights, land development, citizenship, and so on.

The findings from the case studies in this book argue against simplistic assumptions of the relationships people have with floods, and the desirability or not of mobility in response to floods, in policies and programs aimed at reducing the risks of disaster and assisting migrants at risk. Public policy needs to acknowledge the range in floods, relationships people have with floods, and the capabilities and needs of migrants.

To reduce the negative impacts of floods on the lives of migrants, special efforts need to be made to ensure *warnings and guidance on flood preparedness is accessible and understandable*. Postflood, relief programs should also take into account the added constraints faced by migrants, for instance, with respect to language of flood advisories. Without reducing the responsibility and accountability of the state, support should be provided for local initiatives that strengthen community-based safety nets.

Reactive, humanitarian aid after flood disasters is important to migrants, but it is not sufficient. Programs are needed that provide *systematic support to migrants at risk from and affected by floods*. In many locations, there is still too much reliance on patron-client networks that exclude needy individuals based on class, ethnicity, gender, kinship, or other prejudices. Migrants are vulnerable in patron-client systems; they do not trust those providing assistance, and they in turn are not understood or trusted by those providing it. Need, not personal relationships, should determine access to services or support. Gender and class considerations within migrant communities need to be actively addressed.

Governments should resist blaming the victims or reacting with threats of eviction. *Policies aimed at reducing vulnerabilities of migrants to floods need to pay special attention to livelihood security and not just issues of exposure*. Plans to relocate households from places of high risk will not be successful at reducing vulnerabilities if they do not also provide good opportunities for employment and income generation. *Forced displacement is a major cause of serious and compound vulnerabilities and should be avoided and opposed*. Support for victims of such programs in the past should be comprehensive and make use of the expertise of civil society organizations as appropriate. International organizations also have roles in such situations.

In rural, peri-urban, and rural areas, good relationships between local government and communities are important to migrant vulnerabilities to floods. At the same time, effective responses to flood risks and the vulnerabilities they engender requires strengthening *vertical coordination among local, citywide, or regional and national government agencies*. Many of the longer-term barriers to reducing vulnerability arise from the inability to properly link well-meaning responses at one level of government with decisions and plans at other levels.

International cooperation on reducing the disaster risks faced by migrants in the Southeast Asian region needs to be strengthened. International disaster risk-reduction initiatives have only recently begun to pay significant attention to migrants. The 2005 Hyogo Framework for Action does not mention the terms 'migrant', 'migration', or 'mobility' (UNISDR, 2005). A decade later the Sendai Framework for Disaster Risk Reduction makes several references to the needs of migrants and notes that '[m]igrants contribute to the resilience of communities and societies, and their knowledge, skills and capacities can be useful in the design and implementation of disaster risk reduction' (UNISDR, 2015). It also encourages policies that address 'disaster-induced mobility to strengthen the resilience of affected people and that of host communities' (*UNISDR, 2015*). Within the Southeast Asian region this shift has yet to take place. The ASEAN Agreement on Disaster

Management and Emergency Response does not mention 'migrants', 'migration', or 'mobility' (ASEAN, 2013).

The *importance of voluntary migration as a livelihood strategy and part of social development should be acknowledged in policy*. Much energy and resources have been wasted on programs that discourage migration without considering the benefits to migrants, recipient communities, and source communities. A more balanced analysis would lead to new strategies, for example, making it easier to choose where you want to live; register where you live; and thus maintain rights to access education, health, and other public services. This in turn, would help governments plan ways to improve flood and disaster management for all residents, including newer arrivals.

References

ASEAN. (2013). *ASEAN agreement on disaster management and emergency response: Work programme 2010–15*. Jakarta: Association of Southeast Asian Nations (ASEAN).

Ayeb-Karlsson, S., van der Geest, K., Ahmed, I., Huq, S., and Warner, K. (2016). "A people-centred perspective on climate change, environmental stress, and livelihood resilience in Bangladesh." *Sustainability Science* 11: 679–694.

Black, R., Arnell, N.W., Adger, W.N., and Geddes, A. (2013). "Migration, immobility and displacement outcomes following extreme events." *Environmental Science & Policy* 27(Suppl1): S32–S43.

Felli, R., and Castree, N. (2012). "Neoliberalising adaptation to environmental change: Foresight or foreclosure?" *Environment and Planning A* 44: 1–4.

Hendow, M., Pailey, R., and Bravi, A. (2016). *Migrant in countries in crisis: Emerging findings: A comparative study of six crisis situations*. Vienna: International Centre for Migration Policy Development.

Husby, T., de Groot, H.L.F., Hofkes, M.W., and Filatova, T. (2015). "Flood protection and endogenous sorting of households: the role of credit constraints." *Mitigation and Adaptation Strategies for Global Change*. https://link.springer.com/content/pdf/10.1007%2Fs11027-015-9667-7.pdf.

IOM. (2016). *Hazard exposure and vulnerability of migrants in Thailand: A desk study for the capacity building programme "Reducing the vulnerability of migrants in emergencies"*. Geneva: International Organization for Migration (IOM).

King, D., Bird, D., Haynes, K., Boon, H., Cottrell, A., Millar, J., Okada, T., Box, P., Keogh, D., and Thomas, M. (2014). "Voluntary relocation as an adaptation strategy to extreme weather events." *International Journal of Disaster Risk Reduction* 8: 83–90.

Lebel, L., and Sinh, B. (2009). "Risk reduction or redistribution? Flood management in the Mekong region." *Asian Journal of Environment and Disaster Management* 1: 23–39.

Marks, D., and Lebel, L. (2016). "Disaster governance and the scalar politics of incomplete decentralization: Fragmented and contested responses to the 2011 floods in Central Thailand." *Habitat International* 52: 57–66.

Murali, J., and Afifi, T. (2014). "Rainfall variability, food security and human mobility in the Janjgir-Champa district of Chhattisgarh state, India." *Climate and Development* 6: 28–37.

Nauman, E., Van Landingham, M., Anglewicz, P., Patthavanit, U., and Punpuing, S. (2015). "Rural-to-urban migration and changes in health among young adults in Thailand." *Demography* 52: 233–257.

Sakdapolrak, P., Promburom, P., and Reif, A. (2014). "Why successful in situ adaptation with environmental stress does not prevent people from migrating? Empirical evidence from Northern Thailand." *Climate and Development* 6: 38–45.
UNISDR. (2005). *Hyogo framework for action 2005–2015*. World Conference on Disaster Reduction, 18–22 January. United Nations International Strategy for Disaster Reduction (UNISDR): Kobe, Hyogo, Japan.
UNISDR. (2015). *Sendai framework for action 2015–2030*. World Conference on Disaster Reduction, 18 March. United Nations International Strategy for Disaster Reduction (UNISDR): Sendai, Japan.

Index

Abu Dhabi Declaration on Overseas Employment and Contractual Labour for Countries of Origin and Destination in Asia 170
agriculture 26–27, 32–34, 94–95
Association of Southeast Asian Nations (ASEAN) 2, 195–196
Ayutthaya province 89–91, 93, 99–100

Bali Process 170
Bandar Lampung, Indonesia: background 146–148; Bumi Waras subdistrict 154; ethnic networks 159–162; floods 147, 153–163; Kangkung village 150, 155, 158; Kota Karang village 150–151, 155, 160; Lampung province 151; land-use change 152–153; migration 147–148; migration networks 159–162, 163; migration to 150–154; Pasir Gintung village 148–149, 151, 156, 158, 160; research methodology of case study 148–150; social geographies and vulnerability to urban floods 154–159; social networks 161–162, 163; Tanjung Karang Pusat subdistrict 154, 156; Teluk Betung Barat subdistrict 154; urban development 150–154; vulnerability in 150–154
Bang Ban district 93
Bang Chanee village 93
Bangkok 96–99
Ban Lao village 69, 72, 75–76
Bumi Waras subdistrict 154

Cambodia *see* Tonle Sap Lake, Cambodia
Colombo Process on the Management of Overseas Employment and Contractual Labour for Countries of Origin in Asia, 170

conditional cash transfer (CCT) 121
coping strategies 75–76
Cyclone Nargis 1

debt 23–25, 27, 32–37, 50–52, 54
destination countries 34, 36, 72, 77, 82, 168, 170, 190
disaster management 169
disaster response 28–29
domestic migration 36, 47–48
Dong Yang village 68, 72, 75–76, 83
Don Mueang Airport 97
Don Phud district 93
Don Phud municipality 93

ethnic networks 159–162

fisheries 26–27, 29–32
'flexible citizenship' 7, 13–14, 51
flood management: Myanmar 55–59; Thailand 98–99
flood-migration nexus: mobile political ecology 10–11; tracing vulnerability in migration-flood contexts 11–14
flood-prone places 192–193
Flood Relief Operations Centre (FROC) 97–98
floods: Bandar Lampung, Indonesia 147, 153–163; consequences of migration on vulnerabilities to 190–192; coping strategies deployed by Laotian households during 75–76; development policies and 4, 11; in Hanoi, Vietnam 127–141; historical contextualisation, 12; impact on farming in Cambodia 33–34; impacts on migration 188–191; institutional mechanisms dealing with 13; in Laos 63–64, 70–77, 84; in Malaysia 167–168, 175, 178–186; in

Metro Manila, Philippines 105–124; migrants and 188–196; migratory responses to 77; in Myanmar 42–60; 'nature' of event 12; political ecology of 8–10; social production of 11; as source of vulnerability 54–55; in Thailand 89–103; Tonle Sap Lake, Cambodia 22–38
forced resettlement 57, 190

government policies: development policies in Cambodia 38; development policies in Southeast Asia 4; ethnicities policies in Laos 81, 83–84; flood management policies in Myanmar 55–59; flood management policy in Myanmar 55–59; flood management policy in Thailand 98–99; illegal fishing activities in Cambodia 30–31; infrastructure policies in Laos 81; land-use planning in Myanmar 57–59; migration policies in Cambodia 36–37; peri-urban growth-centered approach in Myanmar 59; real estate development in Philippines 116; recommendations for future 194–196; response to flooding in Philippines 116, 118–122; as sources of vulnerability 193–194; urbanization policies in Myanmar 57–59; water policies in Thailand 101–103

Hanoi, Vietnam: background 127–128; drainage system project 127–128, 137–138; floods in 127–141; impact of floods on work mobility 134, 190; migrant livelihoods/residency in flood-stricken areas 131–135; migration in 130–131; nonregistered migrants in 137–141; official flood responses 137–139; research methodology of case study 128–130; responses to flooding 135–137; Tan Mai 128–137; Tan Trieu 128–137; urban change in 130–131
health care: in Cambodia 28, 38; in Malaysia 169, 178; in Metro Manila, Philippines 121; in Myanmar 44, 54, 57, 60; in Southeast Asia 190
health hazards: in Hanoi, Vietnam 127, 140; in Indonesia 147
Huay Man village 68, 72, 75–76
humanitarian aid 195
Hyogo Framework for Action 195

Indonesia *see* Bandar Lampung, Indonesia
Informal Sector Relocation Program (ISRP). 118–121
informal settlements: in floodways 110–112; government response to flooding in 118–122
internal migrants 170–171
international migration 34, 36, 77, 170–171
intra-urban migration 50

Kampong Kor Krom village 24–34
Kangkung village 150, 155–156, 158
Khammouan province 84
Khanham community 99–100
Kota Karang village 150–151, 155–157, 160

Lampung province 151
"land grabs" 31
land ownership 27
land-use planning 57–59
Lan Takfa village 93
Laos: background 63–64; Ban Lao village 69, 72; case study sites 67–70; coping strategies deployed by households during floods 75–76; domicile status of case study villagers 73–75; Dong Yang village 68, 72, 83; educational attainment of case study villagers 78; education of case study villagers 70; ethnicities policies 83–84; ethnicities policies in Laos 81; ethnicity of case study villagers 69–79; government policies on infrastructure and ethnicities 81; Huay Man village 68, 72; income source of case study villagers 78; intersection between flooding and migration in study sites 73–76; Khammouan province 84; Luang Prabang province 67–68, 76, 77; migration networks 82; nature of floods/flooding 70–72; occupations of case study villagers 70; Pha Vieng village 67–68, 72; research methodology of case study 64–67; Saravan province 84; Savannakhet province 68–69, 76, 84; social networks of case study villagers 78–81; status of migration in 72–73; village transnationalization 82–83
livelihoods: agrarian 11, 27; diversification 2, 36; family-scale fishing 4, 26–27; in flood-stricken areas of Hanoi, Vietnam 131–135; migration-based 3–4, 10–11;

of Mingalar Kwet Thet settlement, Yangon, Myanmar 44–45, 54–55; multilocal 11; regulations impacting 2–3; resilience thinking and 8; smallholder farming 4; sustainable 5–6, 8–9; trajectories of Laotian households 77–81

Luang Prabang province 67–68, 76, 77

Malabon City, Philippines: background 105–106; conditional cash transfer (CCT) 121; disaster adaptation response by government 124; government policies 116, 123–124; government response to flooding in informal settlements 118–122; immediate local government flood-related responses 118; internal migration in 105–125; land area/use 108–110; migration and informal settlements in floodways 110–112; national government-initiated programs 118–121; population 110; reasons/conditions for settling in floodways 112–118; relocation programs 123–124; sustainable livelihood program (SLP) 121–122; urban growth and flood hazards 106–110

Malaysia: background 167–169; disaster management 169; economic vulnerabilities 178–182; engineering vulnerabilities 182–183; findings of case study 175–176; floods 167–168, 175, 178–186; migrant populations 168, 170–171, 178; migration context 34, 169–171, 185–186; migration to 36; peoples' adaptation and vulnerabilities 178–183; peoples' perception/sense of governance and responsibilities 183–185; policy context 169; political vulnerabilities 183; research methodology of case study 174–175; Segamat district 169, 171–174, 182–183; social capital 182; social vulnerabilities 181–182; sociodemography 176–178; study area of case study 172–174; undocumented migrants 168; vulnerabilities due to flooding in 167–186

migration: as/for adaptation 81, 85; to Bandar Lampung, Indonesia 150–154; domestic 36, 47–48; flooding and 77; to flood-prone places 192–193; impacts of floods on 188–190; incentives for 23–25, 35–36, 77; international 34, 36, 77; intra-urban 50; in Laos 72–73; linkages between flooding and migration in Thailand 102–103; 'livelihoods approach' to 6; as manifestation of 'capability' 6–7; networks 82, 159–162, 163; peri-urban 48–50; policies 36–37; processes associated with 3–4, 10–11; rural-to-rural 34; rural-to-urban 34; rural-urban migration 191; social dynamics of 7; of Tonle Sap Lake, Cambodia residents 34–37; undocumented migrants 168

Mingalar Kwet Thet settlement, Yangon, Myanmar: background 42–43; development of 59–60; domestic migration 47–48; employment 45; flood management policies 55–59; flood regime 42–43, 45–47; housing 44–45; intra-urban migration 50; land-use planning 57–59; livelihoods 44–45; national policies 56–58; peri-urban growth-centered approach 59; peri-urban housing 44, 50–52; peri-urban migration 48–50; research methodology of case study 43–44; urbanization policies 57–59; urban/rural migration to 47–50

mobile political ecology 10–11
mobility, everyday 1–2, 105–106, 134, 156
multi-local livelihoods 16, 105–106, 110–111, 114–115, 117, 119–122
Myanmar see Mingalar Kwet Thet settlement, Yangon, Myanmar

Nakhon Chai Si district 93
Nakhon Pathom province 93
National Housing Authority (NHA) 118–119

Pasir Gintung village 148–149, 151, 153, 156, 158, 160
peri-urban growth-centered approach 59
peri-urban housing 44, 50–52
peri-urban migration 48–50
Pha Vieng village 67, 72, 75–76
Philippines see Malabon City, Philippines
Poonsup community 97, 189
Prek Trob village 24–34

relief programs 195
resilience 7–8, 102–103
rice production 26–27, 32–34, 94–95
Rojana Industrial Park 99–100

rural-to-rural migration 34
rural-to-urban migration 34
rural-urban migration 191

Sai Mai district 96
Saravan province 84
Savannakhet province 68–69, 76, 84
Segamat district 169, 171–175, 182–183
Sendai Framework for Disaster Risk Reduction 186
social capital 182
social networks 161–162, 163
South Korea 34, 36
squatters 43, 50
sustainable livelihood program (SLP) 121–122

Tanjung Karang Pusat subdistrict 154, 156
Tan Mai 128–137
Tan Trieu 128–137
Teluk Betung Barat subdistrict 154
Thailand: Ayutthaya province 93; background 90–91; Bang Ban district 93; Bang Chanee village 93, 94–96; Bangkok 96; Don Mueang Airport 97; Don Phud district 93; Don Phud municipality 93, 94–95; experience of 2011 flood in semiurban/industrial area 1, 99–100; experience of 2011 flood in urban 96–99; experience of seasonal flooding in rural 93–94; Flood Relief Operations Centre 97–98; Lan Takfa village 93, 94–96; linkages between flooding and migration in 102–103; migration context 36; migration to 34, 42, 72, 77, 82; Nakhon Chai Si district 93; Nakhon Pathom province 93; Poonsup community 97; research methodology of case study 91–93; rural social structure 95, 102; Sai Mai district 96; Tung Songhong housing estate 96–98; U-Chareon community 96–98; vulnerability to flooding, 101–102; water policies 101–103
Tonle Sap Lake, Cambodia: agriculture 4, 32–34; background 22–24, 189; brief overview of life in Prek Trob and Kampong Kor Krom villages 26–34; development policies and 38; disaster response 28–29; fisheries 4, 29–32; flood regime 22, 37–38; governance of 28, 30; government policy 38; government reforms 30–31; "land grabs" 31; migration 34–37; migration policies 36–37; regional-scale policies, 38; research methodology of case study 24–26
translocality 122–123
Tung Songhong housing estate 96–98
Typhoon Haiyan 1

U-Chareon community 96–98
urbanization policies 57–59
Urban Poor Network 96
Uthai district 99–100

Vietnam see Hanoi, Vietnam
voluntary migration 196
vulnerability: concept of 5–7; considering through social exclusion and 'flexible citizenship' 13–14; differential 105–106; economic 178–181; engineering 182–183; flooding as source of 54–55; flood management as source of 55–56; flood-migration-vulnerability assemblage 14–17; impact of government policies on producing 38; political 183; social 181–182; tracing in migration-flood contexts 11–14; ways forward to reduce 58–59

waste management 190
water management 57
work mobility 190